DRUG USE AND
CULTURAL CONTEXTS
'BEYOND THE WEST'

DRUG USE AND CULTURAL CONTEXTS 'BEYOND THE WEST': Tradition, Change and Post-Colonialism

Edited by
Ross Coomber and Nigel South

Free Association Books

First published 2004
by Free Association Books
57 Warren Street W1T 5NR

British Library Cataloguing in Publication Data
A catalogue record for this book is available from the British Library

Produced by Bookchase (UK) Ltd
Printed and bound in EU

ISBN 1 853437 43 3
L.D.: SE-76-2005

ACKNOWLEDGEMENTS

We wish to thank Trevor Brown at Free Association Books for taking on this project; our contributors for making it possible; and Debbie Stewart for assistance.

Also, love and special thanks for their usual patience to Liza, Jake and Ellie and to Alison and Daniel.

CONTENTS

NOTES ON CONTRIBUTORS

Susan Beckerleg is currently an Honorary Lecturer at the London School of Hygiene and Tropical Medicine, University of London. Having graduated in Social Anthropology from the London School of Economics in 1976 she has since worked as an applied Anthropologist in health-related research and intervention projects in a range of settings in Africa and Asia. As a student of the School of Oriental and African Studies, she conducted her PhD field research into Swahili medicine at the Kenya Coast. In 1994 she co-founded the Omari Project, a self-help group with the aim of tackling the problem of heroin use in Kenya. The Project opened the first free residential heroin rehabilitation centre in East Africa in 2000. Recently she has been carrying out ESRC-funded research into women heroin users and their reproductive health in Malindi, Kenya.

Barry Chevannes is Professor of Social Anthropology and Dean of the Faculty of Social Sciences, University of the West Indies at Mona. He was a senior visiting scholar at the Institute of Social Studies in The Hague and the recipient of a Rockefeller Fellowship. He is the author of *Rastafari: Roots and Ideology*. He recently chaired the Jamaican National Commission on Ganja which reported to the Jamaican Government and recommended 'the decriminalisation of ganja for personal, private use by adults and for use as a sacrament for religious purposes'. A Joint Select Committee has recommended that Parliament adopts the proposal.

Ross Coomber is Principal Lecturer in Sociology at the University of Plymouth, England. He has been involved in drug related research for over seventeen years, has written numerous journal articles and edited various

9

books relating to drug use, drug markets and drug policy. He is currently writing a book on misconceptions surrounding drug markets and drug dealers. Recent research has concentrated on looking at the minutiae of drug dealer and drug market operations in England, the US and Australia with particular concern regarding the 'cutting' of street drugs, how drug dealers are initiated into drug dealing and how dealing activity differs in different locations.

Kalyan Ganguly is Assistant Director General (Social Sciences) in the Indian Council of Medical Research. He was formerly Assistant Professor in Medical Anthropology at the Institute of Human Behaviour and Allied Sciences, Delhi University from 1999–2002. He has an M.Sc in Anthropology, an M.Phil and a Ph. D. in Social Medicine and Community Health from Jawaharlal Nehru University, New Delhi. He has received the Prof. B.C. Srivastava Foundation Award in Community Medicine for works in Public Health including issues around drug use, given by ICMR. He has been involved in the evaluation of a number of National Health Programmes in India, most specifically the Pulse Polio Immunisation Programme 1997–2000 and the Family Health Awareness Campaign 1999–2000. He has published extensively in both national and international journals. His latest book is: *Health and Culture of a Metropolitan Resettlement: Issues and Challenges*, (2002), New Delhi, India.

Dwight B. Heath is Professor of Anthropology at Brown University, Providence, RI, USA. Having earned degrees from Yale and Harvard Universities, he has conducted research and served as consultant on a broad range of topics, including land reform and revolution, ethno-history, economic development, cultural change, and ethnographic research methods, as well as alcohol and drug use and their outcomes in tribal and peasant communities around the world. He pioneered in the description and analysis of drinking patterns, and demonstrated that a sociocultural perspective often discredits official policies in the field of alcohol and drugs. He is the author of numerous major books including: *Contemporary Cultures and Societies of Latin America, Journal of the Pilgrims of Plymouth, Land Reform and Social Revolution in Bolivia, Cross-Cultural Approaches to the Study of Alcohol, International Handbook on Alcohol and Culture*, and *Drinking Occasions: Comparative Perspectives on Alcohol and Culture*.

Edward MacRae is Lecturer in Anthropology at the Federal University of Bahia, Associate Researcher at the Centre for the Study and Treatment of Drug Abuse of the Federal University of Bahia and represents the Brazilian Ministry of Culture at the National Anti-drug Council where he is also member of a special expert comission to study the use of ayahuasca in Brazil. He is also vice president of the Brazilian Network for Harm Reduction. After receiving his BA in Social Psychology from the University of Sussex and an MA in Sociology of Latin America from Essex University he returned to his native Brazil where he was awarded a Doctorate in Cultural Anthropology at the University of São Paulo, in 1986, with a thesis on the Brazilian Gay Movement. He has written extensively on the ritual use of entheogens, sexual politics, drug regulation, AIDS prevention among gays and among injecting drug users and harm reduction strategies for users of injecting drugs, crack cocaine and cannabis.

Silvia Rivera Cusicanqui is Professor Emeritus in Sociology at the Greater University of San Andrés, La Paz, Bolivia and also Professor of Andean Programme of Human Rights at the Andean University of Simón Bolívar, Seat, Ecuador. She is the author of several books, such as "Oprimidos pero no Vencidos" Luchas del Campesinado Aymara y Qhichwa de Bolivia, 1900–1980, which has been translated into English and Japanese; Ayllus y Proyectos de Desarrollo en el Norte de Potosi, co-authored with the team of the Andean Oral History Workshop; Los Artesanos Libertarios y la Etica del Trabajo, co-authored with Zulema Lehm. She has also directed several videos and one short film, documentaries and fictional. The videos Las Fronteras de la Coca (a series) is her most recent work in documentary video (2003).

Colin Samson is Director of the American Studies programme at the University of Essex, Colchester, England. He has been working with the Innu peoples of the Labrador-Quebec peninsula since 1994. Much of his work has been linked to a human rights campaign on behalf of the Innu with Survival International. This resulted in the publication of the widely-cited report *Canada's Tibet: the killing of the Innu* in 1999. In addition to several journal articles and book chapters on the Innu, he has just completed a book on the impact of forced sedentarization called *A Way of Life that Does Not Exist: Ethnocide, Canada and the Innu* (Verso, 2003). Among his other interests are Native American art and literature, having published essays on the Tarascan-Chicano artist Ruben Trejo and the Anishinaabe writer Gerald Vizenor.

Stacy B. Schaefer is Associate Professor of Anthropology and Co-Director of the Museum of Anthropology, California State University, Chico. She was formally associate professor of anthropology at the University of Texas-Pan American. She has been researching and publishing on the cultural knowledge, rituals and traditions that Huichol Indians have regarding the use of Peyote for more than twenty years and is the author of numerous articles, book chapters and books. Her most recent book is: *To Think with a Good Heart: Wixárika Women, Weavers, and Shamans*, (2001) University of Utah Press.

Nigel South is Professor in the Department of Sociology and Research Professor in the Department of Health and Human Sciences at the University of Essex, Colchester, England. He joined the University in 1990 and was previously (1981–90) a Research Sociologist at the Institute for the Study of Drug Dependence (now Drugscope). He has interests in multi-disciplinary and comparative approaches to drug use and misuse and to criminology and health studies more broadly. He has published widely on drugs and related issues and books include: Dorn, Murji and South (1992) *Traffickers: Drug Markets and Law Enforcement*, Ruggiero and South (1995) *Eurodrugs*, and South (ed; 1999) *Drugs: Cultures, Controls and Everyday Life*.

Alison Spedding is currently Lecturer in Anthropology at the Universidad Mayor de San Andres in La Paz, Bolivia. An anthropologist and novelist, she was born in Belper, Derbyshire in 1962. She studied at Cambridge and later at the London School of Economics where she gained her PhD. Her principal field of study has been traditional coca producing communities in the Yungas of La Paz, Bolivia, where she has lived since 1986.

Daniel Martin Varisco is currently chair of the Department of Anthropology at Hofstra University in Hempstead, New York, USA. He is a cultural anthropologist and historian who has lived in Yemen, Egypt and Qatar. He conducted an ethnographic study of highland spring irrigation in North Yemen in 1978–79 and returned a dozen times to Yemen as a development specialist. From 1991–2001 he edited *"Yemen Update"* for the American Institute for Yemeni Studies and currently maintains *"Yemen Webdate"* as an online archive devoted to Yemeni studies. He has published widely on the history of Arab agriculture and folk astronomy, especially for Yemen. Currently President of the Middle East Section of the American Anthropological Association, his latest book is *Islam Obscured: The Rhetoric of Anthropological Representation* (Palgrave, in press).

Chapter One

DRUGS, CULTURES AND CONTROLS IN COMPARATIVE PERSPECTIVE

Ross Coomber and Nigel South

Drugs destroy lives and communities, undermine sustainable human development and generate crime. Drugs affect all sectors of society in all countries; in particular, drug abuse affects the freedom and development of young people, the world's most valuable asset. Drugs are a grave threat to the health and well-being of all mankind, the independence of States, democracy, the stability of nations, the structure of all societies, and the dignity and hope of millions of people and their families. (United Nations General Assembly Political Declaration, 1998:3)

INTRODUCTION

Overly simple and one-dimensional definitions of a problem are likely to produce an overly simple and equally one-dimensional understanding of how that problem should be resolved. In September 1997 the incoming United Nations Drug Control Program Executive Director, Pino Arlacchi declared '*A Drug Free World – We can do it!*' This position was taken forward less than a year later with the decision by the United Nations General Assembly to re-affirm the principles of the 1988 Vienna Convention that had taken a relatively hard-line towards eradicating all illicit drug use, production and distribution. The basic underlying premise on which this approach was based is broadly outlined by the quotation used at the head of this page: drugs are inherently evil, their use inevitably undermines indi-

13

vidual health and inexorably leads to the disintegration and destruction of community and society. Put simply, the contributors to this book show that (a) all of this need not be so; (b) such universalising statements ignore diversity and contrary evidence; (c) while drug-related problems undeniably do arise it will always be important to consider 'context'.

Article 14 of the 1988 Convention did contain a statement suggesting that appropriate control measures to eradicate illicit production and reduce demand should take 'due account of traditional licit use' yet this was done without the provision of further explanation or context and any recognition (or indeed, understanding) that forms of drug use may take place that do not result in the outcomes suggested by the aforementioned quote. Moreover, whilst it may well be the case that the aim to harmonise control efforts of all governments against drug use is not being achieved at the level some would hope for it is certainly the case that the 146 countries that in 2003 once again signed up to a further re-affirmation of the Vienna Convention also signed up to the broad principles on which it is based. At the very least, these principles provide a platform from which policies consistent with that position can be vigorously pursued. For crops such as coca, opium and cannabis (see Chapters 3, 4, 5 and 10) the following line of action is strongly urged:

> States in which illicit cultivation of drug crops exists should develop national strategies for the reduction and elimination of illicit crops, including concrete measurable goals and objectives taking into account existing drug control master plans. National drug crop reduction and elimination strategies should include comprehensive measures such as programmes in alternative development, law enforcement and eradication. (UNGASS, 1998)

This book shows that a predominately westernised[1] view of drug use prevails within the international drug control conventions. The formative agreements that emerged in the early years of the 20th century, mainly at the behest of the USA, had a very particular view of the kind of problems produced by drugs and, in response, the need for punitive and prohibitionist control measures (McAllister, 2000). More recently, the US Government and its enforcement agencies have tended to be fierce critics of other governments (such as the Netherlands) and their policy frameworks that have implemented the conventions more liberally. The USA has also consistently rejected adoption of many harm reduction approaches (such as needle-exchanges) as antithetical to the US approach, although pioneering schemes have been established in various cities. Overall, the US-led trend has been one based upon a particularly western, ethnocentric version of 'progressive' and humanist thinking that (without irony) has led to declaration of a 'war' on drugs.

This war however has been a bloody one and casualties result not only from drug use but also from the pursuit of prohibition. Huge populations, often otherwise law-abiding citizens, have been criminalised for using one or another of an ever-widening range of substances, sometimes to a punitive extreme that has few parallels. Prohibition in its varying manifestations is fundamentally based upon the fear of drugs, the fear of intoxicated states, the fear of the individual transformed into something less moral. Understanding drug use faces problems of definition and anomalies regarding what is acceptable versus unacceptable – why are alcohol and tobacco legal while cannabis and opium are not? Why does it seem odd to describe all of these as 'drugs' even though they all have pharmacological effects on the mind and body? Given lack of agreement regarding even the terminology in use ('drugs', 'substances', 'intoxicants', 'narcotics' – the latter with a history of use in US law even when stimulants are actually being referred to) it is clear that the Prohibitionist agenda rests less on scientific consensus than on ideological claims and moral sentiments. This position shores up what Young (1971: 156 and *passim*) called 'the absolutist monolith' and does not allow for the real-world existence of diversity, contra-indicators or experiences that do not conform with western normative expectations (or at least, the 'official' version of these: see below). This book provides a balanced repudiation of the 'monolithic' perspective. The chapters included suggest that if we adopt a cross-cultural approach we will find that in some countries or cultures, drugs are not a problem but a long-established socio-cultural asset, form of support, and basis for morally-grounded socialisation and belief-systems, while in some other contexts where drugs *have* become a destructive force this has followed from western influences.

This book is *not* about 'defending' drug use. It *is* about understanding such use, seeing 'the other side' and exploring the overlooked cultures of use that occur around the globe and that experience the malign, iatrogenic (Illich, 1977) effects of the imposition of western models of drug and crime control (Cohen, 1982). In some cases the misery and harm of forms of drug taking are revealed but again context is important and can provide understanding of how people are pushed into despair and how drugs can come to represent escape from a world that no longer offers what it used to.

FORMS OF DRUG USE AS INTEGRATIVE AND POSITIVE TO COMMUNITY AND SOCIETY

One way of proceeding is to ask whether a one-dimensional understanding of how drugs impact on individuals and societies is a reliable one for all substances (such as those on the list covered by the international covenants) and at all times (Sherratt, 1995; more generally on the western one-dimensionality of concepts like 'health' and 'culture' see Fassin, 2001). Even if we were to accept applicability in some circumstances but not others would we not need to consider further those circumstances where this was not the case – particularly where prohibition has unreasonable effects on whole populations? Many of the signatories to the various international conventions are governments of people who take part in various types of traditional and/or religious drug use and they have had to tread a path of conciliation between international pressure (often involving 'carrot and stick' measures of financial aid and/or economic sanctions) and the heavily invested practices of sections of their indigenous population. As this book shows (and there are numerous other examples that we are unable to include here) there are forms of drug use that simply 'do not fit' the supposedly progressive, western notion of all drug use as *essentially* damaging. In fact, rather than understanding drug use as undermining of individuals, communities and societies, some of the examples presented here are better understood as illuminating positive, integrative and functional contributions of drug use to the social-health of particular communities of people. For many in the various communities described in this book, use is integrated into many facets of everyday life as well as having ceremonial or ritual meaning, often central to spiritual or religious activity. For these peoples, drug use is normal and rather than causing inevitable harm in fact contributes to group solidarity and reaffirmation of traditional roles and community structures. Yet the pressure of international conventions weighs down upon this kind of positive drug use just as much as it does on the prevalence of more destructive use in the urban developed nations – the problem that really lies at the heart of the anxieties of western drug control warriors. Much of the drug use in the non-western settings described is not of the kind that international agreements were originally founded upon nor originally sought to pursue. Furthermore, it is evident that there is nowhere near the kind of uniformity (even in western states) in the interpretation and/or enforcement of international conventions that the prohibitionist establishment would like. Nor is it clear, as we shall see below, that there is uncontested consensus about the desirability of criminal-law based prohibitions and solutions as suggested by the conventions.

NORMAL AND NORMALISED DRUG USE

It is not only drug use in 'traditional' settings that confounds the one-dimensional view of drug use. In the west and other 'modern' nations there are forms of recreational drug use that are increasingly perceived as 'normal' (Parker et al, 1998; Pearson, 2001; South, 2004/5) while some of the harms historically attributed to illicit 'drug use' *per se* (but particularly to recreational use) can be questioned and laid at the door of over-zealous prohibition (Becker, 1963; Nadelman, 1989; Parker, 2000). Arguably, it is a recognition of such factors that has led to a relative fracturing – in practice – of the apparent consensus created by wide subscription to the international agreements. Thus, in recent years, various jurisdictions around the world have liberalised the penalties for personal use of at least some drugs. In the UK, this has seen the disputed but, by some interpretations, effective decriminalisation of cannabis *use*, as in Luxemburg. In Spain and Italy, possession of drugs such as heroin and cocaine for personal use is now to be treated as an administrative offence (EMCDDA 2004a). In Portugal, the possession and personal use of *any* drug has been fully decriminalised (EMCDDA 2004b) while in the UK and Canada the use of cannabis for therapeutic purposes is moving towards legislative authorisation whereas in the Netherlands this widely supported position has already been accepted. Switzerland has introduced heroin prescribing and in other European countries (but also Canada, Australia, New Zealand) the introduction of diverse harm-reduction approaches has been significant over the last twenty years. Such liberalisation partly results from recognition that criminalization of large numbers of the population for an activity (particularly cannabis use) that continues to expand despite years of prohibition, and where little harm results from moderate use, is no longer warranted. That countries such as Portugal, Spain and Italy choose not to punish personal use of heroin and cocaine is also indicative of a strong argument that drug use is a public health issue and not a criminal justice matter (Maher and Dixon, 1999).

CROSS-CULTURAL EXPERIENCES

This book was conceived to make a modest contribution to the understanding of drug use in different cultures and settings. The aim is to stimulate debate about how to achieve more appropriate accommodation of such difference and diversity within the context of international controls.

As indicated above, the forms of drug use that are localised or nationally commonplace in various societies around the world but that remain over-looked are significant and wide-ranging. There are many 'other voices' telling the 'other side' of the drugs story that are deserving of a hearing and that we would have liked to include here but could not. Eventual choices for inclusion were determined by a number of factors. Initially, for example, we were keen to include a chapter on the use of Tabernanthe iboga in Occidental Equatorial Africa, a plant used for a range of medicinal purposes but also for ritual hallucination by adherents to the religion of the Bwiti. A chapter on the Bwiti would have been particularly illustrative for this volume because the use of hallucinogens by the Bwiti has been misunderstood by many and their members have had to confront opposition to its use by the Catholic Church as well as some national and local governments. In Gabon today however, Bwiti religion has become highly integrated into society up to the very highest levels (many government ministers, police officers and soldiers are adherents) and it is seen by many as fundamental to the new republic. Unfortunately no English-speaking authors were available to write for us as we prepared this collection. There are many other cases we would have liked to present – the use of Yaqona (Kava) by Fijian villagers who use the drug for purposes ranging from the social and the ceremonial to the spiritual but in highly integrated and non-problematic ways; or the use of Ebene, a hallucinogenic snuff, by the Yanomamö of the Amazon Basin of Venezuela and Brazil where a state of extreme intoxication is attained in order to reach the spirits important to that group and who provide them with protection from the world. We were nonetheless fortunate to gather contributors with specialist knowledge concerning a wide range of substances: some hallucinogenic and exotic; some familiar to the west but used in ways that are unfamiliar; or, rather more negatively, some very familiar in the west but now used in contexts where their damaging impact is unfamiliar and hence particularly destructive. All these differing accounts help to illustrate that drug use around the world can be understood in terms of normal behaviours rather than requiring diagnoses of pathology or social disease, or interpretation in terms of 'backwardness' or 'underdevelopment'. That these standard forms of explanation of the drug cultures of 'elsewhere' reflect stereotypes, condescension and xenophobia is a key theme of this book but it is also worth noting how they perpetuate the colonialist view of 'other' societies as sick or immature, like children in need of strong guidance.

Drug use *per se* is far from predictive of problematic behaviour or problematic social outcomes. Many of these examples of normal drug use are sufficiently important and/or sacred to those that practice them that one-dimensional international conventions aiming to prevent their use on the basis that they do not fit into a wider notion of human progress and/or the western notion of drug use, can be seen to be both myopic and unreasonably ethnocentric. Conversely, we also illustrate that there are cases where problematic behaviours and social outcomes follow from drug use that reflects, sometimes in stark relief, the consequences of post-colonial intrusion of western governmental and market economic power into formerly stable and harmonious cultural environments.

OVERVIEW OF THE CHAPTERS

Various forms of 'traditional' drug use have their roots in practices that are hundreds, if not thousands, of years old (the use of opium by rural dwellers in India or the coca chewers of Bolivia and Peru) but what is also interesting about some of the examples of traditional use revealed here is how they relate to much more recent practices. Indeed, as is the case with the aforementioned Bwiti of Africa, the three religious groups described by MacRae (Chapter 2) in Brazil are of only relatively recent origin. These (along with a number of other religious movements of American Indians who have adopted the use of peyote – a hallucinogenic cactus) are representative of various syncretic religions (usually a mix of Christianity and traditional local religions) that have emerged in numerous locations around the world and continue to do so. Moreover, it is the case that as 'modern' society becomes more receptive to 'alternatives', as with the disenchantment with modern medicine, the growth of such movements may become more common not only in less-developed communities but also in urban and developed worlds. MacRae's discussion of the use of Ayahuasca (a psychoactive brew made from indigenous plants) outlines how this has become a reality for many in urban, middle-class Brazil. In the USA, where American Indians are given dispensation to use an otherwise prohibited substance, debate is now taking place as to whether non-American Indians who join the religion may also use peyote (Salt Lake Tribune, 2003) while in Mexico, as Schaefer (Chapter 9) shows, the tradition of peyote use is threatened by the popularity of such religious movements in the USA. Various complex issues are raised here that should inform a more sensitive future policy on prohibition.

Prohibition is, by definition, a politically-inspired system of opposition to the use of drugs as a feature of everyday life (South, 1999). Hence, what is striking about many users in the societies considered here is the 'ordinariness' of the use of the substance in question within their practical routines and cosmologies of the world. Spedding, (Chapter 3) emphasises this when drawing the analogy between the common Bolivian' peasant invitation to 'drop round for chew' (of coca leaves) and the western 'come round for a cup of tea/coffee'. That most consumers will chew up to around half a pound of leaves a week (some much more) is indicative of levels of use. Although highly integrated into particular social groups in Bolivian society, Spedding notes how there is little social pressure to chew coca leaves, a contrast to alcohol consumption cultures in the west. Rivera's study (Chapter 4) is complementary and also notes this individual control over coca use. Spedding shows that while coca presents few social problems for Bolivian society, there are both national and international pressures to reduce its production and use. Predominately associated with stereotypes of Indians, rurality and the peasantry, for many Bolivians these are concomitant symbols of backwardness. A middle-class perspective that degrades coca use has been emergent for some time. In the past, spurious claims about coca's ability to 'retard' populations (and thus development) saw it included in the early international conventions and as a result of its association with cocaine, coca is seen as an international problem. However, for many growers and users it is not seen as 'their' problem but one created by the west. Like growers in the hemp industry who are trying to expand the commercial possibilities surrounding 'cannabis' plants, the coca growers wish to expand the commercial use of coca but see their attempts thwarted by policy that can see no social nor economic benefits arising from coca. Similar issues are raised in Rivera's evocative 'road-trip' ethnography but this also examines the more relaxed approach taken toward coca in Northern Argentina in contrast to that taken in Bolivia.

Whereas MacRae reveals how Ayahuasca is used in a highly ritualised fashion, circumscribed by formal procedures of when and how to act in order to access a more spiritual plane, Ganguly (Chapter 5) shows how opium is integrated into almost all facets of rural Indian society. Both Ganguly's depiction of highly integrated but non-problematic use of opium in Rajasthan and Varisco's (Chapter 6) portrayal of qat (khat) use in Yemen, are two examples of casual usage circumscribed by social custom and tradition, reflecting hundreds of years of common use.

Opium – viewed as addictive, dangerous, dehumanising and destructive to individuals and communities by the west – is used multifariously in the region of India described by Ganguly.

> The neonate is nurtured with a dosage of opium and thereafter males graduate to infancy and adolescence by taking the substance in family gatherings and, at times, with peers, on occasions of joy, celebration and conviviality. It is a social lubricant, has a symbolic place in birth, marriage and other ceremonies, and a great deal of its usage has been recognized as medicinal for generations in rural and urban Rajasthan. The multifarious uses to which opium is put only add to its social acceptance.

Ganguly acknowledges that opposition to opium use in India does exist and notes that not all Castes in those areas where use is common participate but opposition to use appears to arise from neither the health problems that follow (these being few) nor the social problems caused by the small number of 'addicts' (who appear to cause little in the way of social harm and are not seen in any way analogous to western 'dope-fiends'). This is normalised drug use in one of its most nonchalant forms.

Varisco relates a highly normalised activity which focuses mainly around the afternoon social gathering where qat (a plant with tender shoots and leaves that release a mild stimulant) is chewed by 'the majority of Yemeni men and a considerable number of Yemeni women' on a daily basis. Introduced to Yemen in the 14th or 15th centuries, qat is experienced as an aid to alertness, concentration, discussion, clear thinking, confidence and friendliness, and becomes part and parcel of a Yemeni's life around the age of puberty. In many senses, to chew is to do something quintessentially Yemeni. According to Varisco, this idea that 'to chew is to belong' has even more resonance today, as qat use has increased since the 1970s rather than declined. Varisco argues that qat chewing is a symbolic form of cultural or national resistance against other more powerful and 'modern' Arab and western states that have viewed Yemen as backward and in terms of disparagement. Given the historical importance of qat in Yemeni culture as well as its role as an article of trade, Varisco argues that it has now become a marker of national identity. As with opposition to opium use in India, attempts to curtail production in Yemen have largely come from 'above'. Westernised images mimicking anti-alcohol messages have become common but find little receptive support among farmers or users.

Many cultures are seen to lie beyond the western-defined 'frontier' separating the 'modern' and the 'backward', the 'developed' and the 'underdeveloped'; failures are attributed to 'laid-back attitudes' (Chevannes, Chapter 10), use of various drugs, and traditional as opposed to organised and innovative orientations to labour and markets. But, for better or worse, modernisation has been influential, it just has to articulate with other deeply embedded practices and values. As Varisco relates: 'In 1999 President Ali Abdullah Salih of Yemen announced that he was personally giving up qat and would use the time to learn computers. Yet it appears that most Yemenis are more wired to their old habits than the internet.'

Of further interest to this discussion is the way that each of the examples outlined so far all depend upon informal social constraints on what are considered to be inappropriate and appropriate uses of the substance in question. In each of the communities described, social sanctions abound as to what level of intoxication is reasonable and how to behave when intoxicated. That accepted drug use has its constraints (even within communities where formal controls are minimal) is significant to note, for in these communities informal controls seem both acceptable and effective. In the west, where controls tend to be highly formalised and where prohibited drug use is (at least in part) about breaking rules, it may be the case that social constraints mean less to those involved and thus the willingness to become intoxicated within reasonable limits is reduced. In the UK, the phenomenon of 'binge drinking' and readiness to mix alcohol with other drugs (Hobbs et al, 2003) suggests that the superiority of one cultural approach to intoxication over that of another is a matter for debate.

In this respect, while some cultures experience excessive problems relating to alcohol use, others appear to experience few problems despite drinking binges which may last several days and where levels of intoxication are reached that are uncommon in the west. Samson (Chapter 8) illustrates how the very real alcohol problems experienced by the Innu of Northern Labrador are inextricably co-related to the disintegration of their cultural *raison d'être* and the lifestyle problems this has left in its wake, but to scapegoat alcohol as a primary cause of the problems of the Innu is as facile as laying the problem of petrol inhalation by Australian aborigines at the door

21

of that intoxicant. The value of drawing upon cross-cultural evidence comes to the fore when it can show differing experiences of phenomena thought to be simple in their effects. Many years ago, Heath related the experience of the Camba of Bolivia, showing that rather than producing disinhibition and all the behaviours associated in western observations of alcohol intoxication, the Camba when drunk, at no time behaved very differently to their normal, non-intoxicated state. Heath's work was at first doubted and criticised but today, alongside other evidence from cross-cultural observations, this path-breaking work is accepted. Importantly, such work signals serious problems for those wishing to blame the simple *availability* of alcohol and other drugs for many of society's ills, for availability only matters in terms of how individuals *then use* what is available and, in turn, this is only understandable in terms of their relevant cultural norms and belief systems surrounding substances. Because this work continues to have such importance, Heath (Chapter 7) provides an update on both the Camba and their drinking but also on the implications that their lived experiences with alcohol have for the kind of research exemplified in this collection.

Providing a dramatic contrast, Samson describes how the post-colonial imposition (or emulation, see Beckerleg, (Chapter 11) of western models of 'progress' can have devastating impacts on traditional cultures, leading to the widespread take-up of destructive forms of substance use. The forced sedentarisation of the Innu and their removal from their land and traditional way of life is a violation of their human rights and yet it is they who are blamed for their plight and labelled as inadequate and ungrateful. Samson shows how heavy alcohol use becomes a two-fold expression of despair but also of power.

In the final three chapters, the themes of challenge and change are explored further. Schaefer (Chapter 9) relates how the centuries old, non-problematic culture of peyote use by the Wixárika in Mexico is based on their legends and the ritualised practice of hallucinogenic communication with the gods. The role of peyote in family rites of passage and community bonding has been vital for centuries. However, like the Innu, the Wixárika are literally experiencing the disenchantment produced by the toll of modernity and progress. In Chapter 10, Chevannes describes the rather more recent (comparatively-speaking) history of a culture of ganja use in Jamaica and the contemporary politics of domestic attempts to legally recognise the everyday and ordinary nature of use while being confronted by the political forces aligned behind the prohibitionist movement. Chevannes writes here as both a scholar of ganja history but also as an 'insider' in the government Inquiry into ganja use. Finally, Beckerleg (Chapter 11) provides an in-depth case-study of the impact on a Kenyan community of western legal investment and illegal criminal enterprise, both generating tourism, social divisions, and a thriving heroin trade. Of interest is how the problems of this heroin-damaged community mirror the family dilemmas and urban drug markets familiar in the west. Here, heroin has been the 'agent' of modernisation of a very undesirable nature.

LEARNING FROM NON-WESTERN, NON-PROBLEM FORMS OF DRUG USE

There may well be significant lessons to be learned from the study of non-western forms of drug use, both in relation to cultures which do not manifest western-style drug problems and from where problems do follow from insensitive and inappropriate western influences. This has been recognised by several recent commentators. For example, a cross-cultural approach can help to illuminate why 'international conventions and national laws can be inappropriate and ineffective in preventing traditional substance use' (Saxena, 1995: 14) or tradition-based drug-crop cultivation; while knowing more about other societies can 'teach us much that is relevant to prevention in our own' (Gossop, 1995: 16). From the western perspective, in their studies of recreational heroin users in the USA, Harding and Zinberg (1979) have argued that informal social sanctions can generate appropriate constraints where heroin use *per se* is not necessarily considered harmful and that these could be highly effective. More recently Harding (1998) has argued that western nations could reduce many harms associated with drugs (including alcohol) use if more appropriate sub-cultural norms and rituals could be encouraged and developed.

The chapters in this book recount examples of drug use in cultural contexts where much that is valued is threatened and much that is threatening has come about because of the loss of what once was valued. All of this is occurring in contexts that are 'beyond the west' in the sense that whether we consider developing nations or remote native communities, or the Innu, Aboriginal or Maori peoples of Canada, Australia or New Zealand, the point is that drug use in these contexts disrupts the western-centred perception of 'order' and 'values'. Put in a different way, what western eyes see as 'right' and 'wrong' can be a world away from the perceptions of other cultures or groups. The continuing power of the discursive understandings and operationalised systems of post-colonialism emphasise the need for the control of problems that are seen as residues of the past and impediments to 'modernisation'. Unacknowledged, of course, are the problems of drug use that follow from western interventions aiming to promote economic and cultural 'development'.

We would argue that a post-colonial perspective is emergent in the field of critical drugs research, aware of the distortions wrought by the dominant discourse and sensitive to the defining of 'other' states (in both the political and experiential senses). In relation to a different but not unrelated project, McLaughlin (2001: 214) has suggested that a post-colonial criminology could draw upon the following points, and their applicability for our purposes is clearly evident:

> At its most simple, the term 'post-colonial' refers to the historical period after colonialism and is linked to anti-colonization and de-colonization. A much broader conceptualisation of the term would include the analysis of the on-going relationship between the colonial and post-colonial . . . The post-colonial is vitally important for understanding the shifting cultural relationships between different parts of a thoroughly globalized world. *As a mode of critique and challenge, it provincializes much of what passes for general theory and points to its Eurocentrism.* (our emphasis).

We hope that in future work, a critical, post-colonial perspective will see further development.

In conclusion, there are two good rules about writing on the topic of drugs. The first is to avoid platitudes like 'since the dawn of time, man has taken mind-altering substances . . .' However, in this case, it is difficult not to break this rule as the project represented by this book is partly founded on the need to recognise the longevity of some cultural practices that have done no harm, and the damage caused when tradition and custom are suppressed. The second piece of advice is to avoid signing-up to the 'extremely unlikely', such as (regardless of the optimism of UN declarations) statements like 'we look forward to a drug-free world'. We can manage to avoid this because we do not expect to see such a state of affairs materialising in the near future. We do however think that it is conceivable that we could move toward a world where there are fewer drug *problems* and that this *could* be achieved in the near future. Regrettably the steps that we would need to take are unlikely to be supported by bodies such as the UN or US and UK governments.

1 This is not to say that condemnation of drug use originates in the west. China fought against the exportation of opium by western powers to its shores in the 19th century. Whilst it is difficult to separate sensationalist accounts from reality at any moment in the history of drug use (particularly drugs that come from 'elsewhere') it can be noted that many of the anecdotes reported by the Chinese at that time are none too dissimilar to those that have been common in the media and government education campaigns over the last 30 years in the west.

REFERENCES

Becker, H (1963) *Outsiders*, (New York: Free Press).
Cohen, S (1982) 'Western crime control models in the Third World: Benign or malignant?' pp. 85–119 in S. Spitzer and R. Simon (eds) *Research in Law, Deviance and Social Control*, vol. 4, (Greenwich, Conn.: JAI Press).

European Monitoring Centre for Drugs and Drug Addiction (2004a) *Illicit posses-sion of drugs and the law: Trends in the illicit possession of drugs*, European Legal Database on Drugs. http://eldd.emcdda.eu.int/trends/trends_possession.shtml

European Monitoring Centre for Drugs and Drug Addiction (2004b) *Illicit posses-sion of drugs and the law: Situation in the EU Member States*, European Legal Database on Drugs. http://eldd.emcdda.eu.int/trends/trends_possession_EU.shtml

Fassin, D (2001) 'Culturalism as ideology' pp. 300–317 in C. M.Obermeyer (ed) *Cultural Perspectives on Reproductive Health*, (Oxford: Oxford University Press).

Gossop, M. (1995) 'Counting the costs as well as the benefits of drug control laws', *Addiction*, 90, 16–17.

Harding, W. M. and Zinberg, N. E. (1977) 'The Effectiveness of the Subculture in Developing Rituals and Social Sanctions for Controlled Drug Use' in Brian M. DuToit, (ed). *Drugs, Rituals and Altered States of Consciousness,* (Rotterdam: A.A. Balkema)

Harding, W. M. (1998) 'Informal Social Controls and the Liberalization of Drug Laws and Policies', in Ross Coomber (ed.) *The Control of Drugs and Drug Users: Reason or Reaction*, (Amsterdam: Harwood Academic Publishers)

Hobbs, D., Hadfield, P., Lister, S. and Winlow, S. (2003) *Bouncers: Violence and Governance in the Night-time Economy*. (Oxford: Oxford University Press).

Illich, I (1977) *Limits to Medicine: Medical Nemesis*, (Harmondsworth: Penguin)

Maher, L. and Dixon, D. (1999) 'Policing and public health: law enforcement and harm minimization in a street-level drug market'.*British Journal of Criminology*, 39(4).

McAllister, W. (2000) *Drug Diplomacy in the Twentieth Century*, (London: Rout-ledge)

McLaughlin, E. (2001) 'Post-colonial criminology'. In McLaughlin, E. and Muncie, J. Editors. *The Sage Dictionary of Criminology*, (London: Sage).

Nadelman, E. (1989) 'Drug prohibition in the United States: costs, consequences and alternatives.' *Science*, 245: 939–47.

Parker, H. (2000) How young Britons obtain their drugs: drugs transactions at the point of consumption. In Natarajan, M. and Hough, M. Editors. *Illegal Drug Markets: From Research to Prevention Policy*, (New York: Criminal Justice Press)

Pearson, G. (2001) Normal drug use. *Substance Use and Misuse* 36, (1 & 2), 167–200

Salt Lake Tribune (2003) 'Justices hear peyote arguments', by Elizabeth Neff, http://www.sltrib.com/2003/Nov/11052003/utah/108401.asp

Samorini, G. (1995) 'The Bwiti religion and the psychoactive plant *Tabernanthe iboga* (Equatorial Africa)', *Integration*, 5: 105–114.

Saxena, S. (1995) 'A stroke of distinctive colour', *Addiction*, 90, 13–14.

Sherratt, A. (1995) 'Introduction: peculiar substances' pp. 1–10 in J. Goodman,

Lovejoy P. and Sherratt A. (eds) *Consuming Habits: Drugs in History and Anthro-pology*, (London: Routledge)

South, N. (Ed.) (1999) *Drugs: Cultures, Controls and Everyday Life*. (Sage: Lon-don and Thousand Oaks, Ca.).

South, N (2004/5) 'Managing work, hedonism and 'the borderline' between the legal and illegal markets: Two case studies of recreational heavy drug users', forth-coming, *Addiction Research and Theory*.

United Nations General Assembly Special Session. (1998) *Action Plan on Interna-tional Cooperation on the Eradication of Illicit Drug Crops and on Alternative Development,* from Resolutions adopted at United Nations General Assembly Special Session on the World Drug Problem New York, 8–10 June 1998. http://www.tni.org/drugs/ungass/docs/un1998.htm

United Nations General Assembly Special Session (1998) *Political Declaration: Guiding Principles of Drug Demand Reduction and Measures to Enhance International Cooperation to Counter the World Drug Problem,* from Resolutions adopted at United Nations General Assembly Special Session on the World Drug Problem New York, 8–10 June 1998. http://www.unodc.org/pdf/report_1999–01–01_1.pdf

Young, J (1971) *The Drugtakers: The Social Meaning of Drug Use*, (London: Paladin)

Chapter Two

THE RITUAL USE OF AYAHUASCA BY THREE BRAZILIAN RELIGIONS

Edward MacRae[1]

INTRODUCTION

The native inhabitants of the Western Amazon have used Ayahuasca, a psychoactive brew made from the Bannisteriosis caapi vine and the Psychotria viridis leaf, for many purposes since time immemorial[2]. The psychoactive effects of this drink are reminiscent of those of LSD and vary according to the dosage, set and setting in which it is taken. Dobkin de Rios lists some of them as follows: altered visual perception, greater sensitivity to sound, feelings of depersonalisation, synaesthesia, etc (Dobkin de Rios 1990:178). Conceiving of this brew as a means of opening the human perception of the spiritual world, shamans have used it for a large range of purposes such as: the diagnosis and treatment of a large variety of ailments, divination, hunting, warfare, and even as an aphrodisiac (Dobkin de Rios, 1972). Although its use probably originated among the inhabitants of the rain forest, ayahuasca was taken to the Andean highlands and can now also be found in many of the Brazilian and other South American large urban centres, as well as in the United States, Holland, Spain, Italy and even Japan.

The use of ayahuasca and other so called 'teacher plants', by Amazonian tribal societies and by Mestizo healers on the outskirts of Peruvian Amazonian cities like Puccalpa, Tarapoto and Iquitos, has been well documented by a large number of scholars. The use of this psychoactive brew by Brazilian religious groups has also been the subject of many studies, mainly in the field of the anthropology of religion, dealing with classical anthropological themes such as cosmology and ritual, shamanism and trance. Others emphasise the comparative approach, dwelling on the relation between

27

cultures (Amazonian and urban) and on the comparison of symbolic systems (Labate 2002:266). This article aims to provide a brief overview of this material and to call attention to the elements of this ritual use that make these religions a good example of what, following Norman Zinberg, might be called 'controlled use' of psychoactive substances (Zinberg 1984:5).

Before one can understand the functioning and the cultural significance of this religious group, one must take into account some of the particularities of Brazilian culture and religiosity. Brazilian society is the result of a rich mixture of European, Indian and African elements. The Portuguese colonization of the region concentrated itself mainly along the Atlantic coastline and, although its influence extended into the interior and almost to the Andes, only recently have the distant frontier and Amazonian rainforest areas been fully integrated into the life of the nation. In spite of the fact that Portuguese incursions were often able to break down traditional Indian social organizations, very little was put in their place in an official manner. Even the presence of the Church was sporadic and unsystematic in most of that region, giving rise to the development of many unorthodox religious movements, which mixed Indian, Catholic, African and assorted Esoteric elements (Maués and Villacorta 2001:49).

As a result of this, although the majority of the Brazilian population is nominally Catholic, there is widespread tolerance and even active participation in a wide variety of sects or cults of different origins. In spite of this apparently free and easy attitude towards religion and of the rapacious materialism that governs social interaction, most Brazilians seem to have some feeling for spirituality and, although they may have difficulty in explaining what they actually believe in, few will call themselves atheists. The precariousness of the public health system provides further encouragement for a large proportion of the poor (and even many rich people) to resort to spiritual healers when faced with illness.

THE SANTO DAIME

It is in this context that we must view the founding of the Santo Daime religious movement in 1930, in Rio Branco, capital city of the, then, Territory of Acre. The founder of this religion was a Black rubber tapper called Raimundo Irineu Serra, who had come to the Amazon from the state of Maranhão, in Northern Brazil, in 1912. It is probable that he was first initiated into the use of ayahuasca by a Peruvian Mestizo healer while working in the forest in the mid 1910s. After taking ayahuasca for some time he began having visions in which he saw a female figure, which he later came to associate with Our Lady of the Conception, whom he also called The Queen of the Forest. She gave him instructions on healing and handed him a new religious doctrine which had a pronounced Catholic flavour although it also incorporated certain Amerindian, African, spiritualist and esoteric elements such as the notions of reincarnation, the law of karma and the cult of assorted elemental spirits.

Several years later, after living in different parts of Acre and after taking part in the setting up of an ayahuasca centre in the town of Brasileia, he eventually moved to the regional capital where he started up his own church. Mestre Irineu (Master Irineu), as his followers and patients knew him, became famous for his healing powers and after some time his influence began to spread in Rio Branco. His initial following was made up of displaced rubber tappers who, after the decline of the Amazonian rubber boom, had been forced to migrate to the cities of the region, where they faced great difficulties integrating into urban society. In a few years his influence became widespread throughout the city and even powerful local politicians came to him in search of healing and electoral support. With the help of such well-placed friends, he was eventually able to acquire a plot of land where he built a church and started an agricultural community with his followers. His church and the area around it, which were at the top of a small rise, came to be known as 'Alto Santo' (Holy Heights) and his followers as 'daimistas' (MacRae 1992:61).

Acre was very sparsely inhabited at that time and was yet to undergo the process of colonization that has now made it into an integral part of the Brazilian nation. Rio Branco was a small frontier town and its outskirts, where the Santo Daime movement developed, were still covered by the forest. Some anthropologists argue that the doctrine spread by 'Mestre Irineu', played a key role in the transition from life in the isolation of the forest to urban conviviality, undergone by the local population after the end of the rubber boom (Monteiro da Silva 1983). As such, the Santo Daime doctrine is an integral element in Acrean culture, even though most of its inhabitants may nominally profess to be Catholic.

Mestre Irineu's contribution to a more Westernised use of ayahuasca included the replacing of the ambiguous traditional Amerindian and Mestizo shamanic power ethic for the traditional Christian values of unconditional love for one's neighbours and the veneration of Catholic saints. As for the ayahuasca brew, which he renamed Daime[3] or Santo Daime (Holy Daime); he likened it to the Christian sacrament, considering it to be 'The Blood of Christ'. His doctrine allied beliefs associated to traditional ayahuasca shamanism to old practises of Popular Catholicism, but this mixing of traditions leads to changes in the meanings attributed to them. Thus while the Santo Daime doctrine may be understood by its followers as 'the doctrine of The Virgin and of Jesus Christ', and Mestre Irineu appears as a messenger of Jesus, at the same time Christ is seen to be closely associated to a plant. The old shamanic logic was linked to typically Christian themes like 'eternal salvation' and the rejection of worldly concerns (Goulart 2002:336).

Mestre Irineu also developed a series of new rituals he claimed to have received in his visions. They almost invariably involve the sacramental use of Daime and display marked Christian influence, although Amerindian and African traits are also to be detected. They vary according to the occasion and may be celebratory 'hymnals', meditational 'concentrations', exorcisms, 'healing works', funeral 'masses' and ceremonies during which the sacrament is ritually prepared (MacRae 1998:105). Mestre Irineu left few documents and his church has no official scriptures apart from his hymns, which are considered by his followers to be a Third Testament.

It is said that all of his doctrine is contained in these hymns, and that they only reveal their full message when heard under the influence of Daime. This has led the Santo Daime teachings to be called a 'musical doctrine'. The hymns are conceived of as having been received by Mestre Irineu from God and the Virgin and are remarkably similar to those of the Catholic Church. They reflect a belief in Jesus Christ as the Saviour and reiterate traditional Catholic values and social standards. Every Santo Daime 'work' starts and ends with the Lord's Prayer and the Catholic 'Hail Mary'.

The Church rituals, which are invariably accompanied by the singing of hymns, frequently involve communal dancing as well. In this case they continue to be highly structured performances, with fixed steps and predetermined places for all, with a rigid separation according to sex and age group.

After Mestre Irineu's death, in 1971, his movement suffered defections and splits. Nowadays there are several separate religious organizations that trace their origins to him, but most are quite small with little more than a hundred followers each. Each tends to stress the fact that it maintains Mestre Irineu's teachings in all their purity, accusing the others of introducing illegitimate novelties. Several call themselves 'Alto Santo' and claim to be the only ones to justifiably do so.

Of all the break-away groups the one to have become best known is the Centro Eclético Fluente Luz Universal Raimundo Irineu Serra (CEFLURIS), started by another Amazonian rubber tapper, Sebastião Mota de Melo, now better known as Padrinho (Godfather) Sebastião. He was considered a powerful spiritual healer himself and headed a community, in another part of the Rio Branco outskirts, which was known as 'Colônia Cinco Mil'. In the mid-1960s he went to Mestre Irineu in search of healing for himself. After taking the brew for some time, he was given permission to hold Santo Daime ceremonies among his followers. On Mestre Irineu's death he declared his independence from the new leaders of the Alto Santo community and gradually introduced a series of doctrinal and ritual innovations of his own.

Unlike the other Daime leaders, Padrinho Sebastião was very welcoming towards young newcomers from outside the Amazon area. As a result the size of the congregations increased and from the 1980s onwards a number of centres were then set up in several southern metropolises like Rio de

Janeiro, São Paulo, Florianopolis, Belo Horizonte, as well as in more rural districts. More recently, especially in the 1990s, Santo Daime churches following his spiritual line began to be set up abroad and are now to be found in many South American and European countries, in the United States and Japan. CEFLURIS is now the biggest of the churches that claim to follow Mestre Irineu and has more than 5,000 followers around the world.

Stressing his autonomy in regard to the Alto Santo, but remaining faithful to the old shamanic Amazonian traditions, Padrinho Sebastião occasionally introduced other 'teacher-plants' in his works. He emphasized that in order that they might grant access to spiritual secrets they should be correctly used in a prescribed ritual manner and not as mere profane entertainment. Of these other entheogens[4], the one he most used was Cannabis, which he had been introduced to by some of the young hippie newcomers he received in his community. According to Padrinho Sebastião, the spiritual name of this plant was 'Santa Maria' and he claimed that it corresponded to the feminine spiritual force of the Virgin Mother, counterbalancing the masculine Daime, which corresponded to God the Father[5].

For some time, Santa Maria was used in 'concentration works', with a specific ritual aimed at healing[6]. Although the more casual profane use of the herb came under frequent criticism in the community it nevertheless continued to occur. In October 1981 the Federal Police invaded the Colônia 5.000 and its sacred 'Santa Maria Gardens', as the Cannabis plantations were known, were burned and some of the leaders, including Padrinho Sebastião, prosecuted. This also gave rise to a series of official measures against all groups using ayahuasca, even those who strongly disapproved of the use of Cannabis and considered it to be a mere 'drug'. This persecution culminated with an explicit prohibition of the use of ayahuasca, which for a few months was placed on the Brazilian official list of illicit substances. However, political pressure led to the setting up of a special official research group to look into the use of the brew which ended up by recommending that its use be liberated for religious purposes. Since then the ayahuasca religions have enjoyed official toleration on the part of Brazilian authorities (MacRae 1994:31). This led Padrinho Sebastião to suspend the use of Cannabis in official rituals and to recommend his followers to do likewise.

He later led his followers to a distant area in the neighbouring State of Amazonas where they founded the village 'Céu do Mapiá', in the heart of the rainforest. For CEFLURIS, Santa Maria, although banned, continued to be regarded as sacred and its semi-ritualised use persists to this day in informal gatherings of some of his followers. Although certain ritual elements are normally observed, as there are few formal occasions for its fully ceremonial use, the prescriptions governing its use cannot be firmly established. Thus, it becomes difficult to set ritual limits with regard to correct time and place for smoking and its use often verges on the merely recreational. The existing prohibitionist official drug policy also tends to bring together the religious devotees of Santa Maria and members of the drug trafficking underworld.

On occasion their persistence in the sacred and profane use of Cannabis has led certain of his followers to have trouble with the police and even to be sent to jail, thus helping increase the prejudice and ill will with which his church is frequently seen by the other ayahuasca religions in Brazil (MacRae 1998:325–338). In Holland, on the other hand, where Cannabis use is not subject to repression, the local followers of Padrinho Sebastião hold Santa Maria rituals regularly, and during a period when the use of ayahuasca was banned in the country, even used it very successfully as a substitute sacrament (Groisman 2000).

Every Daime ritual or 'work' is conceived of as an opportunity for learning and healing, as well as for the indoctrination of the spirits present either in the 'material' or in the 'astral' planes. Although there are specific rituals for different occasions or different needs, they all involve taking the brew and entering into an altered state of consciousness in a social and physical setting designed to contain and guide the 'voyages'. The emphasis on self-control has led anthropologists to consider them to be 'rituals of order' promoting group and hierarchical cohesion and a search for harmony both within and without (Couto, 2002).

Many factors contribute to this controlling effect, such as:

a) Dietary and behavioural prescriptions that must be observed during the three days that precede and that follow the taking of the drink, thus setting the stage for an unusual event that escapes the daily routine.

b) A hierarchical social organization in which a 'commander' or 'godfather' is recognized as the leader of the session, aided by a body of 'controllers', who are responsible for the maintenance of order and obedience to the leader.

c) Control over the dosage of the brew to be taken by participants. The drink is poured by an experienced member of the group who takes into account the participant's state of consciousness, size, age, sex and any other relevant information.

d) Ritual spatial organization and behavioural control. There is a central table/altar where the double armed Cross of Caravacca and other religious symbols mark the sacred nature of the event. All those taking part are given a specific place in the room, usually a rectangle drawn on the ground, where they must remain, grouped by sex, age, and, in certain more traditional areas, sexual status (virgins and non-virgins).

Uniforms of a sober cut, to be worn by all, stress the unity of the group and help maintain a mood of seriousness. The movements of those taking part are rigidly prescribed and one of the main duties of the so called 'controllers' (fiscais) is to ensure obedience to the posture recommended for the seated 'works' (raised heads and relaxed and immobile arms and legs) or the correct performance of a few simple steps during the ceremonies that include dancing.

Another important controlling element is the music, sung and played during most of the ceremonies, which helps harmonize the group, through marked rhythms and voices in unison. This use of music, although inspired by Catholic ceremonies, also harks back to ancient shamanic customs from which the ritual taking of ayahuasca originates. Singing, dancing and the use of percussion instruments with a strong, repetitive beat, are powerful aids in bringing about altered states of consciousness, and are thought to act as a way of invoking spirits. The words of the 'hymns' that are sung direct the 'voyages' in the desired directions and help relieve mental or physical ill feelings.

The hymns also help in the interpretation of the 'mirações' (visions or experiences people have during the Daime 'works'). They help to create connections between the lived experiences and the magical or mythical symbols, with which they become invested, something of great importance in maintaining the unity of the group. The Catalan anthropologist Josep Maria Fericgla, working on the Indian use of ayahuasca, considers this to be a psychic or spiritual function of symbols that was lost by Western societies when they abandoned their traditional ways of organizing unconscious drives and of using these 'sources of renovation' for individual and collective benefit (Fericgla 1989:13).

Whereas the Alto Santo churches usually have small followings, mostly drawn from the poorer sectors of society, the CEFLURIS churches nowadays are more middle class and relatively more prosperous. In recent years they have reserved some of their financial resources to develop plantations of Bannisteriopsis and Psychotria, so as to diminish somewhat their dependence on predatory gatherings in the wild, a practice still prevalent among the smaller Amazonian churches. Nevertheless, in spite of their veneration for the 'Queen of the Forest', it is still common for 'daimistas' of all groups to adopt the method of predatory harvesting methods used before the original vegetation was burned down to make room for cattle raising. Thus they still occasionally organize parties to enter the forest and bring back the vines and the leaves needed to produce a batch of Daime large enough to last them for a number of weeks.

CEFLURIS, however, has made a serious effort to concentrate most of its ayahuasca production in the Céu do Mapiá village, around which they have made fairly large plantations of Bannisteriopsis caapi and Psychotria viridis. Although not yet enough to make all the brew needed to supply the numerous followers of the group, spread around Brazil and the world, these measures have, nevertheless, relieved CEFLURIS from the need to constantly search for new sites in the forest where the plants might be found growing wild. Due to the policy of concentrating most of its production of ayahuasca in this area, there are now a number of people living there who have specialized in this activity and derive their livelihood from it. Although the ritual production of Daime and its distribution around the country consume much time and labour, leaving a relatively small profit margin, and this method is more efficient and less damaging to nature, nevertheless, CEFLURIS is left open to accusations of 'ayahuasca trafficking', on the part of other ayahuasca groups that are better able to produce their own supplies locally.

THE BARQUINHA

This is another religion whose origins may be traced back to Mestre Irineu, although its founder is considered to be Daniel Pereira de Matos, the son of former slaves and a master of many trades (including sailoring, boat building, tailoring, carpentry, bricklaying, shoe-making, poetry and music making). In his youth he was a sailor and left his native State of Maranhão, to travel, like many others, along the Amazonian waterways in search of a better life in Acre and eventually settled in Rio Branco.

When he first arrived there, he led a very irregular life and was noted for his bouts of drunkenness and for composing and singing songs about love, friendship and desire. All this changed after he experienced two episodes of revelation. The first one occurred when he fell into a drunken slumber not far from the River Acre and had a vision of two angels who brought him a blue book with instructions. The second revelation came some time later, while he was undergoing healing in the Santo Daime church led by Mestre Irineu, and received a similar message.

This led him to start his own religious group in 1945, using ayahuasca that was given him by Mestre Irineu. Initially he set up a small chapel in the forest on the outskirts of Rio Branco, where he attended the poorer members of the community such as rubber tappers and huntsmen (Figueiredo 1996:41). He called this chapel 'Capelinha de São Francisco' (The little Chapel of Saint Francis) and when, shortly after his death, it was rebuilt and enlarged it became known as 'Barquinha' (Little Boat). It has continued to grow but remains in the same place and in 2002 was considered to have about 500 followers (Araujo 2002: 501). After his death, in 1958, as happened with Mestre Irineu's followers, his congregation split up and at present six different religious groups in the Rio Branco area trace their original inspiration to his teachings[7]. Other new groups are in the process of consolidation in the State of Acre and there are also affiliated centres in Rio de Janeiro and Bahia States. Altogether at the moment there must be some 1,000 Barquinha followers.

Whereas Mestre Irineu's church modelled itself somewhat on the military organization he had known in his youth, former sailor Daniel Pereira de Matos imparted a more nautical imagery to his. One example of this is the idea that the followers of the religion are 'sailors in the holy sea' aboard the 'little boat of the Holy Cross'.

Of all the ayahuasca religions, this is probably the richest in terms of imagery and ritual. Like the others, it demands that regular participants in its ceremonies follow a series of dietary and behavioural prescriptions and wear uniform, in this case of a vaguely nautical style. There are five different types of uniform to be worn in different rituals (Figueiredo 1996:113). Music plays a great part in the rituals but, unlike what happens in the Santo Daime rituals, where all those taking part are expected to join in the communal hymn singing, it is the leader who sings alone the long Barquinha 'psalms', invoking the assistance of Catholic saints, Afro-Brazilian and Indian-Mestizo spiritual beings.

True to the shamanic origins of its doctrine, much of the Barquinha activities are directed towards the healing of assorted ills that may range from severe physical diseases to problems of a more psychosocial nature such as alcoholism or unemployment. Unlike the other ayahuasca religions, there is also a strong emphasis on removing evil spirits and countering witchcraft.

The Barquinha is the ayahuasca religion that deals most comfortably with episodes of spirit possession, attributing a central role to this type of trance in some of its rituals and in its general doctrine. This in turn lends a special importance to certain members of the group who perform as mediums during the ceremonies and exert varying degrees of authority in the centre's spiritual and profane affairs.

In Barquinha ceremonies one may simultaneously come across spirit possession and shamanic flight, as well as intermediate forms of altered consciousness. This counters the position, held by Mircea Eliade (see Lewis 1977:56) and followers, that these two different types of trance, one considered to be of African origin and the other Siberian and Amerindian, are essentially different and mutually exclusive. In Barquinha ceremonies spirit possession may occur while at the same time the medium undergoes a shamanic flight and loses neither consciousness nor memory, as would be expected in more orthodox cases of possession trance. In other cases, some of the participants may go through a shamanic flight while others undergo spirit possession.

One of the main Barquinha rituals, the 'Trabalhos de Caridade' (Charity Works) is a good instance of this. Here Daime is taken by a number of participants who then seat themselves, either around a large cross-shaped table by the altar (senior members) or on pews or chairs ranged in traditional church style. They then proceed to enter into deep meditation to the sound of prayers and 'psalms', recited and sung by the presiding leader. Meanwhile, in a back room another group of participants, made up of well-trained mediums, having taken ayahuasca, undergo spirit possession and, in their new personae, proceed to attend to people who come in search of healing.

They claim to do this by dominating and indoctrinating the dark suffering spirits who are conceived to be the cause of the patients' ills. The spiritual beings operating through the mediums are thought to tap the energy emanating from the front of the church to use in these spiritual struggles.

In another type of ceremony, performed in an open area adjoining the church building, participants dance under the effect of Daime in a fairly free manner, as if inviting spirit possession. Most of those present will go through classical shamanic flight experiences, while some may eventually pass on to a possession trance. This also implies shifts between expanded consciousness and total unconsciousness and forgetfulness. So wide is the range of states of consciousness that may occur that these ceremonies are recommended as good training in self-knowledge and mediumship.

The Barquinha centres, although generally independent of each other, are all located in the Rio Branco region and their followers are drawn predominantly from the local poor. This may help to explain the prevalence of certain characteristics, of African and Indian origin, which are often ignored or rejected by the middle-class ethos now prevailing in some of the other ayahuasca religions. Their relative smallness and poor social and economic status also make it more difficult for them to organize less predatory manners of producing the brew, which they too call Daime. Since they do not own expanses of land in which they might have extensive plantations of Bannisteriopsis caapi and Psychotria viridis, they must resort to gathering them in the forest where they grow wild. As a result of the severe deforestation occurring in the region, and the growing demand for the ayahuasca ingredients, the ritualised gathering expeditions must now go increasingly further afield[8].

THE UNIÃO DO VEGETAL

This is the newest of the Brazilian ayahuasca religions but it is also the one with the largest following, counting an estimated number of 8,000 associates. Its founder was José Gabriel da Costa or, as he later came to be known, Mestre Gabriel, a rubber tapper who migrated from his native North Eastern State of Bahia to Guaporé (now State of Rondonia) in 1943. During his many travels in this Amazonian area by the Bolivian border, he underwent much hardship and privation. Eventually he made a name for himself as a spiritual leader and healer and, for a time, was head of an Afro-Brazilian religious group where he also performed as a medium undergoing spirit possession. In 1959 another rubber tapper, who belonged to a tradition of Mestizo shamanism, introduced him to ayahuasca. After taking the brew three times he felt ready to make his own ayahuasca and to use it in religious ceremonies of his own (Brissac 2002:536).

Some time later, in 1961, he renounced his activities as a spirit possession medium and declared that he was recreating an ancient order that he had known in previous incarnations and which he called the União do Vegetal. The following year he moved to the regional capital Porto Velho where he continued his spiritual practices till 1971 when he died (Brissac 2002:537).

The new religion took on the official name of Centro Espírita Beneficiente União do Vegetal (Benevolent Spiritist Centre Union of the Vegetable) and during the following years a number of new affiliated centres were set up in many different parts of the country, notably in urban centres outside the Amazonian region and, more recently, in Europe and North America.

A new type of member began to be recruited and the organization took on an increasingly urban middle-class character, which was further stimulated by a policy of rigid selection of those who were to be allowed to take part in the ceremonies. Since all members are expected to contribute with a fixed proportion of their income, the organization soon became quite prosperous and their concern to make socially acceptable their religious use of what was commonly viewed as a hallucinogen led to the adoption of fairly conservative political stances and to the official rejection of any healing activities. Their desire to keep on good terms with the medical profession has also led them to develop a more scientific stance and to support research efforts to study the physiological effects of the brew[9]. They are also quite zealous about establishing a clear difference between themselves and other ayahuasca users who not only maintain the old shamanic claims about the curative properties of the brew, but, in some cases, accept spirit possession in their ceremonies or admit the concomitant ritual use of other plants, namely tobacco and cannabis.

The União do Vegetal (or UDV as it is commonly known) considers itself to be an initiate order and its doctrine is transmitted orally in a highly selective manner. This establishes a hierarchy of initiates consisting of four ranks, of which the highest, that of the 'Mestres', has five further subdivisions (Gentil 2002:518). This reflects their belief that spirits undergo a process of evolution during a succession of incarnations. It has an eclectic doctrine where African and Indian notions mingle with European Spiritism and Popular Catholicism. During different types of ceremonies, religious teachings and secrets are gradually revealed to the followers (Andrade 2002).

Much attention is given to language and there are strong prescriptions regarding words that may or may not be used. Thus the brew is known as 'Hoasca' or 'Vegetal' and it must be 'drunk' (bebido) and never 'taken' (tomado), the more common usage in colloquial conversation in Brazil. This also means that when the ceremonies take place in other countries, they must be carried out in Portuguese.

Members of the 'União' may progress through the ranks of the hierarchy according to their ability to memorize the teachings in exactly the same words as they were imparted, and in accordance to their compliance to the religious statutes and to their maintenance of 'appropriate' behaviour in their everyday life. Members are subjected to constant 'monitoring' and misbehaviour, regardless of the culprit's rank, is frequently punished with demotion, suspension or expulsion. Parameters governing appropriate behaviour are fairly conservative and include abstinence from drink, tobacco, sexual misdemeanours, as well as dancing or attending the ceremonies of other ayahuasca religions. In order to reach the higher echelons members must be married and, with the sole exception of the founder's widow, must be male.

During the ceremonies all members must wear uniform. This consists of a green shirt for most, with letters or a star embroidered on the pocket to identify the different ranks. A very few high-ranking members wear blue shirts. While all men must wear white trousers, women may wear either skirts or trousers, as long as they are the appropriate yellow.

The ceremonies are fairly simple and tend to follow a general pattern. There is a central table around which sit the higher-ranking members. At the head of the table the presiding 'Mestre' often sits under an arch. There are few religious symbols and, apart from an occasional cross, candle or vase with flowers, the table is usually kept bare. Other participants of the session sit in a wider circle around the table, regardless of rank or gender.

The brew is distributed among all those present, each having his own cup, but it may only be drunk once all have been served and a ritual formula pronounced. The following half hour, while the brew has not yet begun to take effect, is taken up by the reading of the rules and statutes of the União do Vegetal. At the end of this time a 'call' is usually made to summon spiritual guides to preside over the ceremony. The 'Mestre' then proceeds in the anticlockwise direction the 'force' is deemed to take, asking each individual participant if he is feeling the effects of the brew and then the session is considered to have really begun. During the next few hours the leader intones different 'calls', verses meant to attract different spiritual beings and to affect the course of the voyage embarked on by the participants. During the session the 'Mestre' may order one or more further distributions of the drink.

The effect of the brew is known by the followers of this religion as 'burracheira'[10], which was considered by Mestre Gabriel to be a 'strange force', or the presence of the 'force' and the 'light' of the Vegetal in the consciousness of those drinking the brew. It is a trance in which there is no loss of consciousness but enlightenment and the perception of an unknown force. There is a heightening of the person's feelings, perceptions and consciousness (Gentil 2002:537). At a given moment during the session, the presiding 'master' announces that he is willing to answer questions. The participants may then ask him questions about different doctrinal points that may be puzzling them. 'Speaking under the force', the master usually proceeds to give fairly elaborate answers, often couched in vivid and poetic imagery and occasionally adopting a sermonizing or chastising tone. Under the state of consciousness brought about by the brew, these questions and answers take on a multidimensionality that endows every word and every image with many layers of meaning able to reach the most unconscious recesses of the mind.

The ceremonies alternate between such moments of teaching and indoctrination and others of introspection and meditation. At certain points the silence may be broken by the 'callings' intoned by the leader or by recorded music, which aim at deepening or lightening the voyage. The music is generally New Age or popular songs whose rhythm and words are deemed appropriate. On occasion, recordings may be played of Mestre Gabriel himself giving lectures, or União do Vegetal secrets may be revealed to those deemed fit for promotion to the higher echelons.

As often happens in all ayahuasca religious ceremonies, during the session some participants may feel unwell or suffer from bouts of diarrhoea or vomiting. They may then be helped by more experienced members of the group, previously appointed for this task who may accompany them out of the room to go to the toilet or to wash up. These episodes are quite common and are usually considered to be a form of spiritual and physical cleansing.[11]

After about four hours the session is deemed to end and the 'Mestre' again proceeds in an anticlockwise direction, this time asking each participant how his experience had been. The answers are laconic and follow a standard formula. He then returns to the head of the table and pronounces a closing prayer. After this the participants are free to talk to each other and spend the next half-hour informally, discussing the ceremony among themselves, while they partake of some light food and refreshments (Henman 1986:229).

The União do Vegetal is particularly careful about the production and the distribution of the brew. Since its members take very seriously the injunction that ayahuasca must not be commercialised, there is a strong emphasis on every regional centre attempting to be self-sufficient as regards producing the brew. In order to rise to the higher ranks of the hierarchy, members must learn the intricacies of planting, harvesting, cleaning and cooking the ingredients. Every centre strives to have its own plantation of Bannisteriopsis caapi and Psychotria viridis, although on occasion they may receive supplies from other regional centres or from the Amazon itself. This self-sufficiency makes members of the União do Vegetal very critical of the way the other religions are dependent on shipments of the component plants or, more commonly, of the brew itself, coming from their regional religious centres close to the forest.

AYAHUASCA RELIGIONS AS AIDS
TO SOCIAL INTEGRATION

As long as the use of ayahuasca was confined to the distant Amazonian region it was out of sight and out of mind for the metropolis-oriented Brazilian authorities and opinion makers. However, the spread of these movements among the urban middle class youth soon had the local moral entrepreneurs on the rampage. In 1986, pending further studies, the government decided to ban the use of ayahuasca. However a set of favourable occurrences led to the setting up of a liberally oriented official study group which after six months research produced a paper calling for the repeal of the ban on a nationwide level (Sá 1996). Among other arguments they pointed out that the members of the different religious groups had been found to be orderly and to lead their lives according to the accepted social values and that there had been no proven damage to health caused by taking the brew. Such findings have been further confirmed by several other studies conducted since then by Brazilian and foreign scientists who continue to consider the brew to be relatively harmless (Andrade et al. 2002, Aranha et al. 1991, Callaway et al.1994, Costa et al. 1995, Grob et al. 1996, Mackenna et al. 1998). The use of ayahuasca has remained legal in spite of occasional attempts to ban it on the part of more conservative sectors of Brazilian society and now, after long judicial disputes, is also officially recognized as a *bona fide* religious practise in Holland and in Spain.

The orderly functioning of these religious organizations helps validate a more tolerant approach to the drug question which places less emphasis on the purely pharmacological aspects of the question and gives more attention to the physical, social and cultural setting in which the use of psychoactive substances occurs. In spite of occasional problems that may always be expected to occur when large numbers of people come together for religious purposes, whether or not these include the ingestion of consciousness altering substances, the ayahuasca religions seem to confirm the effectiveness of social control in determining the consequences of drug use.

When they were originally started in the Amazon, these ayahuasca religions played an important role in helping migrants from the forest adapt and integrate into their new urban environment. Nowadays, however, most of their followers come from a different socio-cultural background. They are, generally speaking, young urban adults with secondary or university level education and usually lower middle-class incomes. Although they may face different problems from the original members, who were, in their majority, very poor rubber tappers newly settled on the outskirts of Amazonian towns, they have their own economic and existential problems. In Brazil today the young of all classes face a rapidly changing society, growing unemployment and a breakdown in the old family structures. Sexual and work ethics have undergone deep changes and traditional religion has lost much of its cohesive function[12].

Young people in Brazil have to cope with the very quick cultural changes occurring around them with regard to the sexual and work ethics as well as the breakdown of traditional family organization and values. In this somewhat hostile milieu belonging to these ayahuasca taking religious groups may provide them with a sense of social, psychological and spiritual identity, which for many is very familiar and reminiscent of their early introduction to traditional Christian doctrine.

The disciplined use of ayahuasca also provides congregates with a safe, well-mapped route to the kind of transcendental spiritual experience that many people seem to be searching for in the compulsive use of alcohol and drugs. Thus, taking part in these religious groups apparently provides some individuals with a structure and practice that effectively helps them to deal with problems of alcoholism and drug addiction, as frequently attested in statements made by members who claim to have overcome serious difficulties of this kind.[13]

In this regard, rather than trying to forbid any kind of induced alteration of consciousness, the ritual use of ayahuasca allows certain experiences of this kind. But at the same time it provides a powerful structuring religious framework within which the congregate may work through personal and difficult life issues in a safer setting. One could, quite appropriately, say that the ayahuasca religious doctrines and practices intrinsically provide very desirable and effective harm reduction strategies which have shown themselves to be of great social and psychological value to the congregates.

The American psychiatrist Norman Zinberg proposed a model for controlled drug use in dealing with issues of drug and alcohol abuse which emphasized the important role played by social sanctions and social rituals that reinforce given sets of values, rules of conduct and standardized ways of producing, consuming and dealing with effects (Zinberg 1984:5). Zinberg's proposal can be viewed not simply as a model, but rather as a standard for defining or redefining the underlying assumptions regarding 'drug use'. Thus, to the extent that certain substances are considered 'drugs' when used under a given set of circumstances, and as 'non drugs' in other circumstances, the drinking of ayahuasca as a sacrament would be the classic example of the 'non drug' use. The sense of purpose with which the brew is taken, alongside the ritualistic and highly structured ceremonies reflecting the Christian doctrine with its indigenous nuances, all ensure that the social taboos that accompany the typical drug user must function in a different manner in this case.

More recently, the Dutch anthropologist Jean-Paul Grund, carrying out research among heroin and cocaine users in the Netherlands, further developed Zinberg's theory by proposing what he calls a 'feedback model of drug use self-regulation' that may help us establish the demarcation between what is commonly called a 'drug' and a sacramental use of plants that contain psychoactive properties. His model takes into account two further elements: the availability of the substance and life structure (Grund 1993:247).

The ayahuasca-using religious organizations seem good examples of these models. Not only do they also adopt ritual procedures for the taking of the brew that fulfil all the prerequisites laid out by Zinberg, but they also regulate their followers, access to the substance and provide them with doctrinal guidance on the structuring of their lives, the further controlling elements added by Grund to his model (substance availability and life structure).

It is interesting to compare the religious use of ayahuasca with the use that is occasionally made of Datura preparations in Brazil. Although this plant has an important place in Indian religious and medicinal practices, it is also commonly taken in a haphazard fashion by non-members of these groups merely in search of 'kicks'. The consequences of this wild use are often unpleasant and may lead to damage to physical and mental health and even deaths due to accidents or suicide.

The prohibitionist zeal that leads government authorities to exert pressure and, on occasion, even ban rituals involving the taking of entheogens, is counterproductive for, as Zinberg maintained, controlled use is a result of social learning and requires suitable social and cultural conditions to develop fully. In the cases we have been describing, dealing with rituals which are not only social but religious as well, we see how informal social controls can be quite effective when allowed to develop in a licit manner, even when involving the use of potent psychoactive substances like ayahuasca. On the other hand, when their banning makes it difficult for them to become fully institutionalised, as is the case with Santa Maria among the members of CEFLURIS, their controlling influence is weakened and it becomes more difficult for them to prevent undesired effects.

1 I wish to thank Beatriz Labate and Ross Coomber for reading the first version of this article and for their very helpful suggestions.
2 Chemical analysis shows that Bannisteriopsis caapi contains the beta-carboline alkaloids: harmine, harmaline and tetrahydroharmine. Diploterys cabreana and the Psychotrias have the hallucinogenic alkaloid N-dimetiltriptamine (DMT). This substance, when taken alone and orally, is inactive, even in high doses, owing to the action of the monoamine oxidase (MAO). Analysis has shown that, although the beta-carbolines found in the mixtures are in too low a dosage to manifest their hallucinogenic properties, they seem to play a role in the inhibition of MAO, thus freeing the DMT from its action and allowing it to show its psychoactive properties. Users of the brew explain this process by saying that the vine (Bannisteriopsis caapi) carries the 'force' while the leaf (Psychotria viridis) brings the 'light'. This is a phenomenological understanding of the way the brew works. Things become less clear when one takes into consideration certain claims that the Bannisteriopsis may reveal hallucinogenic properties when brewed alone, or when smoked or chewed. Apart from their psychoactive effects, the components of ayahuasca have a large range of emetic, antimicro-

bial and anti-helmintic effects, which make them effective in the fight against ascarid worms, as well as protozoaries such as trypanosomes and amoebas. This would explain the use of the brew as an emetic and as a laxative, to cleanse the organism of all impurities. The brew is also said to be useful against malaria (Luna 1986: 57–59).

3   Although there is some dispute about the origin of this name, most scholars accept the native explanation that it refers to the Portuguese expression 'Dai-me', meaning 'Give me', frequently found in the hymns sung during the ceremonies when requests are made to the spiritual world for light, strength, and love. For an alternative view see Monteiro da Silva (2002:367–398).

4   'Entheogen' is an alternative expression suggested by Gordon Wasson and others to avoid the pejorative connotation implicit in 'hallucinogen'. Deriving from the Greek 'entheos' it means 'that which generates the experience of the divine within' and in a strict sense should be used for those drugs that produce visions and which can be shown to have been used in religious or shamanic rites. In a broader sense the word may be used to designate other drugs, be they natural or artificial, that induce alterations in consciousness similar to those produced by the ritual ingestion of traditional entheogens (Wasson et. Alii.1980:235)

5   It is interesting to note that Amerindian and Mestizo shamans usually consider ayahuasca to have a feminine energy (Luna 1986).

6   It is said that 'Santa Maria is not marihuana', and great care is taken to ensure that the sacramental nature of the use is preserved, even when the pressure from everyday life for a more informal profane use of the plant is very strong. One of the ways to ensure the distinction between the two different usages is through the adoption of a special vocabulary to deal with Santa Maria that is different from that normally used in the marihuana subculture.

7   It is difficult to be precise abut the number of Barquinha churches and followers since some of the groups are relatively small and new ones keep cropping up.

8   This information has been imparted to me on several occasions by members of different ayahuasca religions.

9   See McKenna, D. J., et al (1998), Grob, C. S., et al (1996), Callaway, J. C. et al. (1998), Callaway, J. C. et al (1994), Aranha, C., et al (1991), Andrade, E. N. et al (2002).

10   'Burracheira' seems to be a Portuguese corruption of the Spanish 'borrachera', meaning 'inebriation'. However, members of the União do Vegetal have another understanding of the matter.

11   The emetic effects of ayahuasca are so common that in Spanish speaking countries it is sometimes called 'la purga' (the purge)

12   The recent growth of Neo-Pentecostal churches, imported from the USA or spawned locally, is a much more marked phenomenon in Brazilian society than the development of the ayahuasca religions, but both developments seem to serve similar functions, as ways of helping people from different social classes to cope with the acute economic and cultural challenges of modern life.

13   In Tarapopto, in the Peruvian Amazon there is a centre run by Jacques Mabit and Rosa Giove Nakazawa that claims much success in treating drug abusers with ayahuasca and other traditional Indian medicines (Nakazawa 1996).

REFERENCES

Andrade, A.P. (2002) 'Contribuições e limites da União doVegetal para a nova consciência religiosa' in B.C. Labate and W.S. Araújo (eds.), *O Uso Ritual da Ayahuasca* (Campinas,SP:Mercado de Letras; São Paulo: Fapesp), pp543–567.

Andrade, E. N., Brito, G. S., Andrade, E. O., Neves, E. S., Mckenna, D., Cavalcante, J. W., Okimura, L. J., Grob, C. S., Callaway, J. C. (2002) 'Farmacologia Humana da Hoasca: estudos clínicos' in, in B.C. Labate and W.S. Araújo (eds.), *O Uso Ritual da Ayahuasca* (Campinas,SP:Mercado de Letras; São Paulo: Fapesp) pp 621–630

Aranha, C., Travaini, G; Correa, M. A. (1991) 'Aspectos botânicos e taxonômicos das plantas Banisteriopsis sp. e Psychotria sp' Presentation at the Primeiro Congresso em Saude do Centro de Estudos Médicos – União do Vegetal. São Paulo, Brasil, 30th May–2nd June.

Araújo, W. S. (1999) *'Navegando sobre as ondas do Daime-história, cosmologia e ritual da Barquinha'*. Campinas, Editora da UNICAMP.

Araújo, W. S. (2002) 'A Barquinha: espaço simbólico de uma cosmologia em construção' in B.C. Labate and W.S. Araújo (eds., *O Uso Ritual da Ayahuasca* Campinas,SP:Mercado de Letras; São Paulo: Fapesp pp 495–512.

Brissac, S. (2002) 'José Gabriel da Costa: trajetória de um brasileiro mestre e autor da União do Vegetal' in B.C. Labate and W.S. Araújo (eds.), *O Uso Ritual da Ayahuasca* Campinas,SP:Mercado de Letras; São Paulo: Fapesp pp525–542.

Callaway, J. C.; Airaksinen, M. M.; Mckenna, D. J.; Brito, G. S. and Grob, C. S. (1994). Platelet serotonin uptake sites increased in drinkers of ayahuasca. Psychopharmacology 116: 385–387.

Callaway, J. C.; Mckenna, D.J. et al. (1998). Pharmacokinetics of Hoasca alkaloids in healthy humans. *Journal of Ethnopharmacology* 65 (1999): 243–256

Couto, F.R. 92002) 'Santo Daime: rito de ordem', in B.C. Labate and W.S. Araújo (eds.), *O Uso Ritual da Ayahuasca* (Campinas,SP:Mercado de Letras; São Paulo: Fapesp) pp339–366.

Dobkin de Rios, M (1972) *Visionary vine-psychedelic healing in the Peruvian Amazon*, San Francisco, Chandler Publishing co.

Dobkin de Rios, M. (1990). *Hallucinogens-Cross-cultural Perspectives,* Bridport, UK,Prism Press.

Fericgla, J.M.(1989) 'El Sistema Dinâmico de la Cultura y los Diversos Estados de la Mente Humana – Bases para un Irracionalismo Sistêmico' – *Cuadernos de Antropologia* – Barcelona – Editorial Anthropos.

Figueiredo, E.G., Trajano, V. A. Almeida, MF,Azevedo, J.D.O. (1996) Mestre Antônio Geraldo e o Santo Daime. Rio Branco: BOBGRAF: Ed. Preview, 1996.

Gentil,L.R.B. (2002) 'O uso de psicoativos em um contexto religioso: a União doVegetal' in B.C. Labate and W.S. Araújo (eds., *O Uso Ritual da Ayahuasca* (Campinas,SP:Mercado de Letras; São Paulo: Fapesp) pp 513–524.

Goulart,S.L. (2002) 'O contexto do surgimento do culto do Santo Daime: formação da Comunidade e do calendário ritual' in B.C. Labate and W.S. Araújo (eds., *O Uso Ritual da Ayahuasca* (Campinas,SP:Mercado de Letras; São Paulo: Fapesp) pp313–338.

Labate, B.C. (2002). A literatura brasileira sobre as religiões ayahuasqueiras' in B.C. Labate and W.S. Araújo (eds., *O Uso Ritual da Ayahuasca* (Campinas,SP:Mercado de Letras; São Paulo: Fapesp) pp229–274.

Lewis, I.M. (1977) *Êxtase Religioso*(São Paulo: Editora Perspectiva).

Luna, L. E. (1986) *Vegetalismo:Shamanism among the Mestizo Population of the Peruvian Amazon,* (Stockholm,Almquist and Wiksell International).

Gentil,L.R.B. (2002) 'O uso de psicoativos em um contexto religioso' in B.C. Labate and W.S. Araújo (eds., *O Uso Ritual da Ayahuasca* Campinas,SP:Mercado de Letras; São Paulo: Fapesp pp513–524.

Gordon Wasson, R.,Hofmann,A., Ruck, C.A.P (1980) .*El Camino a Eleusis-Una solución al enigma de los misterios*, Mexico, Fondo de Cultura Económica,

Grob, C. S., D. J. McKenna, J. C. Callaway, G. S. Brito, E. S. Neves, G. Oberlender, O. L. Saide, E. Labigalini, C. Tacla, C. T. Miranda, R. J. Strassman, K. B. Boone (1996). 'Human psychopharmacology of hoasca, a plant hallucinogen used in ritual context in Brasil', *Journal of Nervous & Mental Disease*. 184:86–94.

Groisman,A. (1999) *Eu venho da Floresta. Um estudo sobre o contexto simbólico do uso do Santo Daime*. Florianópolis, Editora da UFSC.

Groisman,A. (2000) '*Santo Daime in the Netherlands: An anthropological study of a New World religion in a European setting*' – Dissertation submitted for the degree of Doctor of Philosophy to the Department of Anthropology, Goldsmiths College, University of London, pp 295.

Grund, J.P.C (1993) *Drug Use as a Social Ritual-Functionality, Symbolism and Determinants of Self-Regulation,* Rotterdam, Instituut voor Vesslavingsondeerzoek.

Henman,A.R. (1986) 'Uso del ayahuasca en un contexto autoritario. El caso de la União doVegetal en Brasil, *America indígena* vol XLVI, num1, enero-marzo, pp 219–234.

MacRae, E. (1990) *Guiado pela Lua-Xamanismo e uso Ritual da ayahuasca no culto do Santo Daime,* São Paulo, Brasiliense.

——(1994) 'A importância dos fatores socioculturais na determinação da política oficial sobre o uso ritual da ayahuasca', in *Drogas e Cidadania-Repressão ou Redução de Risco* , Zaluar, A. (ed.), São Paulo, Brasiliense, pp.31–45

——(1998) *Guiado por la Luna-Shamanismo y uso ritual de la ayahuasca en el culto de Santo Daime*-Quito, Ediciones Abya-Yala, pp. 175

——(1998) 'Santo Daime and Santa Maria-The licit ritual use of ayahuasca and the illicit use of cannabis in a Brazilian Amazonian religion', *International Journal of Drug Policy*,9: 325–338.

Maués, R.H. and Villacorta, G.M. (2001) 'Pajelança e encantaria amazônica' in R.Prandi (ed.)*Encantaria Brasileira-O livro dos mestres, caboclos e encantados*, Riode Janeiro, Pallas, pp.11–58.

McKenna, D. J.; Callaway, J.C. and Grob, C. S. (1998) 'The Scientific Investigation of Ayahuasca – A Review of Past and Current Research'. *The Heffer Review of Psychedelic Research* (1):65–77

Monteiro da Silva, C. (1983) '*O sistema de Juramidam, culto do Santo Daime no Acre; um ritual de transcendência e despoluição* , Recife , master of arts dissertation presented to the Institute of Human Sciences, Federal University of Pernambuco.

——(2002) 'O uso ritual da ayahuasca e o reencontro de duas tradições. A miração e a incorporação no culto do Santo Daime', in B.C. Labate and W.S. Araújo (eds., *O Uso Ritual da Ayahuasca* Campinas, SP:Mercado de Letras; São Paulo: Fapesp, pp367–398.

Nakazawa, R.A.G. (1996) *Medicina Tradicional Amazonica en el tratamiento del abuso de drogas-Experiencia de dos años y medio* Tarapoto, Peru, Centro Takiwasi.

Sá, D.B.G.S. (1996) 'Ayahuasca, A consciência da expansão' *in*; *Discursos Sediciosos (Crime, Direito e Sociedade),* Ano 1, número 2, 2° semestre, Rio de Janeiro, Instituto Carioca de Criminologia

Zinberg, N. (1984) *Drug, Set and Setting: The basis of controlled intoxicant use,* New Haven, Yale University Press.

Chapter Three

COCA USE IN BOLIVIA: A TRADITION OF THOUSANDS OF YEARS

Alison Spedding

INTRODUCTION

The recreational use of cocaine hydrochloride has been known in the West since the 1880s and since the 1970s has achieved widespread popularity. However, the coca leaf, from which cocaine is extracted, has been consumed for recreational and ritual purposes in South America for several thousand years. While the Catholic Church combated it in the sixteenth and seventeenth centuries due to its use in native religious rites, a status quo was established which left the leaf free of persecution until the twentieth century, when its position as the source of illegal cocaine led to international legal prohibitions on its circulation and increasingly violent persecution of the peasants who cultivate it, although the leaf itself, its production and use continue to be legal in Peru and Bolivia, which up until the 1990s were the principal producing countries. This chapter reviews the history of coca, the ways in which it is traditionally consumed in Bolivia today and concludes with a summary of the repressive policies directed at coca producers in the Andes which are currently applied as part of the 'War on Drugs'.

A BRIEF HISTORY OF COCA, FROM PRE-COLUMBIAN TIMES TO THE PRESENT

The coca bush (*Erythroxylon coca*), whose leaves are consumed for their psychotropical and medicinal properties, is originally an Amazonian species (Plowman 1986) and presumably was domesticated in that region. Climatic conditions, and the difficulty of identifying archaeological sites amidst the dense forest coverage, signify that there are no concrete proofs of primitive coca use or cultivation from Amazonia. The oldest evidence of coca use in the south-central Andes is from the Peruvian coast, where the desert conditions have preserved organic materials which rot away both in the tropical forest and in the more humid highland areas. Coca leaves, and containers of lime to provide the alkali with which they are chewed (see below), have been found at the site of Huaca Prieta on the north coast of Peru and dated to the pre-ceramic period (between 2500 and 1800 BC; Antonil 1978:40). Other remains of coca and lime have been radiocarbon dated to around 1300 BC, and diverse coastal cultures such as Moche and Nazca have left plaster representations of people apparently chewing coca, that is with a bulge in one cheek, as well as bags of coca leaves buried along with their dead, at times together with remains of other leaves which appear to be tobacco (Rostworowski de Diez Canseco 1977:247–8).

For climatic reasons, archaeological remains of coca have not been discovered in what is today highland Bolivia, although it is evident that 'Bolivian' cultures, in particular Tiwanaku whose capital is located on the northern Altiplano near Lake Titicaca, had wide contacts with Nazca and other places on the coast where coca use has been demonstrated in the first millenium after Christ. One of the problems relates to the fact that whilst coca is produced in ecological regions where ancient paraphernalia for other (hallucinogen) drug use is found, the less durable paraphernalia associated with coca use is unavailable. Early colonial records however, show that there were coca plantations in modern-day Bolivia at the beginning of the sixteenth century (Meruvia 2000, Murra 1991). In summary, it is certain that coca use was current in modern-day Peru more than 4,000 years ago, and the same may well be true of Bolivia, but concrete proofs are lacking.

The first written references to coca date from the early colonial period (sixteenth century; the first conquistadors arrived in Peru in 1532). The authors of chronicles, geographical and administrative reports, and the compilers of dictionaries in native languages, all mention coca use in basically the same modes as today: 'chewing' (sucking on a wad in the mouth), in combination with an alkaline preparation known as *llipta* in Quechua or *llujta* in Aymara, and divination by 'looking' at the leaves.

There is no doubt that the ritual and festive use of coca was central to its role in the pre-hispanic world, and it can be assumed that this coexisted with an everyday use which had more to do with its chemical that its symbolic properties. What is not so clear is how widespread this latter use was in the past. The idea persists among some Bolivian and Peruvian intellectuals, and others, that the Inkas had a 'monopoly' on the distribution and use of coca in such a way that only the aristocracy had permanent access to the leaf. The general population, it is argued, only received coca on special occasions when their overlords organized rites or festivities and distributed coca among the public, together with food and alcoholic drink (principally *chicha*, maize beer, which is still popular today). Prescott, for instance, comments that 'under the Incas, [coca] is said to have been exclusively reserved for the noble orders' (Prescott 1847/1961:108). It is not clear what proofs exist of this 'monopoly'; Garcilaso de la Vega, dedicated spokesman of the Inka nobility makes no mention of it in the chapter dedicated to coca in his *Royal Commentaries of the Inkas* (Book 8, Chapter 15). The ethnohistorian John Murra, whose studies revolutionised conceptions of the Inka empire from the 1950s onwards, considers that no such monopoly existed. The earliest colonial sources do not mention it, and it only appears as part of the efforts of colonial administrators to control the highly profitable trade in the leaf (Murra 1991:659–660).

Coca leaf was one of the first native Andean products to find a commercial market, and the profits to be made from its production, transport and sale, above all to the booming silver mines of Potosí, led to a huge expansion in the areas cultivated and the levels of consumption in the course of the first century of colonisation (Glave 1989). The first areas of commercial production were close to Cusco, but they were soon joined by the Yungas, to the north of the city of La Paz, which is the principal region of traditional coca production in Bolivia today. The option of purchase with money and the development of new routes of distribution presumably allowed a lot of people – mainly the indigenous population, but including Spanish colonists (Antonil 1978:15–17) – to chew coca more often and/or in larger quantities than before. Some Bolivian commentators interpret this as a Spanish imposition, designed to allow greater explotation of mine workers, but the Spanish achieved similar levels of exploitation in their mines in Mexico and elsewhere without need of coca. An alternative view, supported by twentieth century studies of Bolivian mine workers such as Nash (1979), is that the opportunity to get together to chew coca during work breaks allows workers to maintain solidarity and assert their own cultural and political positions, thus enabling them to resist exploitation rather than being consumed by it. Whichever position is correct, the mining market continued to dominate coca production and trade in Upper Peru (its colonial name) and Bolivia right up to the collapse of the tin market and the massive redundancies of miners in the 1980s.

Apart from the demand from the mines, there was a permanent and relatively stable demand for coca leaf among the general population, in particular the peasantry and also the urban lower classes, but this last group was very small in Bolivia, whose population was overwhelmingly rural up until the middle of the twentieth century. From the colonial period onwards, the coca trade was stratified in two grades: the coca produced by haciendas, known as *coca gatera* in the Colony and *coca de hacienda* after independence, considered of superior quality, and *coca mercadera*, later known as *coca de rescate*, produced by small peasant cultivators. These might be residents of free comunities or serfs on haciendas, who were allowed to produce their own coca on usufruct plots ceded by the landlord in exchange for labour services (generally three days a week each on the part of a man and a woman). The hacienda owners' political clout allowed them to obtain tax concessions for their coca and access to the largest and best capitalised markets (the mines). In the first decades of the Colony, almost all the production was in peasant hands (although its trade tended to be managed by the native aristocrats); by the eighteenth century, the haciendas had taken over a large part of the market (Klein 1993), but in the course of the nineteenth century peasant production came to occupy an ever larger share, and by 1902 80% of the coca sold out of Yungas was *de rescate*, that is peasant production (Soux 1993:145). When the Agrarian Reform of 1953 put an end to labour tenancy and distributed hacienda lands among the peasants, the landlords found that without unpaid serf labour it was no longer profitable for them to produce coca on the lands which they retained and the totality of Bolivian coca production passed into the hands of the peasants. This political factor is a central reason for the difficulty encountered by successive Bolivian governments in their attempts to reduce or eliminate coca production, under international pressure from the 1980s onwards (see below).

The period after the Agrarian Reform coincided with a reduction in coca production, mainly due to hacienda coca fields going out of production and the time lapse required for them to be replaced by peasant plots (a coca field generally requires about two years from the initial land preparation to come into production, and another three years before it reaches maximum productivity), but also due to an apparent reduction in use in the late 1950s and 1960s, associated with the propagation of 'modernising' values, which rejected coca chewing as a sign of 'backwardness'. However, this is only an impression; the first study which attempted to detail in quantitative and qualitative terms the profile of coca use in Bolivia was carried out in the 1970s and published some years later (Carter and Mamani 1986). This study has been criticised for assuming from the start a profile of the 'traditional' consumer limited to peasant communities and mining centres, and ignoring other social classes and the urban population in general. There is no doubt that the peasants continue to chew coca, although some factors (chiefly conversion to evangelical protestantism, which rejects coca along with alcohol) may have reduced this use, while it is difficult to guess how much urban use may have changed since the study was carried out.

Massive rural-urban migration in the intervening decades has increased the number of potential urban consumers but cultural changes associated with urban life may have induced them to reduce or abandon their coca chewing. On the other hand, from the late 1980s onwards, coca chewing has been taken up by university students and other intellectuals as a sign of political affiliation to pro-indigenous or indian nationalist currents, and fashionable bars have adopted the practice of putting out baskets of coca on their tables (as in other countries they might put out peanuts or crisps) at the same time as they hire groups of musicians to perform Andean folk music. Huge numbers of Andean peasants have migrated to the eastern lowlands, taking their coca chewing habits with them, and the lowland indigenous groups, who in past centuries did not chew coca, have also taken it up, although the numerical impact of these last is not significant. At the time of writing (2003) there is a national political debate in Bolivia concerning the actual levels and social profile of coca leaf use, although the promised national studies destined to provide definitive data on the topic have not so far been put into practice.

TRADITIONAL FORMS OF COCA USE

'Traditional' coca use in Bolivia refers to three modalities: 'chewing' or *aculli* (from the Aymara *akhulliña*), also known as *pijchar*; as tea (*mate de coca*), plus other medicinal uses; and ritual uses (as part of offerings; it is also usual to chew coca while taking part in these offerings and other ritual occasions, such as the all-night vigils of 1–2 november for Todos Santos, when the souls of the dead return to visit their families). It is generally assumed that the quantities required for the second and third modalities are small in comparison with those required for the first case, chewing as a more or less daily habit associated with work (principally, but not exclusively, manual work in agriculture and mining) and recreation (in peasant circles at least, one says 'Drop round for a chew of coca' instead of 'Come round for a cup of tea/coffee'). The association of coca with work is so general that *aculli* is also used as a synonym for a break from work, equivalent to the British 'tea-break', even when the people concerned do not themselves chew coca. *Aculli* is also used to measure periods in the work day – 'I could finish that in an *aculli*', that is in the accustomed time between two such breaks (two to three hours, according to context). First of all I will describe the activity of 'chewing', before considering its social significance and the distribution of it among different social groups.

The habitual coca chewer usually carries around his or her *coca chino* ('coca wrap' or 'coca tie') which contains coca leaves, *lejía* (in local Spanish; literally 'lye' or 'bleach', but in practice an alkaline paste which, combined with the leaves, releases the active alkaloids), cigarrettes and matches. Traditionally, men carry their coca in a handwoven bag called *ch'uspa* whereas women use another kind of traditional weaving, a square woven in one piece called *tari* or *unkuña*, but these days almost everyone uses plastic bags, except on special occasions (though some continue to use the ch'uspa or tari to wrap the bag in). One sits down to chew and begins by selecting leaves one by one and putting them in the side of the mouth, between the gums and the inside of the cheek. Some people strip out the entire spine of the leaf with the aid of their teeth, others just bite off the stump of stalk that remains attached to the leaf, so that it will not poke their bucal tissues. When a cushion of leaves has been created, one pinches or bites off a piece of lejía, wraps it in more leaves or else inserts it directly into the wad, and continues to add more leaves and perhaps one or two other pinches of lejía until a wad of the desired size has been created. Generally one only creates a wad on one side in one aculli (on the right or the left, according to taste; only on certain ritual occasions it may be obligatory to chew on one side and not the other), although miners, who are notorious for chewing more than almost anybody else, are said to create wads on both sides of the mouth at once. At the same time, it is usual to smoke one or more cigarrettes, commercial or locally fabricated by women artisans, but with black tobacco and not blond tobacco like Marlboro (blond tobacco is said 'not to grab hold' with coca, its flavour doesn't seem to coincide in a pleasurable fashion). The chewer then wraps up their coca chino and gets down to work, sucking on the wad from time to time. 'Chewing' is thus a misnomer; in fact one has to learn *not* to chew, that is to suppress the reflex which leads one to masticate anything held in the mouth, but to hold the leaves there and suck on them. After two hours or more it has lost its flavour[1] and is removed from the mouth and thrown away; this is the *jach'u* referred to by Bertonio. In a recreational context one simply continues chewing until the wad has reached a sufficient size, thows it away and starts over again. It is acceptable to drink alcoholic drinks while chewing and with the coca wad still in the mouth, but to consume any other drink or food the wad is disposed of first.

In peasant circles it is acceptable to chew coca at any time of day and in any situation (in the house, before or after eating, at work in the fields, while visiting or receiving visits, during a party, etc.); the only space where it is not acceptable is inside a church. In Bolivia there are no gender limitations; women and men can chew.[2] Some observers consider that women actually chew more than men, but this impression may be due to the fact that more women than men are prepared to chew in public, outside the community (e.g. while travelling on a bus). The only limitation is age. Some people began to chew when they were children, but almost always because they were orphans and obliged to work hard by the people who adopted them. As a rule, people begin to chew when they start to take on adult work tasks and responsabilities, that is in late adolescence and, above all, once they are married. Thus some may begin to chew at 16, others at 25 or older. In old age the habit is virtually universal in the countryside, limited only by accessibility (money to buy it and coca on hand to be bought, except in producing communities where it is always on hand). The quantity consumed varies greatly, according to personal preference. People in the Yungas consider that 'the greatest chewer' (who does it all day, every day) might get through two pounds of leaf in a week, and miners in Potosí said they could chew a kilo in a week. I myself was able to confirm almost a pound and a half a week per person for some dedicated peasant chewers. Most consumers will use much less than this, probably half a pound per week or less. A pound of best quality leaves costs US$2–3 in street markets in La Paz, according to the season, whereas inferior qualities cost about US$1.50 per pound or less.

There is no particular social pressure to chew coca in everyday contexts, even in communities where almost everyone chews on a regular basis, and some people never acquire the habit. Others do it only for work and not as a recreational activity (in the evenings or when taking a day off). This is a notable difference in comparison with alcohol. Just about every special occasion in Bolivia involves drinking alcohol (except when the participants are evangelicals) and all the adults present are more or less obliged to drink and, indeed, to get drunk, often very drunk. If one doesn't want to drink, or drink any more, the only alternative is to leave the party. However, the obligation to drink only applies to special occasions, and drinking on ordinary days is frowned upon and when it becomes a habit, strongly criticised. Chewing coca is a part of peasant parties (here it may be laid out in a special cloth for all present to help themselves, or someone goes around with a large bag handing it out) but if someone refuses it, no-one will insist that they 'serve themselves' anyway, as they will do when drinks are being offered. The only contexts where one might say that it is obligatory to chew are ritual ones, but no-one who was not already disposed to chew would take part in the sort of rituals where it is an essential part of the procedure.

The specific limitations on coca chewing have to do with social class and ethnicity. The debate on the nature of social stratification, class and ethnicity in the Andes is enormous and never ending, and I shall not attempt to summarise it here. Sufficient to say that 'peasant' is taken to be a synonym for 'Indian', and coca chewing is an 'Indian' habit; hence, members of those social classes not considered to be Indians, or people who aspire to such membership, will not chew. Typical coca chewers are therefore peasants, or lower class urban dwellers such as mine workers, street sellers, market porters or building labourers, who maintain a more or less 'Indian' ethnicity and/or have no aspirations to pass themselves off as middle class, even lower middle class. Middle class chewers tend to limit their use to private situations (in their houses, or in the company of friends who sympathise with the habit), or do it in public to express political and cultural sympathies with Indians and indigenist or indianist postures. The fact that women in general, at any social level, are seen as being more 'Indian' than men, thus explains why women may be somewhat more disposed to chew in public situations than men of the same social group. This association betwen coca chewing and 'Indianness', with all the consequent prejudices and political debates involved with the 'Indian problem' in the Andes, has pervaded the debate on the possible benefits or damage of coca chewing, and often reduces, when it does not entirely eliminate, the 'objectivity' of the arguments or data proposed to support one or another position.

The ethnic/class associations also apply to the ritual uses. Coca is totally out of place in official Catholic ceremonies, and in evangelical protestant ceremonies of any kind; the rituals where it is used correspond to what is usually classed as 'Andean religion', although in practice these rites should really be seen as part of the syncretic complex of popular Catholicism, since they include prayers and offerings directed to Catholic entities such as Tata Santiago (St James) or various avocations of the Virgin, as well as Andean entities such as the mountain spirits or the Pachamama (the Earth Mother). Once again, the most enthusiastic practitioners of these rites are usually peasants and the urban lower class, and middle and upper class people with indigenist sympathies. The only modality of use which has no ethnic/social class limits is in the form of coca tea. This is generally recognised as a good remedy for stomach troubles and all the afflictions associated with *soroche* (altitude sickness), and it has been served in the Presidential Palace to official visitors as diverse as Fidel Castro and the King and Queen of Spain. Other medical uses, however, continue to be 'Indian': for instance, the use of the coca *jach'u* (taken from the mouth, saturated with lejía and saliva) which is bound on to infected wounds or swellings to suck out the pus and reduce inflammation.

The other 'traditional' use, which is part of the general category of ritual use but which deserves to be considered apart, is divination in coca leaves. This is only one of various traditional ways of divining and divination through other rituals/methods and with other materials is not uncommon. In all cases involving coca leaves, the procedure is the same; variations are due to regional traditions or personal preferences of the curer, not the nature of the problem to be resolved. The leaves to be used should be provided by the client and, ideally, he or she should have slept with them under his/her pillow the night before, or at least put them in the breast of their clothing for a while before beginning the session. The bag of leaves should also contain an 'eye', that is a coin, which is payment for the service and will be used in the divination itself. They are then handed to the curer with the request 'Please look at this for me' (*uñjarapitaya* in Aymara), followed by an explanation of the problem. The curer prepares his/her tari, a handwoven cloth of the type women carry their coca in. In La Paz, at least, taris for divination should be woven from llama wool and not sheep wool or synthetic fibre. He/she places the 'eye' coin in the upper part of the cloth and may also set out various selected leaves, which represent people or places involved in the problem or some other important element. Some curers revise the leaves provided and select only some of them (undamaged ones in particular), others simply take a handful of the leaves just as they are. These are then scattered over the cloth from a certain height. The curer observes how they fall (the last ones to fall are often of particular importance), the pattern they form over the cloth, and the nature of the leaves themselves.

There are some natural deformations of the leaves which have meaning (in particular, 'money' and 'drunkenness'); holes due to the attack of certain insects are also significant (small holes due to the *ulu* caterpillar indicate illness sent by or anger of the Pachamama, the bites of the *chaka* leafcutting ant indicate negative gossip or rumours). Discolourations, any deviation from a uniform bright green colour, are significant. The size and shape of the leaf itself can indicate different categories of persons (a long narrow leaf is a man, a round, wide one is a woman, tiny leaves are children), but other meanings are due to the processing of the leaf, folds and creases that result from it being packed and pressed. It should be noted that most of these meanings are negative (illness, affliction, and if the leaf has both sides folded over symmetrically towards the middle, death); hence it is important that the coca should have been processed with care, because clumsily processed coca, with a lot of broken and crumpled leaves, will inevitably give rise to depressing conclusions. The better the quality of the coca, the more likely is a positive result. It is also significant which way up each leaf falls. The underside of the coca leaf is a much paler green than the upper side. The underside is called 'white' and the upper side, 'green'. Around Lake Titicaca the green side is usually seen as negative and white as positive; it is said that the curer 'looks at white'. North and south of this region it is more usual to 'look at green', that is the darker upper side is taken as positive. All these elements are combined with the distribution of the leaves – which leaves cover others, if they form a 'path' or chain in one or another direction, if leaves cover or touch the eye and in which way, if the stalks of the leaves point 'up' (away from the diviner) or 'down' (towards him or her), if the leaves fall flat or if some stick upright, to provide an interpretation. Those diviners who cast only selected leaves, without discolorations or deformations, rely almost exclusively on the pattern. The curer will usually cast the leaves three times for a particular question, interpreting each cast in dialogue with the client, to arrive at an answer. When the session is over, the curer pockets the 'eye' and the coca, and may receive an additional payment, before proceeding to whatever other ritual is indicated, which will require other inputs and be paid for separately.

CHEMICAL AND BIOMEDICAL ASPECTS OF COCA USE

Divination is evidently the use of coca which is most divorced from its chemical properties. The coca leaf contains fourteen alkaloids, of which cocaine (isolated in 1859) is only the best known. The function of the lime, lejía or other alkaline substance (some urban chewers use bicarbonate of soda) is, combined with the saliva which saturates the leaves, to release the alkaloids which are then absorbed through the tissues of the mouth. Some lejias are relatively mild, whereas others are very strong and should they come into direct contact with the skin of the mouth or the tongue, cause an unpleasant burning sensation and even blisters. The manangement of the lejia is actually the most difficult thing to learn in chewing coca: how much to use, how to place it in the middle of the wad where it is insulated away from direct contact with the mouth, and not destroying the leaves by really chewing them so that the lejia emerges and burns the mouth. These burns are the only bad effect recognised by habitual coca chewers (there is no idea that one can chew 'too much' coca, much less get 'strung out' on it). Mineral lime is used for chewing in northern Peru and Colombia, but all the lejías used in southern Peru and Bolivia are made from vegetable ashes and there is a great variety of them, although by no means any ash (e.g. from common firewood) is suitable for this end. Cigarette ash is suitable, although not at all strong. The quinua stalks mentioned by Bertonio in 1612 continue to be the most common source of commercial lejias sold in La Paz. The taste of the coca wad, rather anodyne and slightly bitter at the beginning, changes notably when the lejía begins to act, and habitual chewers generally have very strong opinions as to which lejía they prefer, which 'grabs hold' (has a good effect and/or flavour) and which does not. In rural areas they may burn their own lejía.

The folk version of the biochemical effects of coca chewing which is current in Bolivia generally begins by saying that it 'takes away hunger and sleep'. This is true to the extent that coca allows one to tolerate hunger and helps to stay awake all night, whether to take part in a nocturnal ritual or because one is a long distance driver (one often observes bags of coca next to the steering wheel of buses or lorries). It is not a radical appetite suppressant like cocaine or amphetamines, and the user simply throws away the wad and gets down to eating when food is on hand. No chewers reject available food in favour of coca if both are to be had; the only cases I know of coca substituting food refer to poor families where the parents chewed coca because the food was only enough for their children, or orphans who were not given enough to eat. The custom of chewing coca after supper and before going to bed likewise indicates that it maintains wakefulness but does not cause insomnia. The other observation is 'I use it for [manual] work'. The stimulant effect may possibly allow increased muscular effort or endurance, and there are some biomedical studies which claim 'increased endurance under stress' for coca chewers (Hanna 1974), although peasants in the Yungas who did not chew but often worked alongside those who did considered that chewers did not have a notably higher productivity. In so far as it has a positive contribution, this may be due to improved concentration and more attention to the task at hand, which would explain why it may be used by students preparing for examinations, and why it is considered to have a beneficial effect on the quality of the conversation and promotes mutual understanding and communication in recreational contexts.

However, these subjective effects are notoriously difficult to prove according to objective criteria, because so much depends on the context of use and the expectations, set and setting (Zinberg 1994) of the user. Pharmacological studies have tended to focus on measurable physiological effects, such as the constriction of blood vessels in the extremities (Hanna 1974), which serves to protect the user against cold and would therefore be beneficial at high altitudes. The folk version also includes protection from the cold as a benefit of coca, but this does not explain why it is also chewed at lower altitudes and even in Amazonia, where cold is not a problem. Other studies have pointed out that coca chewing raises blood glucose levels and have related this to facilitating digestion of the traditional Andean diet, consisting mainly in carbohydrates, and the digestive problems caused by high altitudes (Bolton 1976, Burchard 1975; there is a summary of medical and cultural positions in Allen 1988:220–226). Once again, the folk version also recognises that coca, chewed or as tea, is a remedy for 'stomach ache' in general (a euphemism for diarrhoea and related afflictions). According to Antonil (1987:30), modern studies which are concerned to divorce coca chewing from cocaine snorting and thus free it from the diabolic connotations of 'drug abuse', purposefully ignore or even deny the euphoric effects of use. There is no doubt that even the best coca chew never has the sort of impact on mood that a line of cocaine can have, but the folk version does recognise that it is a mild euphoriant – another reason for use cited by some chewers is 'for sorrow, because of my worries': chewing coca helps one to get over the sadness or think better about the worries, and then get up and get on with doing something about them. A good comparision is the 'nice cup of tea' which is the traditional British remedy of first resort for anyone suffering a crisis. Antonil also emphasises the anaesthetic effect in the mouth as the cocaine is released. This does occur, but it is not always particularly notable (once again, it seems to depend a great deal on the type and quantity of lejía used) and although it may help one to endure a toothache, by no means does it do away with it as the purified derivatives will. Above all, the anaesthetic effect is never mentioned as something sought after by traditional users, and some people even cite it as a disagreeable feeling, which put them off coca when they first tried it.

What users emphasise as desirable is the *flavour*. They seek coca which seems to them to be 'sweet' and not 'bitter', and which maintains its flavour in the mouth for as long as possible before turning 'tasteless' which means it's time to throw it away and start another wad. The quality of 'sweetness'[3] no doubt has something to do with the alkaloids released, but is determined in large part by the aromatics contained in the leaf, and these are what are affected by the conditions of production (altitude and exposure to sunlight, soil composition) and processing (the leaves should be dried within 48 hours of being harvested, and not touched by rain while they are spread on the drying floor).

LEGAL AND POLITICAL PERSECUTION
OF COCA LEAF

The studies of coca use which have been most questioned are those which, on the basis of social correlates between being a coca chewer and other characteristics such as being a poor illiterate peasant, proceeded to draw the conclusion that coca chewing actually causes illiteracy, ignorance, poverty, malnutrition and so on. The most infamous of these investigations is that carried out in Peru in the 1940s (Gutiérrez-Noriega 1947/1975), which declared that coca chewing caused mental deficiency, demonstrated not only by illiteracy but also by a negative attitude towards the superior culture (that is, middle-class Peruvian urban culture) and indifference to economic problems. The population which was studied consisted of Quechua-speaking peasants living in rural areas where little or no public education was available, and that in Spanish, and economic opportunities were limited to traditional agriculture and herding, while the psychological tests used were those designed for North American urban populations. Today, no-one would accept these conclusions, but unfortunately for the legal future of the coca leaf, they were published when the United Nations, in the first flush of enthusiasm for 'development' on a world scale, was seeking to promote 'modernisation' on all sides and to combat any habits or customs, like coca chewing, which seemed to be an obstacle to progress. The result was the inclusion of coca leaf in the first international conventions designed to combat drug abuse, on the grounds that it was addictive and damaging. In 1962, Bolivia signed the 1961 Single Convention on Narcotic Drugs, promising to put an end to coca chewing within 25 years, together with the eventual elimination of coca plantations.

By the 1970s another reason for prohibiting coca had appeared on the scene: the new wave of cocaine use in the cities of the North. Direct pressure to reduce or eliminate traditional coca use (in so far as such pressure ever existed; in Bolivia, it appears that the government trusted to social change to reduce *aculli*, and took no active measures to achieve this) had disappeared in all the Andean countries by the end of the 1980s, but has been replaced by fierce programmes directed at eliminating the cultivation of coca because it is the raw material of cocaine. The 1988 Vienna Convention on drug abuse, also signed by Bolivia, recognised 'illicit traditional uses' but declared that the cultivation of coca for the purpose of producing narcotics was a crime, and that all 'illegal' coca plantations – that is, destined for cocaine production – should be destroyed (Gironda 2001:273). In the same year, the Bolivian government promulgated the notoriously draconian Law 1008 (Regime of Coca and Controlled Substances) which replaced the less strict anti-narcotics legislation already in existence. The new law defined three zones of coca cultivation: limited areas of 'traditional cultivation' where coca growing would be allowed to continue, 'excess zones in transition' where coca plantations were to be gradually erradicated and substituted by other crops, and the 'illegal zone' which was all the rest of the country. Coca leaf 'in its natural state' and destined for consumption in 'traditional forms, such as the 'acullico' and chewing, medicinal and ritual uses' is declared legal, but coca *'iter criminis'*, that is destined to he processed for cocaine, is illegal and subject to repression. Coca chewing as such is not a target, although the legal controls on coca trading, aimed at preventing the leaves reaching drug traffickers, may raise prices and make it more difficult for some chewers to obtain the leaf. All these problems have to do with the processing of coca into cocaine. Given that the War on Drugs dominates the debates about coca in recent decades, and shows little sign of abating, a brief commentary on cocaine and coca in Bolivia is in order.

The two countries which, historically, have cultivated large extensions of coca and possess a relatively large number of traditional consumers, are Bolivia and Peru. Indigenous groups in Colombia, both in the highlands (Antonil 1978) and the lowlands (Hugh-Jones 1979:201–4) also consume coca leaves, but they represent a tiny minority within the country as a whole. When the modern cocaine boom began in the 1970s, Peru and Bolivia were the principal sources. Colombian buyers flew into those countries to purchase cocaine paste[4] which they took to Colombia to process it into crystal cocaine and then smuggled it out to the consuming countries. Coca production increased dramatically from the late 1970s; in Bolivia it expanded particularly in the Chapare, the tropical zone of the central department of Cochabamba. There had been small coca fields on the slopes descending towards the Chapare since at least the sixteenth century (Meruvia 2002) but only from the 1960s, when the large-scale colonisation of the lowlands began, did Chapare coca achieve an important impact in Bolivian markets. Whilst some Chapare leaves are sold for chewing in poor regions of Bolivia, and the best quality, selected leaves may even be exported to Argentina for chewing, giving the lie to the common claim that *all* the coca from the Chapare is used for cocaine making, it is none-the-less undeniable that the massive expansion of coca cultivation in the Chapare was basically due to the cocaine boom.

In 1980, a military government openly associated with the cocaine industry took power in Bolivia, provoking the rejection of the United States which cut off aid and froze funds (Dunkerley 1984:292–344). In 1982 a democratic government returned to power, but proved totally ineffectual on all fronts; the economy collapsed, inflation hit over 10,000% a year, and the only flourishing sector was the cocaine business, which the government made no attempt to control. During this period, the price of coca leaves continued to rise, virtually the only product that kept pace with inflation. This flourishing however, led, by 1986, to a crisis of over-production. As a consequence the price of coca leaves collapsed; anti-narcotics operations were declared and the main traffickers, evidently informed in advance of the plans, prudently retired from the scene. Colombian buyers decided that it was no longer worth the risk of travelling to Bolivia, and also began to abandon the Huallaga valley in Peru which had previously been their favourite source of supply; in the 1990s coca cultivation began to expand enormously in Colombia, and by the middle of the decade there was more land under coca in Colombia than in Peru, previously the largest producer (Vargas Meza 1997, Clawson and Lee 1996). In Bolivia, meanwhile, the government began a programme of 'voluntary eradication' of coca fields, where growers received compensation of US$2,000 per hectare of coca eradicated (Sanabria 1993). This continued until 1998, when the government of Hugo Banzer[5] decided to reduce and eventually eliminate the compensation for eradication. The reasons for this, among others, were that the money was often used to plant new coca fields, and the possibiliy of receiving money in return for uprooting them encouraged people to carry on planting coca. From January 2002, soldiers continued to uproot coca fields, but this was now carried out 'forcibly' – that is, lorry-loads of soldiers with pickaxes and an armed guard with a machine-gun accompanying every squad of ten men, simply drive up to any coca field they can find and proceed to destroy it, without consulting the owner and much less making any payment. Another irony is that these soldiers, young conscripts from the highlands doing their year of national service, can often be seen chewing coca while they uproot it.

It is not surprising that the eradication process has given rise to a constant series of protests, marches, demonstrations and armed confrontations between the Chapare coca growers and the government, with over a hundred dead to date (mainly peasant cultivators, but including some police and soldiers). Eradication is supposed to be complemented by programmes of 'alternative development', providing infrastructure such as roads, schools and drinking water, and promoting other cash crops such as bananas, oranges, passion fruit, black pepper, pineapples, palm hearts and macadamia nuts. The main problem is that the Bolivian market for these crops is very limited and rapidly saturated, while it is difficult to get access to export markets. Many coca growers shifted to these new products but gave up on them when they did not provide the income that had been promised by the programmes. At present (2003) the confrontations continue, with the growers demanding permission to cultivate at least one small plot (a quarter hectare, or less) of coca per family, while the government, in line with the US position in the War on Drugs, continues to insist on pursuing eradication with the target of 'Zero Coca' – that is, no coca at all in the Chapare. The US Embassy in La Paz has, since about 1999, 'discovered' supposedly 'excess' coca in the Yungas as well, and has demanded that this too be eradicated; until then, the Yungas had largely been left alone as a legal 'traditional zone'. The Banzer government sent troops in to start this eradication in June 2001, but they were immediately expelled by the peasants *en masse*. No more attempts have been made to date but in Bolivia at least, the War on Terrorism has not managed to displace the War on Drugs, and more conflicts over coca cultivation may be expected at any time.

A large part of the difficulty of erradication is due to the fact that all producers are independent peasant farmers. If the producers were a small number of large-scale estate owners, it would be relatively easy to target them and pay them off with compensations high enough to be invested in another profitable business. The peasants, however, are much more numerous, and the amount of coca each cultivates is not usually enough to justify compensation high enough to finance another activity with an income comparable to that provided by coca. In addition, Bolivian peasants were organised in 'syndicates' or peasant unions as part of the Agrarian Reform. In the 1950s and 1960s these unions were managed by the government, but as the peasants gained more experience in union organisation they rejected official control and now possess an independent organisation which extends from local to national level. These unions contribute to the effective organisation of coca growers' resistance to eradication programmes, and since they are legal organisations and not 'subversives' or 'guerrillas' the government is obliged to negotiate with them, instead of simply resorting to military or police repression. There have been repeated efforts to present the Chapare movement as linked to a 'narcoguerrilla' (on the lines of Sendero Luminoso in Peru, or the FARC in Colombia) but none have been at all convincing.

International prohibitions are also the principal obstacle to widening a market for coca leaf and its products apart from cocaine. As is well known, the original recipe for Coca Cola included cocaine, and numerous other drinks and patent medicines for 'sinus trouble' and other afflictions were highly popular at the end of the nineteenth century (Ashley 1975). The first US law making the possession or distribution of cocaine a crime was passed in 1914; it was gradually removed from patent medicines and drinks, and in medicine was replaced by synthetic anaesthetics like lidocaine or procaine. It was retained for medical use solely in eye surgery, where the patient requires an anaesthetic which acts immediately, as cocaine does, instead of one which has a delayed effect like the synthetics. The coca growers' movement and its sympathisers in Bolivia propose the 'industrialisation' of coca leaves as an alternative use for that part of the production which is not consumed by traditional chewers. Chewing is seen as a habit rather hard to promote; apart from social prejudices, it is rather anti-aesthetic (producing an unsightly bulge in one cheek and stained teeth and lips) and takes some learning to 'chew' properly, manage the lejía and acquire the taste. Alternatives are toffees or pills containing coca, with a more acceptable taste and easy to suck.[6] Coca tea is available in tea bags all over Bolivia and could have wide market appeal; it has an agreeable taste and, unlike coffee, does not irritate the stomach. Other products with a less immediate appeal include coca-based cough syrups, toothpaste, wine, and even a coca jam.

Unfortunately, the attempts made so far to export these products have been unprofessional, carried out by some members of sympathetic NGOs who did not investigate sufficiently the commercial regulations in the countries for which they were destined. For example, samples of *trimate* (a mixed herb tea containing coca, aniseed and camomile) exported to Belgium were rejected, not for their cocaine content but because they turned out to contain more traces of pesticides than permitted by EEC regulations. Other obstacles relate directly to cocaine – a footballer who drank coca tea before an international match failed the anti-doping test, while a US citizen who had drunk a coca syrup failed the anti-drug test he was subjected to at work. Many countries (the UK is one of them) include coca leaves in anti-drug laws in the same category as heroin and cocaine. In practice, one requires several hundred pounds of leaves to produce a reasonable quantity of cocaine hydrochloride, and the likely price of such a quantity of tea bags or coca in some other processed form in a non-producing country, without considering the additional cost of the chemicals required, would almost certainly be prohibitive. Nevertheless, the export of coca leaves would open up this possibility, and while cocaine continues to be satanized and subject to legal prohibitions, it is unlikely that many countries will admit the import of coca-based products.

Both the movement against coca eradication and the attempts to 'industrialise' the leaf and export its products use the slogan 'Coca is not cocaine'. This is true in so far as coca chewing does not have the same effects as snorting cocaine and much less smoking crack, but false in so far as coca leaves are the source of cocaine. Given that government repression is often justified by claims that the peasant movement is somehow linked with or financed by the 'drug trade' it is understandable that the peasants always declare publicly that they have nothing at all to do with cocaine making and trading, although this is hypocritical; at least during the cocaine boom of the 1980s, there were not many coca growers who did not have at least a relative involved in the fringes of the trade, although the transference of drug-related coca production to Colombia reduced this to a minimum from the 1990s onwards. More honestly, they declare that they just grow the leaves and sell them and what other people do with them after that is not their problem.

Bolivians in general claim that cocaine use is basically a rich country problem which they are not responsible for. This is in large part true. If there were not a demand for cocaine, no-one would produce it, and the number of cocaine consumers within Bolivia itself is very limited (basically a few middle-class users, and some members of the underclass who smoke cocaine paste).[7] There is evidence that cocaine does not produce physical dependence and its use tends to be self-limiting – a user may consume a lot for a time, but after a while reduces the quantity consumed or abandons it altogether because it no longer produces the same euphoria as at the beginning. A serious study of crack dealers in New York concludes that the real problems are due to poverty, racism and social exclusion, and not caused by the drug itself (Bourgois 1995). Despite the lack of empirical proofs – and notable failure in achieving its expressed ends -the rhetoric of the War on Drugs, backed up by conservative moralising about the duty to protect 'young people' and 'the family' from chemical menaces and the criminal mafias that deal in them, is useful to governments everywhere when it is necessary to justify repression of undesirable groups, from the lumpenproletariat (native and/or immigrant) in the inner-city slums of the North to militant peasant farmers in the Andes. It is also useful for increasing border and immigration controls all over the world, and now that communism has ceased to be a threat, provides a reason for intervening directly or indirectly in the internal affairs of Third World countries. More rational debate on drug use may help to combat the prohibitions and promote a gradual relaxation of legal controls, but the sad truth is that drug prohibitions are unlikely to disappear until the forces of repression have discovered another cause which is equally adaptable for their ideological ends – or until repression ceases to be a central element of national and international politics, an even more utopian dream.

1 Top quality chewing coca (from high altitude, clay soils in Nor and Sud Yungas provinces) stays tasty for two hours or more. Coca from Inquisivi province, from similar altutudes, is not so good (probably due to different soils) and local chewers say it turns tasteless within an hour or so. Allen (1988:128) mentions chewers in Cusco throwing away wads after 45 minutes, which suggests inferior coca. The coca I have encountered on sale in Peru was definitely inferior, and frontier provinces obtain Bolivian Yungas coca when they can. This seems to be due to the government monopoly which controls coca trading in Peru and pays a flat price for all leaves, thus removing any incentive to take the extra care required to produce top quality leaves. In Bolivia the trade is in private hands and buyers pay a premium for first quality leaves, less for second or third quality, much less for discoloured leaves, and higher prices for special types such as 'selected' or 'destalked' leaves, which are mainly destined for the Argentinian export market (Rivera, this volume).

2 This is a notable contrast with the Nasa (formerly Paez) in the Colombian highlands, studied by Antonil (1978), where coca chewing is basically for men and only post-menopausal women chew. Likewise, coca chewing is a male practice for the lowland Barasana, in Colombian Amazonia (Hugh-Jones 1979). The

erotic interpretation of 'Mama Coca', the spirit of the leaf, presented by the first author thus lacks validity for the southern Andes.

3   This 'sweetness' has nothing to do with the sweetness of honey; it is an acquired taste, like that of dry wine or black coffee.

4   The usual process for making cocaine in Bolivia and Peru is as follows. Coca leaves are macerated and crushed by treating them in a dilute solution of sulphuric acid. The resulting juice is treated with kerosene and other chemicals to produce an off-white substance known as 'basic cocaine paste', mainly consisting of cocaine sulphate. This is then 'washed' with ammonia and potassium permanganate to remove the impurities. The third step involves dissolving it in acetone or ether and applying hydrochloric acid to produce 'crystal', cocaine hydrochloride. This can be snorted or injected. The two previous stages are insoluble in water, thus easier to store or transport, but cannot be snorted, only smoked mixed with tobacco. The figures on how many kilos of leaves are needed to make a kilo of base are very variable, but all agree that one needs hundreds of pounds of leaves to make a few kilos of even very impure paste. As a result, the first stage is only practical in the producing countries where large quantities of leaves can be obtained without difficulty.

5   Ironically, the same man who, as a military dictator in the 1970s, oversaw and is held in large part reponsable for the takeoff of the cocaine industry in Bolivia. His son-in-law and other family members were involved in scandals involving cocaine smuggling. See Dunkerley (1984: 199–248) for the history of his rule as dictator.

6   Coca toffees can be purchased in the Museo de la Coca (Coca Museum) in the centre of La Paz. They are pleasant to suck and have a slight stimulant effect. Their maker, however, is a psychiatrist who became interested in coca chewing as a treatment for cocaine paste smokers, and has made no effort to find an export market for them.

7   In recent years there have been claims that the use of cocaine and marijuana in Bolivia is rising rapidly, giving rise to an internal 'drug problem'. However, the studies that supposedly demonstrate this have a dubious scientific base (for instance, those who reply 'don't know/don't answer' when asked if they have ever used a substance, are classed as 'evasive users', that is lying about their use, and used to inflate the percentage of users), and even so barely reach figures of 3% for those who have ever tried marijuana and 1.5% who have ever tried cocaine. See Laserna (1996) for a useful criticism of this and other mistaken arguments about coca and cocaine in Bolivia.

REFERENCES

Allen, Catherine (1988) The hold life has. Coca and cultural identity in an Andean community. Washington and London: Smithsonian Institution Press.

Antonil, (Anthony Henman) (1978) Mama Coca. London: Hassle Free Press.

Arriaga, Pablo José de (1621/1999) La extirpación de la idolatría en el Perú. Cusco: Centro Bartolomé de las Casas.

Ashley, Richard (1975) Cocaine. New York: St Martin's Press.

Bertonio, Ludovico (1612/1984) Vocabulario de la lengua aymara. Cochabamba: CERES.

Bolton, Ralph (1976) Andean coca chewing: a metabolic perspective. American Anthropologist 78(3).

Bourgois, Philippe (1995) In search of respect. Selling crack in El Barrio. Cambridge: Cambridge University Press.

Burchard (1975) Coca chewing: a new perspective. In Rubin, Vera (editor) Cannabis and culture. The Hague: Mouton.

Carter, William and Mauricio MAMANI (1986) Coca en Bolivia. La Paz: Editorial Juventud.

Clawson, Patrick and Rensselaer W. LEE III (1996) The Andean cocaine industry. New York: St Martin's Press.

Dunkerley, James (1984) Rebellion in the veins. Political struggle in Bolivia, 1952–1982. London: Verso.

Garcilaso de la Vega, Inca (1609/1985) Comentarios reales de los Incas. Lima: Banco del Crédito del Perú. Biblioteca Clásicos del Perú 1.

Gironda, Eusebio (2001) Coca inmortal. La Paz: Plural.

Glave, Luís Miguel (1989) La producción de los trajines: coca y mercado interno colonial. In Trajinantes.Caminos indígenas en la sociedad colonial, siglos XVI/XVII. Lima: Instituto de Apoyo Agrario.

Gutierrez Noriega, Carlos (1947/1975) Mental alterations produced by coca. In Andrews, George and David Solomon: The coca leaf and cocaine papers. London and New York: Harcourt, Brace and Jovanovich.

Hanna, Joel (1974) Coca leaf use in southern Peru: some biosocial aspects. American Anthropologist 76(2).

Hugh-Jones, Christine (1979) From the milk river. Spatial and temporal processes in Northwest Amazonia. Cambridge: Cambridge University Press.

Klein, Herbert (1993) Haciendas and 'ayllus'. Rural society in the Bolivian Andes in the eighteenth and nineteenth centuries. Stanford: Stanford University Press.

Laserna, Roberto (1996) 20 juicios y prejuicios sobre coca-cocaina. La Paz: Clave Consultores SRL.

Meruvia Bladerrama, Fanor (2002) Historia de la coca. Los Yungas de Pocona y Totora (1550–1900). La Paz: Plural Editores/CERES/Alcaldía de Totora.

Murra, John (editor)(1991) Visita de los valles de Sonqo. Madrid: Instituto de Cooperación Iberoamericana.

Nash, June (1979) We eat the mines and the mines eat us. Dependency and exploitation in Bolivian tin mines. New York. Columbia University Press.

Plowman, Timothy (1986) Coca chewing and the botanical origins of coca (Erythroxylum sp.) in South America. In Pacini, Deborah and Christine Franquemont (editors) Coca and cocaine: effects on people and policy in South America. Cambridge, Mass.: Cultural Survival Inc.

Prescott William H. (1847/1961) The conquest of Peru. New York: New American Library.

Rostworowski de Diez Canseco, María (1977) Plantaciones prehispánicas de coca en la vertiente del Pacífico. In Costa peruana prehispánica. Lima: Instituto de Estudios Peruanos.

Sanabria, Harry (1993) The coca boom and rural social change in Bolivia. Ann Arbor: University of Michigan Press.

Sharon, Douglas (1978) Wizard of the four winds. ·

Soux, María Luisa (1993) La coca liberal. Producción y circulación a principios del siglo XX. La Paz: Cocayapu/CID.

Spedding, Alison (1994) Wachu wachu. Cultivo de coca e identidad en los yunkas de La Paz. La Paz: CIPCA/Cocayapu/HISBOL.

Vargas Meza Ricardo (1997) Colombia y el área andina. Los vacios de la guerra. In del Olmo, Rosa (editor) Drogas. El conflicto de fin de siglo. Caracas: Cuadernos de Nueva Sociedad.

Zinberg, N. (1994) Drug, Set, and Setting: The Basis for Controlled Intoxicant Use, New York, Yale University Press.

Chapter Four

A QUASI-LEGAL COMMODITY IN THE ANDES: COCA LEAF CONSUMPTION IN NORTH-WESTERN ARGENTINA

Silvia Rivera Cusicanqui

'In La Quiaca there aren't Argentinean or Bolivian Indians. There are, simply, Indians' (Jaime Molins, 1916).

INTRODUCTION

Coca leaves have been produced, circulated and consumed in the Andes for several thousand years. Soon after the Spanish conquest of the Inka state in 1532, and overcoming the initial attempts by the *conquistadores* to satanize and ban the trade, coca leaves became in fact, along with minted silver and Andean textiles, grains and tubers, one of the key commodities of the trade circuitry called the *trajin*[1], thus an early sign of the 'modernity' of the Andean colonial and postcolonial markets. The silver mining centre of Potosi (in today's Bolivia) was at the heart of this system, attracting labour and produce from a vast regional space (from Quito, in today's Ecuador to Tucumán, in today's Argentina) not only to enable work in refining and minting silver but to participate actively in the circulation of money that, through its movement, transformed and reconstructed the local economies and productive units in the Andean region. This has been seen as a complex and multifarious process of 'adaptive resistance' through mercantilization (cf. Stern 1987).

The liberalizing and progressive aspects of this market have been overlooked by researchers and historically were blocked by successive attempts at State monopoly, fiscal pressure and expropriation of land and resources from the indigenous communities by the colonial (and later republican

65

criollo) elites. Since the 17th century and up to the agrarian reform of 1953, the coca producing regions of the Yungas of La Paz and Cochabamba were dominated by large haciendas with servile labor, although the trade remained largely in the hands of native and *cholo* (or *mestizo*) entrepreneurs and free communities of the highlands and valleys (Soux 1993).[2] During this same period, the economic agency of Andean peasants and traders, as well as of native and *cholo* merchant elites, established a long-term historical tendency, realized in the materiality of trade as well as in the symbolic and cultural interaction of people-through-commodities (Marx 1946, Appadurai 1988). The intensity and diversity of the demand for indigenous commodities was thus able to open crevices in the rigid caste-like structure of colonial and postcolonial society, in spite of the institutionalized privileges granted to the *conquistadores* and later to their republican *criollo* heirs.[3]

Two events had a profound impact on the long term process of circulation and exchange of coca leaves established in colonial times. First, the independence of Andean nation-states in the early 19th century created a new map of borderlands and fiscal controls over the routes through which commodities reached long-distance consumption centres, suddenly turning internal market exchanges into import-export trade or into contraband. Second, in 1860 a new character entered the scene: cocaine, one among fourteen alkalloids contained in the leaves, was synthesized in Europe and became commercially available worldwide. Soon, this became a popular medicinal and recreational drug, so famous that it would provoke heated medical and political debates involving personalities such as Freud, Mantegazza and others, contributing to enduring myths about the effects of coca leaves that still have followers in the West (Andrews and Salomon, 1975). In the Andean countries, the attitudes toward this debate followed divergent paths, revealing the economic interests involved. Thus, while Bolivian *hacendados* and indigenous entrepreneurs largely remained suppliers for the regional markets of coca-leaf 'chewers'[4], between 1860 and 1950 Peru became the main producer of industrial, legal cocaine for the world market, resisting fiercely, though without success, the international drive towards its prohibition (Gootenberg 1999).

Historian Ruggiero Romano (1982) has analysed this transition from legal to illegal and its impact on the coca-leaf economy, in terms of two 'false equations': from *good coca=good cocaine*, to *bad cocaine=bad coca*. The latter became the official position of the United Nations after the publication in 1950 of the results of the *Commission of Enquiry on the Coca Leaf* based on a bibliographical discussion and a series of interviews in Peru and Bolivia (mainly with the white medical and entrepreneurial establishment) presented during the twelfth period of sessions in New York (ONU, 1950). The conceptual framework of this enquiry was provided by among others, Peruvian scientist Carlos Gutiérrez de Noriega, who in the 1940s claimed to have demonstrated that coca is just a plant carrier of cocaine, and that the coca-leaf chewer is under the permanent toxic influence of this substance[5].

The debates that took place around this issue will not be dealt with here (see Rivera 2003 b) but they can help us to understand the divergent 'life histories' of coca as a commodity in both countries, i.e. the cultural patterns of value and meaning that underlie its production, circulation and consumption, and the changes thereof through time (Appadurai 1988: 12–13). Thus, while the dominant position in Peru was to defend the modern, industrial production of cocaine, rejecting the chewing habit as a dirty, unhealthy and backward indigenous tradition (Gootenberg 2002) the Bolivian elite, particularly the *hacendados* of the Yungas region, well aware of the commercial value, long distance market circuits and trans-cultural consumption patterns of coca leaves, had been involved for decades in a campaign to defend the habit, stressing digestive, stimulant and nutritional value, as well as potential for universal consumption (Fernández 1932, Lema 1997).

Events in the 1950s would put an end to the involvement of the Bolivian elite in the defence of coca-leaf production: the social revolution of 1952, led by the MNR (Movimiento Nacionalista Revolucionario), and the agrarian reform initiated in 1953 transformed the economy of coca producing regions into a landscape of small *cocales* (coca fields, ranging from one sixth to one hectare), in the hands of aymara and qhichwa speaking peasant families. The MNR, a party of elite leadership and popular constituency, took up with missionary zeal the task to 'civilize indians' and eliminate traditions of sociality that were thought to be exclusive to them (Rivera 1993 a, b). A myth that was widely shared by both national and international observers (and still employed today against coca leaves by Bolivian and US government officials) is that they are used as a substitute for food, and that their consumption is linked to conditions of deprivation and hard labour. But it is common knowledge among chewers, as Carter and Mamani (1978) demonstrated through a detailed national survey in rural and mining areas, that coca leaves are consumed after meals, due to their digestive properties, but otherwise, just as coffee and cigarettes are used around the world. The recreational and medicinal consumption of the leaves and their use as an anti-acid, a mild stimulant to prevent drowsiness and fatigue, or to ease digestion (functions that are especially important at high altitudes), has been overlooked as the basis of the contemporary expansion of the habit, not only among the urban population in Bolivia (which was not included in the survey by Carter and Mamani, 1978 [6]) but in neighbouring countries as well.

Eventually, this entire realm of economic realities became totally eclipsed by what was known as the 'cocaine boom' in the late-1970s and 1980s, involving Andean peasant migrants, mainly to the lowlands of Cochabamba, in the expansion of the area under cultivation and in the domestic production of cocaine *pasta,* supplied to local mafias (dominated by elite members of the military and the police, as well as by prominent politicians) and to the Colombian transformation industry[7]. This fact has contributed to the erasure of the other trajectories of the leaf, and has cast a shadow on the subsisting and expanding legal markets, systematically ignoring the increasing number of people (not only traditional Andean peasants) that chew the leaf as a natural medicine as well as in recreational and work-related contexts.

The War on Drugs is one of America's many irrational wars and has been sustained ideologically through a contemporary version of the 'prose of counterinsurgency' (Guha 1983), that implies an epistemological and political effort on the part of those in power, to primitivize and criminalize the *cocaleros* (coca leaf producers) as well as to deny the existence of modern and licit markets for the coca leaf, which tend to grow following the same trans-regional circuits as the colonial *trajín*[8]. In spite of the interdictive efforts, producers, traders and consumers have succeeded in keeping alive a market for the various brands of 'selected' leaves and, by so doing, managing to limit the official attempt to push the cocaleros towards the illegal trade which justifies military intervention and repression against producers by shifting definitions of areas considered 'legal' or 'excedentary'. These definitions are highly political, as they imply a series of conversions (from aerial photographs to hectares, from hectares to metric tons of dried leaf crop, from the latter to cocaine) based in non-transparent and unreliable methods of calculation (Rivera 2002, 2003b). As one analyst put it, 'information is selectively sought and elaborated to justify decisions already made' (Laserna 1997: 210).

In this chapter, I will attempt to describe the social and cultural organization of an economic and geographical space where the biography of coca-leaves most ostensibly diverges from the so-called coca-cocaine complex, and where price differentials (among other factors) constitute an economic force that blocks the use of these leaves for industrial purposes. The core of the chapter is an ethnography but before moving onto this, I will outline the original purposes and context of this research.

EMERGENCY IN THE YUNGAS OF LA PAZ

The historical narrative and 'road ethnography' that follow were prompted by an event that was long announced but not really believed until it happened. In mid-June, 2001, a task force of combined army and police anti-narcotics soldiers invaded the core of the 'legal coca' region in the Yungas of La Paz to erradicate the 'legal' coca crops that were allegedly being cultivated there. After seven days of an impressive mobilization on the part of *cocalero* families, traders, transporters, and townspeople, the *Fuerza de Trabajo Conjunta* (Combined Task Force) had to abandon the region. The producer organizations forced the government of General Banzer to sign

an agreement whereby the Yungas region would be respected and the restrictive regulations on commercialization would be reformed. The cocaleros in the Yungas are well aware of the destination of their coca-leaf crop, and since the late eighties, they have specialized in the production of two types of 'selected' coca leaves for long distance consumption markets, which are expanding in and outside the borders of Bolivia[9].

As Appadurai (1988) has shown in his study on 'the social life of things', one of the issues involved in unequal exchange and in the neo-colonial price differentials that emerge at different points in the 'life history' of indigenous commodities is that trade imbalances involve differential access to knowledge – from producer, to trader, to consumer. Through the power and reality effect of images, hundreds of cocalero producers in the Yungas were able to see for themselves the various forms of consumption and the different cultural meanings attached to coca-leaf in places distant from their small-scale local society, such as North-western Argentina. Moreover, if the black legend[10] of coca attributes to the Spanish *conquistadores* the expansion of the chewing habit as a means to supplement food deficits and secure the increased exploitation of forced labour in the mines, the discovery of modern recreational forms of consumption in Argentina, in which 'whites' or mestizos of European descent were actively involved, gave the producers a strong argument in favour of the de-penalization of the coca-leaf trade and its qualification as a modern medicine and natural stimulant, appropriate for export markets. The cognitive gap is related, as we will see below, to the dominant official view that *akhulliku* (see endnote 4) is a traditional indigenous habit that is being swept away by progress and modernization. The idea of public consumption as natural, the cultural diversity of consumers and the variety of contexts in which Northern Argentineans of all social backgrounds involve themselves in *coqueo* (coca chewing), had a revealing effect that reached the Bolivian public in a moment when crucial decisions on the fate of the legal coca crop were being taken by the Bolivian government under political and economic pressure from the USA, largely without the participation of peasant organizations (see the complete report on our research by the journal *Pulso*, La Paz, October 26–November 1, 2001, and *Coca*, Rivera 2003b).

The following section will deal with the diverse contexts of consumption, as well as with ritual practices that are becoming increasingly popular as 'invented traditions' (Hobsbawm and Ranger 1983) in the Argentinean North-west, considering their implications as signals of regional identity linked to practices and beliefs related to the construed memory of an authentic, indigenous past but, at the same time, taking place in the context of modern forms of interaction and sociality.

CROSSING THE BORDER THROUGH VILLAZÓN

'Argentina is becoming like Bolivia', I said to Félix Barra, as we were travelling towards the provincial capital of Jujuy. We had just faced a series of paradoxes in the border city of La Quiaca. Crossing the border represents a buoyant illegal business for a series of enterprises based on contraband, unequal exchange, and multiple extortions from migrants, particularly from Bolivia and Peru. To begin with, there were moneylenders who loaned around $100US per day, for ten days, in order that their customers could meet the requirement that they demonstrate available funds to qualify as a 'tourist' when questioned by the Gendarmería or Argentinean police at the border. Once in the bus that would take them to the inland cities or agricultural areas, the moneylender sent an agent to reclaim the money but at an interest rate of 30% accrued in little more than one hour! Ricardo Abduca has called this system of calculated exploitation based on international border legislation (and its violation) a 'frontier rent', a sort of colonial tax that is charged to tourists and to migrants on account of the existence of an international border. In practice, an operation of extortion based on the racial and national stereotypes which are the result of a combination of power-knowledge relations. Commercial earnings, illegal exactions, legal constraints and subtle or overt forms of racism have created a series of economic opportunities for actors with unequal access to power (such as *gendarmes*, frontier policemen, smugglers, and prospective illegal migrants (Abduca, ca. 1994: 9–10)).

Such disparities particularly affect transportation of coca leaves, yet due to high demand and cultural acceptance of the coca habit, special *frontier rent* is created, associated with the current application of anti-drug policies, which paradoxically through banning coca leaf actually encourages the smuggling of its rival commodity, cocaine, because this is less conspicuous, low weight and has other political advantages at the border[11]. Needless to say, neither one nor the other were visibly transported through the border and we were not interested in contraband *per se* but in the cultural meaning and economic value of the market for coca leaves in their natural state as an alternative market for the so called 'legal' Bolivian crop of leaves. Thus, although we had seen huge loads of coca *takis* (fifty pound packages) in the terminal at Villazón, as well as in Tupiza, the coca leaf bundles disappeared at the border. However, the further we travelled inland, crossing the high altitude mountain range and down toward the provincial capitals of Salta and Jujuy, the more conspicuous the sale of coca leaves became.

JUJUY AND SALTA

Jujuy is the lively capital of the north-western province of the same name. There is a busy street and bar atmosphere in the popular commercial area around the bus terminal, which got quieter as we approached the centre of town. Attracted by the lights, we stopped at a large billiard room, full of mostly male customers chewing coca as they silently played billiards. We were lured in by this atmosphere, where chewing coca in public didn't seem to carry any sort of prejudice or social shame. The saloon was quite spacious and had high ceilings with fans and neon lights. In groups of two to five, the players concentrated on the precision of the game and were chewing coca leaves as if this was the most natural thing in the world. We noted that consumption seemed to be a strictly individual affair. Nobody offered coca to anybody else and every once in a while, they took some *bica* (sodium bicarbonate) or *llipta* (alcaline substance made from ashes of plants) from special containers and added it to the wad, in order to reinforce the flavour and the strength of the leaves held in their cheeks. Nobody 'chewed' the leaves but they kept the coca wad (*bolo* or *akusi*) in the mouth for hours, gently turning it around and sucking it.

The images I registered gave us an appreciation of a masculine and nocturnal scenario in which the habitual consumption of coca leaves takes place. The clients and the bartenders of this saloon, located in the centre of the city, were using coca leaves in a classic form: as a mild stimulant to keep a lucid mind and to avoid drowsiness and fatigue. Although a few of the players were smoking cigarettes, it was mostly the people seated around the tables who were smoking, as well as parsimoniously drinking locally produced alcoholic beverages such as ginebra, beer and wine, or imported ones, such as whisky. When we left, it was past two in the morning. The atmosphere was still lively and the concentration of the billiard players had not diminished. No doubt, many of them would stay up until sunrise.

Our interview at the journal El Pregón a few days later, as well as the long conversation we had with members of the CTA (Argentinian Central Union of Workers) in the previous afternoon, confirmed the dissemination of the habit of *coqueo* in different contexts, such as the workplace or union meetings. Male and female reporters at the newspaper headquarters chewed the leaves while working and paused their business to chat with us, after we had been interviewed by a journalist. The interview resulted in an article with large headlines and two photographs in the central pages of the journal. It is worth noting the natural way in which coca leaf chewing was represented in the photography. One of the photos showed a woman from the Puna (one of highest and driest regions in the world), with her child putting a coca leaf in her mouth, and the other portrayed Félix taking coca leaves from his *ch'uspa* (a hand woven coca leaf bag) and giving them to me[12]. After the interview, as the photographer received the leaves that Félix offered, he put his hands together in a cup, as is usually done in traditional Andean etiquette: 'Do you usually receive the coca leaves like this?' I asked; 'Yes, of course. It is a matter of respect', he answered. Three other journalists, who were in front of the screens of their computers, took out their bags or boxes for coca leaves, to receive handfuls from Félix. One had recycled an old tobacco box, lining it with a blue plastic bag to keep his leaves fresh: 'It is really good, is it from the Yungas?' he asked Félix; 'From Coripata' he answered proudly. A woman journalist summarized the ambiguities between law and common practice:

'I don't know in which law but there is an article that allows coca leaf chewing, no problem. But what happens? That it is allowed in Salta and Jujuy but not in the rest of the country. My brother-in-law travels a lot, he goes to Buenos Aires and elsewhere. He wants to die when he goes out of the province because, if they catch him with half a kilo of coca leaves, he goes to jail. Just for carrying coca leaves he can go to jail. To jail!!. Because they don't know that there is a little piece, a little article in the law that permits *coqueo*' (Collective interview, journal El Pregón, 30 July, 2001, see video annex, *Las Fronteras de la Coca*).

This information is actually inaccurate, since Law 23737 is a Federal Law and therefore it has decriminalized coca-leaf possession and consumption throughout the entire country. Yet the ideas of the jujeño journalist reveal a lot about the political economy of the coca-leaf trade, marked by cultural valorization and perceived obstacles that are enforced by *habitus* more than by actual legal restrictions (Bourdieu 1991a). This is surely the reason why, as one goes further south, prices increase astronomically. A kiosk owner in Jujuy, who worked in one of the busiest streets downtown, said that in Catamarca and Córdoba (cities further south, midway to Buenos Aires) coca leaves cost 70 pesos per kilo (from 70 to 40 $US, depending on the exchange rate), which compared to Bolivian prices imply a 500% to 800% price increase.

The intensity, geographical scope and seriousness of prohibition were the subjects of a series of speculations in our conversations with various taxi-drivers, bartenders and store clerks in our walks through the city. During the interview with members of the CTA, journalist Raúl Noro, correspondent of La Nación (one of the main journals of Buenos Aires), gave us a postcard where the relevant paragraphs of Federal Law 23737 were printed:

Art. 15: The possession and consumption of coca leaves in natural form, as a habitual practice of *coqueo* or chewing, or as coca leaf tea, will not be regarded as possession or consumption of drugs. Federal Law 23737 was sanctioned on the 21st of September, 1989, approved on the 10th of October, 1989, in application of Art. 70 of the National Constitution and published in the Official Bulletin as of 11 October 1989 (my translation).

Carrying this postcard, which had been printed by the National Congress in August 1994, consumers who wished to travel outside the provinces where *coqueo* was a tolerated habit, could use it to support their legal rights as consumers in case the police tried to arrest them. This information about the law was an important way to cope with long established prejudices and misconceptions about the legal status of coca in Argentina, although for us it also left unanswered the paradox involved in the decriminalization of consumption and possession, while at the same time, the ban on commercial transportation of bulk coca leaves across the border remained untouched. It was no secret that illegally crossing the border carries risk but the current situation seems to criminalize the Bolivian retailers and wholesalers more than their Argentinean counterparts. When in La Quiaca we even saw a *gendarme* chewing coca leaves though we were unable to film him. People told us that the *gendarmes* stationed at the border receive bribes to let coca leaf pass and that they resell confiscated coca in the retail stores of the towns further south. The *gendarmería* occasionally incinerate seized leaves to attract press coverage and publicly demonstrate their zealous enforcement of the law (interview with Zacarías Gutiérrez, La Quiaca, August 7th, 2001). It thus seems that crossing the border with coca leaves implies special risks for stigmatized populations, such as indigenous and mestizo merchants from Bolivia, or jujeño peasants from the Quebrada and the high altitude Puna. Anthropologist Mercedes Costa, a resident in Maymara, a small town on the road to Tilcara, told us that a few years ago a baby had been killed, stabbed in the back bundle (*q'ipi*) of her mother, by a policeman who thought it was a hidden bulk of coca leaves (interview with Mercedes Costa, Maymara, August 3, 2001).

At the end of July, we were invited to a restaurant, whose owner is a middle-aged woman from La Quiaca, of Bolivian descent. It is one of the best typical restaurants in Jujuy, where one can eat hot stews of a mixed Bolivian-Puneño origin while folk music is being played by the best local performers and groups. That night was special because it was the eve of the *pachamama* (earth deity) festivities, and the ceremony of the *ch'alla* (offerings and libations) was announced. What followed was a conspicuous representation of the nocturnal modernity of Northern Argentina; a mix of invented traditions, vague memories of a pre-capitalist past, and a host of un-recognized debts to the rural Andean cultures of both sides of the border. The *ch'alla* to the Pachamama (Andean earth deity) consisted in burying food while expressing desires and prayers using beer or wine ceremonially. Then everybody offered coca leaves covering the buried food, and offered cigarettes to smoke and share with the Andean gods. Variations of this type of ceremony in honour of the *pachamama* are held throughout Jujuy and Salta during the month of August.

This scene is similar to what we saw in Salta, one hour distance by bus from Jujuy. As we were walking through the commercial streets downtown, we were surprised to see painted signs, posters and even neon signs advertising the leaf: 'Don't tell anybody. Coca, Export Type. Selected, *Despalillada* (Stalked), Common'. The poster also announced candy, beverages and cigarettes. Another big store, called Ke Koka, offered all types of coca leaves at different prices, in packages from one ounce to a quarter kilo, 24 hours a day. In its logo, the letters E, O and A were designed as coca leaves, with a big luminous display that could be seen from afar, together with a Coca-Cola advertisement. Another sign at the door of a store, said: 'Selected Coca leaves. Bolivian Bica' (sodium bicarbonate). Further on, at the San Silvestre store, which had branches in other cities, there was a neon sign with the design of green coca leaves over a blue backdrop with its logo. In all these stores, the product was dispensed in special sealed and printed plastic bags. The Secus and Ke Koka stores had stickers with the store's logo and handsome designs with green coca leaves. The fanciest kind of package included a bag of sodium bicarbonate or *llipta*, which came along with the selected *despalillada* variety. This is a special and more expensive leaf, where the stalk has been cut out to avoid hurting the mucous tissues of the mouth. An habitual chewer would do this by hand as he or she puts the leaves in the mouth but the *despalillada* would save one this 'effort'. The display and packaging of the different varieties of coca leaves reveal the various styles and etiquettes of chewing, as well as the preferences of *conoisseur* consumers. This is also the case with handcrafted leather bags for carrying the leaves, or little cases made of horn or silver, which are used to carry sodium bicarbonate or *llipta*. All of these items are very popular in the artisan markets of Salta and Jujuy.

Far from the centre of town in Salta, we also discovered a street market where women from Bolivia were sitting on precarious benches behind wooden boxes, on top of which they displayed ritual items such as alcohol, coca leaves and a variety of *lliptas*, all produced in Bolivia. The coca leaves were already packed in green plastic bags containing as little as a quarter of an ounce, to as much as one ounce. It was a type of small-scale retail market for ritual consumption, where coca leaves are used to do the *t'inkas* or *ch'allas* (coca leaf offerings and libations invoking mountain spirits) of August. For a while we walked through the place and met customers, all of them of modest appearance, probably Bolivian migrants and workers who had to pay the August offerings and share some coca leaves with friends or relatives. They usually chose one ounce bags, at a much lower price than in the retail stores of the busy commercial area: 1 peso per ounce of what seemed to be a small or *taki* variety of a slightly lower quality. In contrast, the retail stores owned by established entrepreneurs from Salta, charged from 2 to 2.50 pesos for an ounce of *taki* leaves, 3 pesos for the selected (big and regular) leaves and up to 4 pesos for the *despalillada* from which the stalks had been removed. The latter usually included a small amount of *bica*, and it is worth noting that Bolivian sodium bicarbonate seemed to have a reputation for good quality.

That evening we went to a folkloric restaurant (*peña*) located in one of the central and busiest streets of Salta. Customers at most tables were using coca leaves, some with sodium bicarbonate and others with *lejía* or *llipta*. As in the billiard saloon in Jujuy, the style of *coqueo* was modern, individualistic and its etiquette showed the habit of connoisseurs. Nobody really 'chewed' the leaves and the big coca leaf wads were bulky in their cheeks, slowly being turned around and supplemented with alkaline substances or more leaves. While there we had a brief conversation with a woman who happened to be a high official of the *Dirección de Prevención de Adicciones* (Bureau for the Prevention of Addictions). While she skillfully mixed the leaves with sodium bicarbonate, she mentioned Law 23737 that decriminalizes *coqueo*, and referred to its current experimental use by local physicians in the treatment of addictions to tobacco, cocaine hydrochloride and cocaine base, a therapy successfully introduced twenty years ago by Bolivian psychiatrist Hurtado (1995). The ground floor of the *peña* was full of people and one image symbolises the type of consumer market we were witnessing. On a table, a woman in her thirties had put her cell phone, the keys to her car and a green bag of coca leaves. There was also a glass of wine and a dish with sodium bicarbonate. To us, she seemed the perfect modern consumer, an independent professional or upscale bureaucrat, who was enjoying herself alone and visibly at ease in this night of partying and live music.

Next day we travelled to the Concert of the Mountain, in a natural amphitheatre carved by water currents from the red rock, on the way to Cafayate, the southernmost town of the Salta province. The scenario was awesome and it served as an acoustic shell for an extraordinary music concert, combining both the folklore of the Argentinean North and classical music, played by various groups, including a chamber orchestra from Germany. *Coqueo* was widespread in the audience. Among the music groups many played Bolivian genres such as the *waynu*, the *kacharpaya* and the carnival dances of Oruro. This sort of 'appropriation' of Bolivian music would have bothered more than one among the chauvinist members of the Bolivian elite but to us, the fact that a group from Buenos Aires was playing *Señora Chichera*, the *Diablada* (Devil's Dance) or *Ojos Azules* (pieces emblematic of Bolivian folklore), did not seem a case of 'cultural theft'[13] but an example of the expansive and hegemonic potential of the Andean culture in the context of a crisis-ridden country whose links with Europe have only served to create a distorted mirror of the West. Along with *empanadas* (meat pies) and *locro* (a local stew), wine and *ginebra*, coca leaves were consumed by a variety of people, from hippie artisans to university professors, bohemians and music lovers from the intellectual elite of Salta. Among them there were many survivors of the military dictatorships that had caused so many disappearances and deaths in the 1970s. In this culturally and politically charged environment, coca leaf chewing had become a symbol of invented traditions and identities that had both emotional and political connotations, connecting modern markets with deeply felt memories and motley cultural practices.

The inclusion of 'sahumerio'[14] or *misa dulce* (sweet mass or table) in the *pachamama* ceremonies currently performed in Salta and Jujuy seems to have spread only recently, through influences from the Bolivian Altiplano of Oruro and Potosi. Yet, the burial of food and coca is linked to local rituals by the indigenous dwellers of the Puna. The ritual practices that were previously confined to the isolated and discriminated communities of 'muleteers, herdsmen and weavers', that folk narrator Fausto Burgos described in the 1920s, have now come down to the cities and expanded transculturally. At the Jujuy market it was quite impressive to see how many *misas* of various sizes were being sold from 1 to 10 pesos ($1–10(US) at the time). The street and market trade of *sahumerios* and other ritual items is intense by the end of July and throughout the month of August (when the earth is hungry). The *pachamama* rituals have been expanding due to the general wave or revitalization of cultural expressions by both local and migrant populations. Along with coca leaves, an intense and somewhat hidden import trade of ritual items from Bolivia (including llama fetuses, llama lard and others) is flourishing, and the demand for authenticity still favours the shamanic and ritualistic knowledge of Bolivian traders.

REFLECTIONS IN THE MIRROR
OF A BORDERLINE

During the course of our ethnographic journey we were unable to gain access to some spaces for first-hand observation or video recording. For example, the Provincial House of Representatives, public or private clinics and hospitals, and the Judicial Courts, require special permits for admission that are not easy to obtain. However, our evidence points to the normality of *coqueo* in such contexts, both among elite officers and doctors and rank and file employees, much as the coffee break has been universally established in other urban and modern contexts. Furthermore, while sharing coca leaves is usual practice in the kind of rituals described above, it is the individualized form of consumption that is dominant within the professional strata of those (both male and female) who chew in public and in the workplace. This is in sharp contrast to Bolivia, where it would be unthinkable to find public employees, judges or medical doctors chewing coca-leaves during work hours (even if they like *akhulliku* in private).

Perhaps the most evident contrast between Bolivia and Northern Argentina regarding the normality of coca-leaf chewing can be found among professionals working in the media. In Northern Argentina, newspaper and radio journalists are champions of *coqueo* and perhaps it is their personal experience with the habit that allows a more balanced representation of the issue in their reporting. But in Bolivian journals of La Paz or Cochabamba, the press-rooms would be full of cigarette smoke and a journalist would seldom be seen chewing coca leaves. The Bolivian press is thoroughly censored and strongly supports government and US campaigns against *cocaleros*. Prejudices are common among government officials but journalists do not seem aware of the distorted information they are helping to spread. The stereotyped perceptions of the Bolivian elite are in sharp contrast with the attitude of public figures and journalists in Salta and Jujuy who have first hand experience of the effects of coca-leaf chewing.

The undergraduate and graduate students in Salta and Jujuy are also an important sector among the practitioners of *coqueo*. While giving talks and courses in the public universities of both cities (1998), I have observed the normality of *coqueo* among students, during and after classes. Many of them also carried to their classrooms the large and ostentatious implements that are used to drink *yerba mate*, the stimulant herb discovered by *guarani* peoples in pre-hispanic America[15]. In Bolivia, the use of coca leaves among university students is also quite usual but as the accompanying social stigma is still strong, the contexts for *akhulliku* are much less visible. Nonetheless, in Cochabamba, as *cocalero* demands have become a public and political issue of general appeal to the public, coca-leaf chewing by university students has become an activity with both recreational and political implications. 'First Friday' ceremonies (*ch'alla* and libations to the *pachamama*, held on the first Friday of each month) and graffiti in defence of coca leaf, are now common in the streets and *chicherías* (bars where maize beer is sold) of Cochabamba and around the University – but we are still far from the normality of *coqueo* that we saw among youth in Salta and Jujuy.

Rabey (1989) has noted the changes in demand in Argentina (1989), particularly the expansion of *coqueo* within the female and younger population. As a female union leader told us, 'Before, it was not a good thing to be seen in public chewing coca, if you were a woman. Today it is normal' (Collective interview, CTA, Jujuy, August 31, 2001). Use among young people is slowly expanding although *coqueo* has to compete with other preferences and tastes which have more appeal (from video games to 'designer' drugs). The slow process of learning how to chew coca leaves and their strange taste may be off-putting for children or young adolescents and in fact constitute a barrier for universalisation of the habit[16].

The paranoid attitude towards 'drugs' prevalent in the West, as well as the 'manufactured consensus' fabricated by the press and the crusaders of the Drug War, have blurred elementary distinctions and transformed public common sense into sheer ignorance.

It seems that the cultural and cognitive gulf between the west and 'the other' has mythologized commodities coming from the South and has only continued to widen since the times of Freud and Mantegazza, in spite (or perhaps because) of the speed and intensity of global communication flows. In the global village, the intensity of prejudice and the flow of misinformation have played their part in obscuring the nature of this particular commodity and erasing its modern history as a mercantile fuel of post-colonial internal and inter-regional relations. The coca leaf boom in Northern Argentina rests upon a dense texture of shared beliefs that permeate labour relations in modern capitalist enterprises as well as the more general sociality involved in entertainment and leisure activities. This chapter has aimed to clarify some of the broader theoretical and political issues involved in these relations, showing how the economic processes to which they give rise are deeply embedded in a network of symbolic and cultural meanings but also of uneven relations of power that share a shifting and dynamic nature. The ethnography of a consumption market presented here has provided reflections on the permeability and flexibility of Andean cultural practices and their hegemonic potential in the modern scenarios of industrial capitalism and globalized urban cultures. In these contexts, coca leaf consumption bridges frontiers of class, nationality and culture, in spite of the rigid barriers imposed by world-wide prohibition and in a local context marked by an international borderline. The situations described here reveal not only the economic importance of the Argentinean market for traditional, licit uses of coca leaf (as Art. 14 of the Vienna Convention states) but also provide some historical and contemporary evidence of the long term processes of mercantile intercultural exchange involved in the expansion of demand. The tacit knowledge that consumers have about coca leaf as a sort of social lubricant in inter-ethnic relations is a key aspect in the political economy of this quasi-legal commodity and might help us to understand the peculiarities of the market, not only as a space for the circulation and exchange of commodities but also as a cultural arena for the negotiation of identities and the interplay of complex and grossly uneven relations of power and domination.

1 See the thoroughly researched historiography of the trajin (local and long-distance trade routes in the hands of aymara – or qhichwa-speaking elites) during the first two centuries of Spanish colonial rule, by Luis Miguel Glave (1989, chapter 2), particularly what he calls 'the production of circulation' referring to the multiple inputs of human labour, knowledge and social skills (not to mention land and pack animals) by native entrepreneurs and communities in the Andes, as exemplified in the coca leaf trade.
2 'Cholo' and 'Mestizo' refer to mixed-blood, white-indians, the former being closer in mores and dress to their Indian ancestor, the latter to their Spanish ancestor.
3 'Criollo' refers to Andean-born Spaniards and, in general, all of the elite of European origin that ruled the country from colonial times.
4 Dry (but fresh) coca leaves are not exactly 'chewed', but gently sucked and kept in the mouth, adding an alkaline substance (in Bolivia, usually ashes from dried and burnt quinoa, sweet potato or other plant stalks) to promote the absorption of the leaf's components through the mucous membranes of the mouth. In

Bolivia, this form of consumption is called *akhulliku* or *pijjchu*, and the verb has been hispanized as *akhullikar* or *pijjchear*. In Peru it is called *chajjchar* and in Argentina coquear; all these terms imply something different from 'chewing'. The absence, in English, of a proper term, has forced me to continue using 'coca chewing' to mean *akhulliku* or *coqueo*, but I will go back to these terms when the context of the sentence allows for it.

5 This is known as a 'pharmacocentric phallacy' and is characteristic of the approach by bio-medical science to all natural plant remedies, not only coca leaves (personal communication, Paul Gootenberg). More recently, the 'ecgonine hypothesis' (Burchard 1978) has emerged to counteract the long lasting cocaine hypothesis (see for example, Saenz 1938 and Morales 1990), stating that in the metabolic process of coqueo the main alkalloid involved is not cocaine but ecgonine, which is crucial for the metabolism of glucose, but eighty times less toxic than the former. If personal testimonies could serve any purpose in this debate among scientists (most of whom probably have never seen a real life coca leaf) let me state, as an habitual chewer for the last 25 years, that I find the stimulating effects of *akhulliku* milder than those of coffee.

6 The study by Carter and Mamani was the basis for the establishment of 12,000 metric tons (dried leaves) in the Yungas of La Paz and in a small area of the lowlands of Cochabamba, as the top limit of the legal coca-leaf crop recognized by the Law 1008 on Coca and Controlled Substances (Republica de Bolivia 1988). This law regulates the production and commercialization of coca leaves for 'traditional licit uses', but only where there is 'historical evidence' of these uses (following Art. 14 of the modified version of the UN Single Convention, Viena 1988). The ambiguous legal status of the coca leaf (which is considered *iter criminis* when en route to become cocaine base or hydrochloride) allows for a severe interdictive control of the legal markets, which has actually promoted the diversion of the coca leaf crop to the illicit trade.

7 The expansion of the area dedicated to coca cultivation in Cochabamba, and the forced erradication that reduced this area to almost zero in 2000 are processes that will not be dealt with in this paper, but the English speaking reader can consult dozens of papers and books on this issue, mainly attempting to show how the 'bad indian' behaves when left on his own economic initiative (a paradigmatic case is the book *Cocaine, White Gold Rush in Peru* by Edmundo Morales, 1990). For more balanced approaches on the Bolivian case, although still unaware of the nature and magnitude of licit markets, see the compilation by Léons and Sanabria 1997 (particularly the introduction by the editors), as well as Painter 1994, Healy 1997 and Laserna 1997. See also *Las Fronteras de la Coca*, Rivera 2003b.

8 See *Las Fronteras de la Coca*, Rivera 2003b.

9 Leaders of COFECAY Dionisio Nuñez and Simón Machaca, have estimated that more than a third of the Yungas coca leaf crop goes to the expanding Argentinean market. The research for Rivera (2003b) included the production of two videos *Junio 2001, La Retirada de los Yungas*, and *Viaje a la Frontera del Sur*; both the book and videos have been used to introduce the question of legal markets into the public and political debate, both within and outside the cocalero regions.

10 Coca has a dark past, being used in abusive and exploitative ways to extract long working days from the mine-workers. Coca was part of their salary.

11 Several informants in the border-town of Yacuiba, claimed that some politicians of the highest rank were believed to be habitual consumers of Bolivian 'cristal' and that senior officers were often sent to procure it at the border bridge of Pocitos-Salvador Mazza. At one point, they say, the demand by the Buenos Aires elite seems to have been so heavy, that a fully-fledged cocaine industry was estab-

lished in and around Yacuiba. (Interviews at the border, August 2001).

12 El Pregón, August 2–2001, p. 6, 'Cocaleros de Bolivia miran con esperanza a Jujuy' (Bolivian Cocaleros have great hopes in Jujuy). The CTA interview and the visit to El Pregon have been edited into the video Las Fronteras de la Coca.

13 The case of the Devil's Dance, performed by a group in La Quiaca and studied by Gabriela Karasik, is only one of many examples in which 'cultural theft' is used as an argument to reinforce frontiers that are culturally fluid but administratively rigid. The paradox here is that the group members are sons and daughters of Bolivian migrants. In turn, nationalist elites in the Jujuy have considered the Devil's Dance as a Bolivian 'cultural invasion' (Karasik 2000). Fantasies about purity and authenticity regarding Bolivian music are in sharp contrast to the universality of *coqueo*, that easily adapts itself to the constructed identities of all sorts of consumers.

14 *Sahumerio* (from the Spanish verb *sahumar*) is an offering to be burnt, and the smoke carries the scents of herbs, sweets, *untu* or llama lard and many symbolic items, to the heights of the mountain Gods. The sweet *misa* or *mesa* (mass or table) is a preparation of sweets, coca and other herbs, and many ritual and symbolic items which are burnt on special occasions to propitiate good fortune, abundant crops or health.

15 As in the case of coca leaves, yerba mate saw an impressive colonial expansion to cater to a vast internal market (including today's Brazil, Bolivia, Paraguay, Uruguay and Argentina); but unlike coca leaves, there was never a 'black legend' about yerba mate and presently it is being freely exported to the world market for natural remedies and stimulants.

16 It is usual that beginners, not knowing how to combine the coca leaves with llipta or sodium bicarbonate, will cause excessive salivation or irritate the mucous membranes of the mouth, even producing blisters when not doing it properly. I know of people who have abandoned the attempt after one or two experiences of this sort.

REFERENCES

Abduca, Ricardo ca. 1994 *De los Yungas Paceños al Noroeste Argentino. Nuevo Enfoque Sobre la Producción de Coca para Consumo Tradicional.* Unpublished manuscript.

Andrews, George and David Salomon 1975 *The Coca Leaf and Cocaine Papers.* New York, Harcourt Brace Jovanovich.

Appadurai, Arjun 1988 *The Social Life of Things: Commodities in Cultural Perspective.* Cambridge, Cambridge University Press.

Benencia, Roberto 1995 'La Horticultura Bonaerense. Medianeros Bolivianos', in Benencia y Gabriela Karasik. *Inmigración Limítrofe: los Bolivianos en Buenos Aires.* Buenos Aires, Centro Editor de América Latina.

Bourdieu, Pierre 1991a *El Sentido Práctico.* Madrid, Taurus Humanidades. 1991b *La Distinción. Criterio y Bases Sociales del Gusto.* Madrid, Taurus Humanidades.

Burchard, Roderick 1996[1978] 'Una nueva perspectiva sobre la masticación de la coca', in William Carter (ed.) *Ensayos científicos sobre la coca.* La Paz, Juventud

Burgos, Fausto 1927 *Coca, Chicha y Alcohol. Relatos Puneños de Pastores, Arrieros y Tejedoras.* Buenos Aires, TOR.

Carter, William E. (ed.) 1996 *Ensayos científicos sobre la coca.* La Paz, Juventud.

Carter, William E. and Mauricio Mamani 1978 *Multidisciplinary Study. Traditional Use of the Coca Leaf in Bolivia.* La Paz, Museo Nacional de Etnografía y Folklore. 1986 *Coca en Bolivia.* La Paz: Editorial Juventud.

Cassanelli, Lee V. 1988 'Qat: Changes in the Production and Consumption of a Quasilegal Commodity in Northeast Africa', in Appadurai (ed.) *The Social Life of Things. Commodities in Cultural Perspective.* Cambridge, Cambridge University Press.

Fernández, Nicanor T. 1932 *La Coca Boliviana. Maravillosas Propiedades y Cualidades de la Coca. Opiniones de Prestigiosos Médicos y Naturalistas Acerca de la Planta Sagrada de los Incas del Perú.* La Paz, Editorial América.

Glave, Luis Miguel 1989 *Trajinantes. Caminos indígenas en la sociedad colonial. Siglos XVI–XVII.* Lima, Instituto de Apoyo Agrario.

Gootenberg, Paul 1999 'Reluctance or resistance? Constructing cocaine (prohibitions) in Peru, 1910–1950', in Paul Gootenberg (ed.) *Cocaine. Global Histories.* New York, Routledge.

——2002 'Between Coca and Cocaine: A Century or More of U.S.-Peruvian Drug Paradoxes, 1860–1980', unpublished manuscript presented at an internal Seminar, New York University, February.

Goffman, Erving 1998 [1971] *Estigma. La identidad deteriorada.* Buenos Aires, Amorrortu.

Grimson, Alejandro 1999 *Relatos de la Diferencia y la Igualdad. Los Bolivianos en Buenos Aires.* Buenos Aires, Editorial Universitaria de Buenos Aires. 2000 'La migración boliviana a la Argentina', in Grimson y Edmundo Paz Soldán. *Migrantes Bolivianos en la Argentina y los Estados Unidos.* La Paz, Programa de las Naciones Unidas para el Desarrollo. Cuaderno de Futuro N° 7.

Guha, Ranajit 1995 [1983] 'The Prose of Counterinsurgency', in *Subaltern Studies II. Writings on South Asian History and Society.* Delhi, Oxford University Press

Healy, Kevin 1997 'The Coca-Cocaine Issue in Bolivia: A Political Resource for all Seasons', in Barbara Léons and Harry Sanabria, *Coca, Cocaine and the Bolivian Reality*, New York, State University of New York Press, pp. 99–115.

Hinojosa, Alfonso, Liz Pérez y Guido Cortéz. 2001 *'Tantas Idas y Venidas'. Campesinos Tarijeños en el Norte Argentino.* La Paz, PIEB.

Hobsbawm, Eric and Terence Ranger 1983 *The Invention of Tradition.* Cambridge, Cambridge University Press.

Hurtado Gumucio, Jorge 1995 *Cocaine, the Legend: About Coca and Cocaine.* Second Revised Edition, La Paz.

Karasik, Gabriela 1995 'Trabajadoras Bolivianas en el Conurbano Bonaerense. Pequeño Comercio y Conflicto social', in Benencia, Roberto y Karasik, *Inmigración Limítrofe: los Bolivianos en Buenos Aires.* Buenos Aires, Centro Editor de América Latina.

——2000 'Tras la Genealogía del Diablo. Discusiones Sobre la Nación y el Estado en la Frontera Argentino-Boliviana', in Alejandro Grimson (comp.) *Fronteras, Naciones e Identidades. La Periferia Como Centro*, Buenos Aires, Ciccus y La Crujía.

Lema, Ana María 1997 'The Coca Debate and Yungas Landowners During the First Half of the 20th Century', in Barbara Léons y Harry Sanabria, *Coca, Cocaine and the Bolivian Reality*, New York, State University of New York Press, pp. 99–115.

Laserna, Roberto 1997 *20 (Mis)Conceptions on Coca and Cocaine.* La Paz, Clave.

Léons, Barbara 1997 'After the Boom: Income Decline, Erradication and Alternative Development in the Yungas', in Barbara Léons and Harry Sanabria (eds.) *Coca, Cocaine, and the Bolivian Reality.* New York, State University of New York Press, pp. 139–167.

Léons, Barbara and Harry Sanabria (eds.) 1997 *Coca, Cocaine, and the Bolivian Reality.* New York, State University of New York Press.

Marx, Karl 1946 [1867] *El Capital. Crítica de la Economia Política.* Vol. I. México, Fondo de Cultura Económica.

Molins, W. Jaime 1916 *Bolivia. Crónicas Americanas.* Libro Primero. Buenos Aires, n.e.

Morales, Edmundo 1990 *Cocaine. White Gold Rush in Peru.* Tucson, The University of Arizona Press.

Organización de las Naciones Unidas (ONU) [United Nations] 1950 *Informe de la Comisión de Estudio de las Hojas de Coca. Actas Oficiales.* Duodécimo Período de Sesiones. New York. 1961 *Convención Unica de 1961 Sobre Estupefacientes.* Versión oficial, Naciones Unidas. 1988 *Convención de las Naciones Unidas Contra el Tráfico Ilícito de Estupefacientes y Sustancias Sicotrópicas.* Versión oficial, Naciones Unidas.

Pacini, Deborah and Christine Franquemont (eds.) 1986 *Coca and cocaine. Effects on People and Policy in Latin America.* Cambridge, Mass and Ithaca, N.Y., Cultural Survival and Latin American Studies Program, Cornell University.

Painter, James 1994 *Bolivia and Coca. A Study in Dependency.* Boulder and London, Lynne Rienner.

1986 'Coca Chewing and the Botanical Origins of Coca (erythroxylum spp.) in South America', in Pacini and Franquemont (eds.), *Coca and cocaine. Effects on People and Policy in Latin America.* Cambridge, Mass and Ithaca, N.Y., Cultural Survival and Latin American Studies Program, Cornell University.

Rabey, Mario 1989 'Legalidad e Ilegalidad del Coqueo en Argentina', en *La Coca . . . Tradición, Rito, Identidad,* México, Instituto Indigenista Interamericano, pp.35–78.

República de Bolivia 1988 *Ley 1008. Regimen de la Coca y Substancias Controladas.* La Paz, 19th July, n.e.

Rivera Cusicanqui, Silvia 2002 'Sobre el estudio del mercado legal de la hoja de coca', in *Pulso,* 22–27 December.

2003a 'El mito de la pertenencia de Bolivia al mundo occidental', in *Temas Sociales. Revista de Sociología, UMSA.* No. 24, La Paz.

2003b *Las Fronteras de la Coca. Epistemologías Coloniales y Circuitos Alternativos de la Hoja de Coca. El Caso de la Frontera Argentina.* La Paz, IDIS and Aruwiyiri.

Romano, Ruggiero 1982 'Alrededor de dos falsas ecuaciones: coca buena=cocaína buena; cocaína mala=coca mala', in *Allpanchis* N° 19, Cusco, pp. 237–252.

Secretaría de Salud del Gobierno de la Provincia de Jujuy 2000 *Encuesta sobre el consumo de hoja de coca en la Provincia de Jujuy.* San Salvador, Secretaría de Salud.

Soux, María Luisa 1993 *La coca liberal. Producción y circulación a principios del siglo XX.* La Paz, Cocayapu and CIDES.

Spedding, Alison 1994 *Wachu Wachu. Cultivo de Coca e Identidad en los Yunkas de La Paz.* La Paz, Hisbol, Cocayapu y CIPCA.

1997a 'The Coca Field as a Total Social Fact', in Barbara Léons and Harry Sanabria (eds.), *Coca, Cocaine and the Bolivian Reality,* New York, State University of New York Press, pp.47–70.

1997b 'Cocataki, Taki-Coca, Trade, Traffic and Organized Peasant Resistance in the Yungas of La Paz', in Barbara Léons and Harry Sanabria (eds.), *Coca, Cocaine and the Bolivian Reality,* New York, State University of New York Press, pp.117–138.

Stern, Steve J. 1987 *Resistance, Rebellion and Consciousness in the Andean Peasant World, 18th to 20th Centuries.* Madison, the University of Wisconsin Press.

Various Authors 1989 *La coca . . . tradición, rito, identidad.* México, Instituto Indigenista Interamericano.

Chapter Five

OPIUM USE IN RAJASTHAN, INDIA: A SOCIO-CULTURAL PERSPECTIVE

Kalyan Ganguly

Indian history is replete with references to the use of opium, cannabis and other intoxicants. What is less well known is that in large areas of rural India, opium continues to be used in ways that signify both the importance of its use to individuals and communities as well as the normality of its use, in the sense that it is highly integrated into the everyday fabric of communities. After providing a brief historical and contemporary account of opium use in India, this chapter will describe opium use today in the desert regions of Rajasthan, where the majority of males (nearly 60 per cent) and 10–15 per cent of females regularly consume opium and its derivatives. The socio-cultural aspects of consumption are also discussed.

A BRIEF HISTORY OF OPIUM

Whether in solid or liquid form, the smoking and intake of opium, cannabis and other intoxicants in India has been a common practice for centuries. The early Hindu rulers; subsequent Islamic invaders, the Moguls, and others influencing custom and culture, from courtesans to commoners, have all appreciated and encouraged consumption of various intoxicants in various forms. Even rulers of a more recent past (pre-British era) used intoxicants like opium or cannabis for the purpose of pleasure and conviviality. Opium in particular has a long and often mythical past of nearly ten thousand years, much of it referring to long-standing, universal appeal and diverse uses. Records also show that opiates have been used for at least 8,000 years for their pain relieving properties. Moreover, the ancient Sumerians spoke of opium's capacity to produce a sense of delight or satisfaction and gave it the name of 'gil' which meant joy or rejoicing, whilst the Babylonians are credited with spreading knowledge of the poppy's medicinal properties east to Persia and west to Egypt. Pictorial representations of the opium poppy are also frequently found in classical Greek culture where opium was used in both medicine and religion (Wijngaart 1989) and as early as 16th century BC, physicians in Egypt were advised to prescribe opium for crying children.

More specifically, the ancient and medieval literature of India commonly provides descriptions of the Chandu Khana (Traditional Bars) that were places for drinking alcohol and smoking opium, and that have often been likened to the infamous 'opium dens' of the West (Chopra, et al. 1965). These were particularly popular with opiate users all over India, particularly in northern states like Rajasthan, Uttar Pradesh and Madhya Pradesh, where they were considered ideal for group consumption of a variety of intoxicants but mainly opium. In the first quarter of the 20th century Chandu Khanas were numerous even in many parts of the Indian subcontinent and served a range of functions. For example, use of the chillum (the earthen conical pipe) that rotated amongst the smoking partners of a particular group not only enhanced the cohesiveness of the group but also reduced the economic burden to the user as the purchasing of opium was largely shared. In its various forms, raw or processed, opium has remained a popular intoxicant and stimulant for the rural masses throughout Northern, Eastern and Central India. It should also be noted (although it is not the focus of this chapter) that cannabis has also been commonly used in India since ancient times and that multiple drug use has been reported in the Indian subcontinent for many years. The earliest Western record of use of opium in India was made by the traveller Duarte Barbosa (1518), who observed that the Indians began eating opium in small quantities as children and increased the quantity consumed until: 'If they leave off eating it, they will die immediately'. Similarly, Alfonso de Albuquerque wrote to the king of Portugal in 1543 'that the Indians are lost without their opium to eat'.

Originally brought to India by Arab traders, opium was attributed with special meaning and accredited with various wondrous qualities. Its use, as suggested above, was multifarious: used in war for instant pain relief from wounding but also as a home remedy to relieve child teething; for intestinal disorders, worms, convulsions, diarrhoea and even for cases of mental disorder. Although widely acknowledged as a life-giver and life-enhancer it was also put to use to aid both suicide and infanticide. Detailed accounts of opium use by various tribal and non-tribal groups for various ailments and other purposes are available, as are reports by later travellers in the 17th and 18th centuries that give an indication of the extent and nature of the 'opium habit' in different parts of the world including India (Mohan et al 1981).

During the 19th century, India under British rule infamously became one of the primary centres of the cultivation and export of opium, its importance for British Empire trade being illustrated by engagement in two wars with China to force it to continue to import opium. In terms of prevalence, the British Government's Royal Commission on Opium in the mid-1890s, and Chopra (1982), who made use of excise records of different parts of the country to appraise the prevalence and geographical dispersion of opiate use, both declared that opium smoking in rural areas was rare. However, Vincent (cf. Dymock et al., 1890) in a study of the Orissa province estimated there to be one opium addict for every 12 adults and further observed that rural dwellers consumed more opium than did urban dwellers. Likewise, Moore (cf. Dymock et al., 1890) reported the popularity of opium among the agricultural classes in Rajasthan. As we shall see, it seems likely that the latter studies were reporting something closer to the truth. After gaining independence in 1947, India incorporated prohibition of all intoxicating substances as part of the Directive Principles of the State Policy under Article 47 of the Constitution adopted in 1950. Following legislative and administrative measures by the Government of India, the non-medical and quasi-medical use of opium was prohibited in 1959, except for persons requiring administration of it on medical grounds (Sharma, 1981). In 1975 the total number of registered opium addicts in India was 80,809 (National Committee, 1977).

REGISTERED OPIUM ADDICTS OF INDIA

Some countries, such as the UK, have an approach to opiate addiction that includes the provision of prescribed opiates to those identified and registered[1] as addicts – something that has been known as the British System. Although India does formally permit the registration of opiate addicts and the subsequent prescription of opiates, it is the case that since 1959 this has been discouraged and as a consequence the numbers registered have fallen. In 1970 there were 87,945 registered addicts, in 1992 this had fallen to 14,993 and then to 10,752 in 1996 with only a few fresh licenses issued in this latter period (Narcotics Commissioner of India, – personal communication, 1997). Such trends in prescribing are usually indicative of the acceptance or not of opiate use and whether it is seen as legitimate practice to maintain an individual's habit or to encourage abstinence[2]. In India, the State governments have become more stringent and some opium users (rural based, the old) often find it difficult to obtain their normal amount. Thus these subjects either report for treatment or change to using other substances, mostly alcohol. (UNDCP, 2000). The decline in registrations of opium addicts has, as suggested, more political and symbolic overtones than anything else. A declining figure of registered addicts not only supports claims that the prevention of addiction is being successfully managed but also portrays the effective handling of psychotropic substances like opium by both the state and central government.

RAJASTHAN: A PROFILE OF PEOPLE AND PLACE

Rajasthan, located in the north-western part of India is spread over an area of just over 340 thousand square kilometres and supports a population of approximately 56 million. It has 33 administrative districts, 11 of which are desert districts covering an area of approximately 209 square kilometres (Govt. of India Census, 2001).

Most of these 11 districts are part of the 'Thar' desert of Rajasthan, the seventh largest desert in the world, spread across the boundary of India and Pakistan covering a length of nearly 700 km from north to south. Two of the eleven districts are quite large in size: Jaisalmer and Barmer respectively, and the density of population in these two districts are 13 and 69 persons per square Kilometre. This compares to a national average of 324 persons per square kilometre. The desert districts have been categorized (linguistically) as Marwar province and the dialect is Marwari a deviation of Devnagari the official language of the country. Both Hindus and the Muslims populate the area. Christians tend not to be found in the rural districts of western Rajasthan; however they do exist as a minority in urban areas.

Although the flora and fauna of this area is very typical of any arid region of the world it only rains heavily approximately every four years. The non-rainy years are called the 'Kaal' period (the drought years) and during these drought years the main activity is the digging of wells and making roads under the 'food for work' scheme of the Government of India. During these periods of relative underemployment the consumption of opium increases. (Malhotra and Trivedi, 1985).

The primary line of work in this region is agriculture and most of the families own, work on and live on the produce of their land. In general, males plough the land and females help in other agricultural activities. One significant aspect of agricultural production districts is that the crop yield is very low per hectare in comparison to the national average, in the main, attributable to below average rainfall and an improper and inadequate irrigation system Such a basic dependence on the land has meant that the Rajasthani people are heavily affected by disturbances in the ecological balance owing to the vagaries of the climate and both drought and famine – Akal (great famine), Jalkal (scarcity of water), Tinkal (scarcity of fodder), Trikal (scarcity of all three items) – have been common. The people have therefore evolved tenacious means and adjustment mechanisms to cope up with such situations (Malhotra and Trivedi 1985).

Given that the rainfall in Rajasthan can vary five to ten fold from one year to another and that such differences may occur between places just a few kilometers apart the farmers can never be sure of harvesting their grain. This necessitates that the size of land held by individual households is quite large and scattered, with several fragments at different parts of the boundary of the village. The Rajasthani's are generally of the opinion that a greater number of fragments of land provide a greater chance of a harvest from some plots in the face of erratic weather (Malhotra and Trivedi, 1985).

December to early June are months of comparatively little activity, the only work being, for example, collection of fodder for the cattle and preparation of crop fields. The elderly roll strands of hemp between their palms to make the ropes needed to tie the crops and for making cots. This proves to be an ideal time for the consumption of opium and its various natural derivatives (Ganguly1995). The monsoon rains however, which generally begin in the middle of July, signal a period when long days are spent in the fields. In the months of September–November, the Kharif crop is harvested. Thus, the two periods of peek activity are late June and July, when Kharif is planted and from September to November when it is harvested (Ganguly 1995).

ECO-CONSERVATION: A WAY OF LIFE

In order to have an effective and balanced use of the ecosystem, and to utilize different types of grasses, shrubs and tree foliage, each household will herd a mixture of animal species including cattle, buffalo and camels and also raise sheep and goat. Many Rajasthani's claim that keeping different types of livestock provides them with some security when diseases affect some species but not others. Trees and shrubs are put to multifarious use by the household; particularly for meeting the requirements of food, housing, fencing, animal feed, making ropes and baskets. Dung burning is also prevalent. Since most of the rural folk live in scattered homesteads and the person to land ratio is relatively low, there is little difficulty in procuring firewood and the demand for firewood has no serious impact on the vegetation cover (Malhotra and Trivedi 1985).

CULTIVATION AND SUPPLY OF OPIUM

Nearly 80 percent of India's opium is produced in Kota, Jhalawar, Bhilwara and Chittorgarh in Rajasthan and in Ratlam, Ujjain and Mandsaur in nearby Madhya Pradesh. This sits alongside the region of Gajipur in neighboring Uttar Pradesh which has long produced the bulk of legal opium for the rest of the world. In recent years however, the amount of opium cultivated has been subject to increased sanction by the Indian Government.

Between 1976–1999 the permitted acreage for opium cultivation per household was reduced from ten acres to just one (Ray 1999).

Poppy cultivation has a symbolic, economic and functional purpose for the farmers of Rajasthan. The pious, for example, kindle incense sticks and remove their sandals before entering the poppy field because the poppy is considered to be a bounty from mother Kali the Hindu goddess of power and ferocity and a destroyer of demons (Sharma 1996). In addition, the poppy helps to condition the soil for other crops, especially for maize. A popular saying goes: 'Rotate maize and opium and you will have both food and income'. For the farmer, an acre given over to poppy cultivation means they should realize over Rs 1000 (US $22) in terms of the opium alone and they should also realize a substantial amount for poppy seeds which fetch up to Rs 2000 a quintal in the open market. This income alone exceeds what the average Indian farmer would achieve in one crop cycle (with the majority of Indian farmers having two crops per year) from the same area under cultivation of other crops.

Some of the locally grown opium (within the state of Rajasthan) is also sold to the black-market where it fetches Rs.8000 toRs.10000 per kilo. In turn, the purchaser of the unadulterated milk of opium will generally retain the bulk of their purchase for personal use and sell on the rest to others, partly compensating for the money spent on their initial outlay. A regular retail purchaser, for example, spends between Rs.50–60 for getting 10gms of opium for his personal use (Manaklao Publication 2000). The best quality opium may even cost Rs.100 per 10 gms to a connoisseur addict. It is suspected that some adulteration often takes place, with the retailer/addict adulterating the opium milk with cheaper synthetic compounds for a 'fast kick effect' although the degree to which this takes place is unknown. In addition, some of the opium produced is used for medicinal purposes and other parts of the poppy towards the making of poppy seed oil. The oil is used as a base for mixing iodine with table salt to make iodized salt and also used as a condiment in Rajasthani cuisine.

The licensing of cultivation through the Excise Department of the State Government enables the government to keep a formal eye on opium production and output but does little to prevent the seeping of some of the produce onto the illegal market, which, in turn, has a cascading effect on the local economy, improving incomes of families. Black-market suppliers either hood-wink the authorities or connive with corrupt officials who also share the profits of illegal trade. The Indo-Pakistani border is porous at many points, easing cross-border trafficking. The districts of Bikaner, Jaisalmer and Barmer are flanked by the Punjab and Sindh provinces of Pakistan and these are areas where both opium cultivation and trade are common.

Overall, the desert climate is not a congenial one and planting of opium poppy and the staple crop of millet is carried out with ritualistic accompaniment to encourage successful growth. Crop failure of opium is not only a monetary loss but also considered to be a bad omen in relation to fail-ure of other crops or some mishap in the family. Given that the produce is an important item, socially, fiscally and ritualistically for many occasions, it is important to gain the best yield possible. When crop yields are low however, some supply of opium is secured from across the border from the Sindh and Punjab provinces of Pakistan and from the adjoining Indian State of Uttar Pradesh.

OPIUM CONSUMPTION AS A WAY OF LIFE

Although epidemiological studies of opiate and other intoxicant use in India are relatively scarce, a number of studies were carried out between 1981–1985 by Sharma and Mohan (1981a,b; 1983) on behalf of the All India Institute of Medical Sciences, as well as in collaboration with the Indian Council of Medical Research. These studies are particularly note-worthy for their focus on the general prevalence and nature of consumption of opium, alcohol and other synthetic drugs in the two Indian metropolises, Delhi and Lucknow, as well as in the in the city of Jodhpur, Rajasthan.

These studies indicated that opium ranked third highest in terms of con-sumption of intoxicants and was only outscored by alcohol and tobacco, both in males and females respectively. In general terms however, preva-lence rates for opium of less than 1per cent in the city studies (except for males in Jodhupur at 1.2per cent) were low and would give even a con-servative government little cause for concern. In Rajasthan as a whole, the prevalence rates were much higher with 13per cent of males and 8per cent of females said to be consumers of opium. If these studies were (and remain) a fair reflection of opium consumption in urban areas then the prevalence rates in the desert areas of Rajasthan might be expected to be higher.

Such a situation was borne out by data from a later study (Ganguly et al, 1995) of opium consumption and its socio-medical meaning in three desert districts of Rajasthan. In these areas the consumption of opium and its natural derivatives was found in startling abundance. Nearly sixty per-cent of males (starting from 15 years to 75 years of age) were found to be addicts. Use was highly gender specific with female consumers (whilst still very high compared to other parts of urban India) ranging from only 10per cent – 15per cent of the total consumers. Female addicts, apart from a small number of physically and mentally ailing females, were often found to be married to addicts. Significantly nearly 90per cent of able bodied addicts were considered to be non-deviant in their behaviour (both socially and economically).

Analysis in terms of caste showed that approximately 60per cent of Rajputs (warrior caste) were consumers of opium and this high prevalence rate largely reflects the fact that these people have been traditional opium users since the time of Rajput regality in the state. The Meena (a scheduled tribe) who were always loyal to the Rajput in every sphere of life since the days of the Rajput kingdom, were also high opium consumers (nearly fifty percent). Overall, the majority of consumers (70per cent) were between 40–60 years of age.

Few social issues with addiction were recorded and it was noted that in general up to 90per cent of addicts were not considered problematic in social or community terms, although around 10per cent were considered to show some kind of deviant behaviour, whether of a socio-cultural and/or economic nature. By and large, the addicts in these communities were not perceived as 'dope-fiends' – on the contrary they were leading a very normal life.

Use levels were relatively high. Initiation into opium use would be with around 10gms a day sometimes later progressing up to 100gm on a daily basis. So far as doda (dried and powdered poppy capsule) consumption was concerned there were addicts who were consuming 300gms of doda per day.

Other studies (Manaklao Ashram 2000) have suggested that the use of opium as an intoxicant is rising in most parts of Rajasthan. In western Rajasthan alone it has been estimated that about 20per cent of adult males can be classified as opium addicts, while another 40per cent abuse it fairly regularly. 20per cent of households are estimated as having a highly addicted member. The average per capita consumption of opium was found to be around 10gm per day (Manklao Ashram2000), with increase in use thought to be attributable to factors such as the gradual denigration of arable land due to chronic droughts causing tremendous mental tension among the villagers, inadequate state support for jobless youth, and overall changes in the life-style of youth in particular.

OPPOSITION TO POPULAR USE

In spite of the popular use of various psychotropic drugs, Indian society as a whole and, in particular the reformers and the law-makers; have never been in favour of the unrestricted use of such substances. At different times in Indian history and in different locations, such opposition has been both muted and influential. Even in Rajasthan, some religious sects, such as the Vishnois since the 16th century, have forbidden their followers to indulge in the use of opium or any other intoxicant. Others however, such as the afor-mentioned warrior cast the Rajput, have been much more proactive in their support for and use of opium.

Some international pressure, and indeed the intentions of some Indian Governments to conform with the various International Conventions seeking to deal with the growth of the heroin trade from the 1970s, have meant that a range of sanctions against opium production and heroin use have been implemented. This is a trend that has been consistent all around the so-called 'Golden Triangle' and 'Golden Crescent' countries neighbouring India, implicated in the global heroin trade. However, although the Narcotic Control Bureau has occasionally introduced strong measures to (in many ways be *seen* to) control addiction and drug peddling there has been little effect on traditional culturally based opium use. In Rajasthan, a region where the consumption of opium is not seen as a social problem, little formal opposition exists to prevent its use, although (as already noted moderate sanctions to reduce and control production have been introduced.

CONSUMPTION OF OPIUM:
SOCIO CULTURAL DIMENSIONS

The study by Ganguly et al (1995) was carried out over a period of two years in three Tehsils (districts) of Rajastjhan. In all, six villages of these Tehsils were part of the main study although the use of opium and its various natural derivatives was also explored in a number of other desert districts at the same time. The study sought not only to record epidemiological data but to also understand the various socio-cultural patterns of use and the meaning(s) consumers attached to such use. In an area where a new born infant is introduced to opium within minutes of birth and where he/she will live with it until he/she breathes their last, this was understandably important.

Initiation to opium takes place very early in this part of Rajasthan through various social customs and rituals. It is also used as a medicinal support in different ailments of the young. New born infants are given a taste of opium by mothers who touch the opium nugget on the tip of the child's tongue (in front of family and friends) in order to socially prime the newborn and thereby bring the neonate into the cultural fold of the western Rajasthan opium-usage culture. In addition to this, the guests present are treated to opium water along with sweet delicacies. In the case of irregular bowel, diarrhoea, stomach pain or mild pyrexia of unknown aetiology, the child is given a small nugget of opium weighing 2/3 gm in a day to ease the discomfort. In this way the prescription of opium is not only a part of traditional ethno-medicine but is also the socially accepted way of alleviating the suffering of the neonate. As they grow, children will observe members of their family, members of the community and the village elderly, mainly the men, spending a substantial amount of time and money in the gathering of opium. Opium is taken with the break of dawn by the addict, at any place, any time, barring the temple or cremation ground.

Opium also has practical and symbolic value for adolescent and newly married males. Considered to have an effective aphrodisiac quality and to enhance sexual satisfaction, opium is very much a part of the rite of passage into sexual maturity. Post-marital consummation and the chivalry of a man are often delicately poised between the art of procuring opium and its successful use at the time of need. This belief was found to be omnipresent and not exclusive to any caste, creed or religion barring few exceptions. That opium also brought pleasure was not denied. Some described the 'nasha' (kick) induced by a few puffs from a communally shared chillum (an earthen conical pot used for smoking) as an experience similar to a voyage to heaven. For others, the feeling of the opium kick was described as being so magnificent that they felt 'on top of the world'.

Although some instances were cited of men who had become addicted to opium through the chewing of pure nuggets, this has recently become so prohibitively expensive that many have to make do with opium substitutes such as opium nuggets mixed other matter. One of those belonging to the warrior-caste, the Rajput, reminisced that in the 'good old days' they would take opium before a battle in order to steady their nerves and to inhibit untimely bowel movements. Another Rajput, of humbler rank, put it more prosaically: 'Yes, they'd issue a lump of opium to every man in those days, and one would be glad to get it – might as well enjoy it now – may not be here tomorrow'.

Depending on the groups involved, opium and its use carries different functions and meanings to that of alcohol. Whereas among the Rajput, alcohol consumption is undertaken as part of group ritual in private spaces and the aim of drinking is to become inebriated as quickly as possible, opium is used more broadly and – unlike alcohol which can lead to 'embarrassment' – was and still is being used in public (Dorschner, 1983). Opium is considered to be an intoxicant which never embarrasses the user (despite the fact that chronic users were known to face social and occupational decline in some rare instances) because the effect of opium is slow and steady and, as a result, a consumer will never be footloose or groggy or behave in an unruly manner.

In striking contrast to the Rajput, members of the other higher caste-group in the village, the Brahmin, unequivocally denounce the use of daru (alcohol) and amal (opium). For them, it is utterly inimical to a religious life – and in matters of religion the Brahmin are considered to speak with authority. This priestly caste abhors meat, non vegetarian diet and wine . In addition to the Brahmin, the Vishnois also prohibit the use of intoxicants.

Whilst there are some forms of opium use common among all the using groups (such as the giving of opium to a newborn or its use as an aphrodisiac), use is also subject to difference, dependent upon the group or caste involved and relationships with other castes. One example of this is in the opium session of the Rajput who are free to consume opium as they like. In such sessions the Rajput will be accompanied by 'lesser mortals' such as the Meena or Bhil and these will be provided with free opium from their

Master in return for providing company and arranging the opium session. In these sessions the Rajput are free to explore the euphoric use of opium fully, taking 'time-out' to enjoy themselves, whilst the 'support team' of Bhil or Meena will be expected to retain greater control as they have to service the needs of others. Opium gatherings of this nature also help to ameliorate some of the inter-caste tensions and in fact help to promote higher caste Rajput interaction with low caste Meena. This type of inter-action also helps to maintain cordial relationships between these families at other times. By comparison, the Jats, the agricultural caste, will be found mostly taking opium within their own group while Muslim's (forbidden to take any intoxicant as per the Shariyat (holy tenets) of the Koran) that do take opium will do so in lesser numbers and less publicly. Where the con-sumption of opium by Muslims did take place it was reported to be mostly attributable to Hindu peer pressure and the perception that, by conform-ing to use and thus appearing to accept the customs of the majority, this helped the minority Muslims gain some degree of social recognition and integration into the Hindu dominated society of Rajasthan.

Choudhary (1995) has suggested that such use of psychoactive sub-stances is related to magico–religious as well as cultural influences and that ethno-medical usage is primarily for '(1) eco-stress adaptation, to enhance physical or mental endurance in response to adverse geo-climatic condi-tions; (2) the positive social acceptance of drug use to escape from eco-social stress. In both these situations drug abuse is a form of indigenous therapy reflecting an attempt at human survival at times of extreme psy-chosomatic stress'. In addition, Choudhary adds that, 'a lesson to be learned from this eco-stress adaptation/escape phenomenon of drug addic-tion is that of unique – ethno-medical cultural dynamics, where drug abuse is not seen as a problem but a self-administered and socially accepted found therapy in disguise' (Ibid). The local Rajasthani healers, for example the Bhopas), were found to be both users and prescribers of opium and to use it in particular as a therapy/cure of symptoms of a neuro psychotic origin. Such use is in fact pervasive through out the desert districts of Rajasthan.

ASPECTS OF TRADE

Opium use serves the interests of various parties, primarily the addict (in relation to eco stress adaptation/escape phenomena) and the dealers. Many peddlers who might otherwise have been involved in more serious heroin and related crime in Rajasthan were satisfied with dealing in opium in the majority of cases. However a further interest in the gains obtainable via the trade in opium lies in the law enforcement department of the govern-ment. Licit benefits come from the considerable revenues that the legal trade in opium continues to produce but the real concern is the illicit connivance of the authorities with the dealers. Corruption, where an ostrich-like attitude is adopted by the authorities at times of opium trading, means that some amount of black-market supply goes 'unnoticed' and fails to come to the attention of the government.

Despite the opportunity of 'easy money' to be made through opium cultivation, it is important to note that this has not been sufficient motivation to entice non-opium producing farmers into opium production. Complimentary to this, the state government has pursued regular surveillance (under the aegis of the 1985 Narcotic and Psychotropic Substances Act) to help check illegal cultivation of opium in this area and has played its due role in maintaining the status quo. In this way, we can see the intricate relation between opium use on the one hand and clear-cut social sanctions by society on the other.

THE OPIUM SESSION

The host (manager) of an opium session is usually regarded with high esteem and enjoys the special pleasure of being the organizer of an event at which participants are equally happy in finding a safe place of like-minded people that (albeit temporarily) removes them from their mundane day-to-day problems. An opium session thus quickly becomes the happiest gathering in the village so long as the consumption of opium continues. Gatherings of this type are quite routinely organized among addict friends in their respective houses or in one corner of the village. The bonding of the group members is not determined by age (it can have members ranging from 25 to 65 years of age) but by the intensity of participation in the gathering. Opium sessions are also highly male-gendered and such groups would never welcome a female addict/user nor do the females have their own group sessions. In the desert regions of Rajasthan, a woman either uses opium alone or in the presence of her addict husband. Generally however, neither adult women nor adolescent girls are observable when using opium; the exceptions to this being women who are chronically ill for whom medicinal use is wholly accepted or those women recently widowed for whom opium is considered an aid in coping with the he trauma of loss. In such situations, neither the children nor other family members would consider this act as something 'unsocial' on their mother's or relatives part.

At the beginning of the opium taking session, the host conducts some rituals (offering opium to Lord Shiva) and then he advances his palm containing the water extract of diluted opium (the concoction offered to Shiva) to other members. The fellow members sip the extract from the palm one by one. This continues until the extract is totally exhausted. The members of an opium group meet, discuss and resolve many things concerning the group members present or matters of common concern related to the village. After an opium session of this kind it is common for the men to return home and continue with the use of opium nuggets (a dry black nugget weighing 1gm to 10 gm depending upon the need of the user) after which the likely outcome is for the user to end up in a sound slumber.

Similar to the opium session, but less formal, one could find groups of villagers sitting within or outside the village in the open or in any courtyard discussing village or national issues with a chillum in hand. The chillum is rotated from one person to the other in the gathering. In the desert, as well as in certain non-desert districts of Rajasthan, these gatherings are known as 'Hathai', a place where the elderly of the village are supposed to sit in their spare time and discuss various issues. The Hathai is never a lively gathering and opium is enjoyed intermittently, punctuated occasionally by the use of tobacco. Outsiders are welcome to such gatherings if they are willing to participate in the use of amal or doda with the hathai members. Group meetings of this kind tend to be characterized not by intoxication, as in the more private opium sessions, for each member of the group is very self-conscious of their individual disposition and a clear head is desired and maintained for the duration of the meeting and the exchange of pleasantries with non-group members.

FAMILY DISCONTENT

Attendance at opium sessions or the meetings by the adult male will not always be received with calm detachment by the family group. Sometimes a background noise of resentment can be heard and the men questioned as to the waste of time and in some cases the waste of precious financial resources due to the use of opium. Importantly however it is the user of opium who is castigated and the blame laid firmly at the door of the individual for such waste. Opium itself is never blamed. Such a situation was commonly observed to result in contradictory outcomes. Whilst chronic users were often blamed for heavy indulgences that impacted upon family life rarely did the user get help from their family to resolve such heavy use? Indeed it was noted that the need for the treatment of opium addiction appeared never to be considered by either family members or those close to the family as a sensible recourse for the addict. This may of course be partly related to the fact that even where such facilities were available, for example at institutions like the Primary Health Centre these were found to be ill equipped to handle serious cases of addiction.

MANAKLAO: A PSYCHO-SOCIAL INFIRMARY

Outside of an opium addict's family and social circle there is very little in the way of state or other provision of social security, treatment or other support in Rajasthan. One of the few resources that is available to those with drug problems however is the detoxification organization Manaklao Ashram. The centre has been active for more than two decades at Manaklao in the Jodhpur district of Rajasthan, approximately 22 km from the city of Jodhpur. The primary aim of this organization is to provide a detoxification programme for people addicted to opium, heroin, cocaine, cannabis and alcohol. The programme works on the basis of short-term (10–12 days) residence in a camp where detoxification is facilitated. At the time of the research, eighty percent of those in residence were consumers of amal and doda in the camp's 'Ashram' (a place where a pious atmosphere is maintained in order to facilitate peace). Access to the programme usually works on the basis of self-referral or at the very least the voluntary agreement of the addict. A defining aspect of the programme is the recognition that the individual must have a genuine desire to detoxify and reduce/end their opium (or other drug) use. It is often the case that such individuals are introduced to this Ashram by others (ex-addicts) that have previously been detoxified there. Some however are compelled to enter the camp, using it as a form of social welfare when they have no money to purchase opium and they are suffering withdrawal. They otherwise have nowhere or no-one to turn to but the camp. Often, those that refer on this kind of basis do not possess the genuine desire to leave their addiction behind and will struggle to be successfully treated. None-the-less, because the approach of the organisation is to create self-confidence among its clients through part-medical, part-social and part-spiritual treatment, some progress is often made even with these individuals, particularly those willing to surrender themselves to the norms, rules and regulations of the Ashram. The Ashram claims a very high success rate – not verified by independent assessment – with over 80per cent of those undertaking detoxification reported to be clear of their addiction and to have avoided relapse. A great many of the successfully detoxified were reported as going on to act as 'torch bearer' for the centre and to work with the needy – of which there are many.

As with resources for the treatment and rehabilitation of drug users, there are few infirmaries providing modern health care in Rajasthan as a whole or in the desert districts of the region. Such scarcity results in a serious short-fall of resources to the really needy and ailing addicts.

ADOLESCENT USE

The use of opium by male adolescents is not simply recreational as there are a number of attendant rites of passage associated with opium use. Female adolescent use is rare. The use of opium by male adolescents in the desert districts of Rajasthan has similarities to the use of cigarettes by adolescents in the west where some adolescents associate such use with 'being tough' or more specifically as being 'grown-up' and wishing to present an image of being more mature than their years. The adolescent use of opium is associated with the establishment of manhood (the men use opium 'to do men's things' such as discuss issues and take responsibility for resolving community issues). Such use may be seen not only as satisfying the young ego but also, at times, it may provide the passport to joining the group of mature addicts. The younger of the adolescent boys indulged in opium taking in a clandestine fashion (as do underage drinkers in the West) often sneaking away to enjoy opium in one or other corner of the village in their free time. Commonly for this group, the opium used is stolen from the father or grandfather. If caught, the standard justification is to deflect blame and cry 'peer pressure' whilst claiming to be non-too-keen on the activity. The adolescent use of opium, contrary to that given to elderly addicts, is not something that is given any social or cultural sanction .

DISCUSSION

The prevalence of opium users is very high in Rajasthan with particular concentrations in the Western desert districts of the state. The use of opium is not distinguished by caste, creed, religion or financial status and it has now established itself as a staple intoxicant. Through a rough estimate on the basis of the study carried out by Ganguly et al (1995) one can extrapolate that the number of addicts (opium and derivatives) in the state of Rajasthan alone is more than the cumulative figure for Germany, France and Spain. The cultural practices surrounding opium use make it an object central to the life of the people of Rajasthan. The users are mostly considered to be decent people, well accepted within their society. The neonate is nurtured with a dosage of opium and thereafter males graduate to infancy and adolescence by taking the substance in family gatherings and, at times, with peers, on occasions of joy, celebration and conviviality. It is a social lubricant, has a symbolic place in birth, marriage and other ceremonies, and a great deal of its usage has been recognized as medicinal for generations in rural and urban Rajasthan. The multifarious uses to which opium is put only add to its social acceptance.

Opium consumption in various forms, at small social or political gatherings and at larger, more public, village gatherings, has an evident symbolic and functional importance deriving from earlier times and now integrated into the contemporary setting. Such interdependency between opium and the people is a characteristic image of typical rural Rajasthan. Rather than opium being understood as a destructive force as it is in the West, the social fabric is understood to be strengthened by its presence and use in a number of ways: its use is instrumental in social gatherings, enhancing the interactions of individuals on a one-to-one level but also -depending on the form and objective of the gathering – local traditions, group inter-relationships and institutions are reinforced. It can be suggested that over many generations this type of use may have helped to maintain a dynamic equilibrium between the negative and positive effects of opium use and consequently to have provided an important niche for the substance in this society.

Although the prevalence of problem opiate use is small – less than 1per cent were reported to have either lost their vocation or shown substantial social decline – that fraction of addicts is none-the-less in need of a state governed health care mechanism combined with social security to fall back upon during time of distress. At present, this support is not forthcoming. Thus there is a need to develop policies and support mechanisms preventative of problem use for those in need whilst at the same time accepting that most opium use is both highly functional and socially acceptable. In this sense it will be unwise (and probably unsuccessful) for intervention policies to ignore the existing customs around opium use and rather than working to subsume and integrate what are relatively successful traditional mechanisms of social control to attempt to do away with such methods. It needs to be recognized that the very existence of opium use, in the form that it takes in parts of Rajasthan, has played a real role in the prevention of more serious forms of substance use that may bring with them much greater problems. By permitting and accepting opium use within its traditional framework and the consequential informal social controls that accompany such use there is a real opportunity to galvanize the 'natural' harm reduction effect that this produces amongst such addicted users. Given this, there is little need at present to prohibit the practice of opium use. There is an opportunity for the state to collaborate with organisations like Manaklao and to also help develop more self-help groups for ex-addicts. Moreover, there is little to be gained by prosecuting chronic addicts who may then languish in custody. Rather, the primary health care system should be developed to enable it to treat such cases. Although any society rightly fears the entry of more problematic substances and more problematic use, it is not appropriate to associate all substance use with problems or to demonize all users, use and substances. The current victim-blaming ideology of the law enforcement authorities warrants a paradigmatic shift to victim-caring, cooperation and counselling. Opium addicts in India are not the same as problem drug users from other countries and they are certainly not of the same ilk as the demonized 'dope-fiend' of the West. Customs do not die easily – particularly those so heavily integrated into so many facets of every-day life. Opium use will remain. In acknowledging this, India will have to adjust the broad-brush laws it has enacted and learn to deal with substance use issues in a way that does not destroy old customs and ways of life and thus potentially be more destructive than the so-called evil it is attempting to wipe out

1   Although the Addicts Index and the formal registering of addicts has now been discontinued. Monitoring now takes place through a different system.
2   As in the UK, the registration or monitoring of addicts only reveals those who have come to the notice of the authorities – such as those entering treatment – it likely underestimates the number of actual addicts many, many times over.

REFERENCES

Andrew, C.F., (1926), The Opium Evil In India: Britain's Responsibility London: Student Christian Movement.

Brian, Inglis, (1975), The Forbidden Game: A Social History of Drugs, London: Hodder and Stoughton.

Census of India (2001). New Delhi: Government of India, Registrar General Office.

Chaudhary A.N. (1996). Commentary on 'An ethnographic account of opium consumers of Rajasthan (India): socio-medical perspective'. Addiction (1995) 90, 13–19.

Chopra, R. N. ,and Chopra, I.C. (1965). Drug Addiction with Special Reference to India, New Delhi: Council of Scientific and Industrial Research.

Dorschner, J.(1983) Rajput alcohol use in India. J. Stud. Alcohol 44(3):538–544.

Dymock, W., Warden, C.T.H., and Hooper, D (1980). Pharmacographica India. London: Kegan Paul, French Trubner and Co.

Ganguly, K.K. Sharma, H.K., and Krishnamachari, K.A.V.R.(1995). An ethnographic account of opium consumers of Rajasthan(India): Socio-medical perspective. Addiction 90(1):9–12.

Government of India; Drug Abuse in India (1976): Report of Expert Committee. Ministry of Health and Family Welfare.

Illegal Drug Market in Delhi 2001: A UNDCP & UNICRI Report. New Delhi.

Malhotra SP & Trivedi HS. (1985). Socio Economic Organisation of the Bishnois – A Typical Agricultural Sect of Western Rajasthan; Annals of Arid Zone, Central Arid Zone Research Institute. Jodhpur. Govt.of India. Jodhpur. Rajasthan.

Manaklao Publication, (2000), 'Manaklao Ashram', Jodhpur, Rajasthan.

Ministry of Welfare, Government of India (1992). Drug Abuse Summary of Research Studies. New Delhi.

Mohan D, Sethi HS & Tounge E Edts. (1981a). Current Research in Drug Abuse in India. Gemini Printers; New Delhi.

Mohan, D, Sharma, H.K., Advani, G.B. & Sundram, K.R. (1981b) Prevalence and Pattern of drug abuse in rural area of Rajasthan. Report submitted to Ministry of Social Welfare, Government of India, new Delhi.

Mohan, D., Sundram, K.R. (1983). A Collaborative Study on Non-Medical Use of Drugs in the Community. Base line survey Report. New Delhi: Indian Council of Medical Research.

National Committee(1977). Drug abuse in India. New Delhi: Ministry of Health and Family Welfare. Govt. of India.

Ray R (1998). Current Extent and Pattern of Drug Abuse. Soth Asia Drug Demand Reduction Report UNDCP (ROSA). New Delhi.

Ray R & Omprakash (1999) In World Drug Report 1999–India Country Profile. Draft Report UNDCP (ROSA). New Delhi.

Roy, S., and Rizvi. S.H.M.(1996). Nicotine Water to Heroin, Delhi: B.R. Publishing Crop.

Royal Commission on Opium (1893), Report, Simla: Government of India, Central Printing Office.

Sharma H.K. (1996). Socio-cultural Perspective of Substance Use in India, substance and misuse, U.K.

Sharma, M. C. (1981). Narcotics control in India. In D. Mohan, H.S. Sethi, and. E. Tongue (Eds.), Current Research in Drug Abuse in India. New Delhi Gemini Printers.

Shah G.R. (1998) Encyclopedia of Narcotic Drugs and Psychotropic Substances; Vol-I, Psychology-57; Gyan Publishing House: New Delhi.

Witters W, Venturelli P and Hanson G (1992); Drugs and Society: Jones and Bratlett Publisher. USA.

Wijngaart, G. Van de, (1991) Competing Perspectives on Drug Use: The Dutch Experience, University of Utrecht, The Netherlands,

UNDCP South Asia report on Drugs (2000), UN publication; New Delhi, India.

Westermeyer, J. (1976) The pro-heroin effect of opium laws in Asia, Archives of General psychiatry, 33, pp. 1135–1142.

Chapter Six

THE ELIXIR OF LIFE OR THE DEVIL'S CUD?
The Debate over Qat (*Catha edulis*) in Yemeni Culture

Daniel Martin Varisco

INTRODUCTION

'. . . but the social nexus within which the chewing takes place is one of enforced and routinised lethargy as groups of men lie around chatting from two to eight. In this way qat, by blocking off the whole of every afternoon with institutionalized idleness, i.e., unemployment, greatly contributes to Yemen's problems.'

(Halliday 1974:89)

'In both the learned class from which the officials used mainly to be drawn and with the ordinary man in the street qât chewing is associated with that good fellowship the Englishman finds in beer drinking.'

(Serjeant 1983:175)

The country of Yemen is closely associated with the early cultivation and trade of coffee, a stimulant that spread in the 17th century to the major European capitals and also the furthest reaches of the emerging colonial empires. To refer colloquially to coffee as a cup of mocha is a telling reminder that at one time the Red Sea port of Mocha was once the major supplier for the coffee trade. There is another Yemeni stimulant that did not catch on outside the country; this is the shrub *Catha edulis*, know in Arabic as *qât* but commonly referred to in English translation as khat. The qat plant is cultivated in Yemen solely for its leaves and tender shoots, which are picked fresh and chewed in social gatherings at times on a daily basis by the majority of Yemeni men and a considerable number of Yemeni women. For the past four centuries or so qat has been an important local cash crop and its widespread usage has had a profound impact on local culture.

For Yemen the similarities between use of the two stimulant plants – coffee and qat – are striking, which makes the differences in perception both within Yemeni society and from the outside all the more interesting. Most foreigners echo the sentiment of Fred Halliday that qat use is a hindrance to development or a bane to sound health. An earlier British traveler, G. Wyman Bury (1915:154) called qat chewing a 'social evil' and suggested it was 'the foe alike of thrift and industry'. This outlook, although not necessarily for the same reasons, has been adopted by several prominent Yemeni scholars and politicians since modern nation-building began in the 1960s. The poet 'Abd al-'Aziz al-Maqalih (1983:8) likened the continued use of qat to an unpatriotic form of wounding the Yemeni self. From such a perspective it does not really matter if qat proves to be an addictive drug or not; it is viewed mainly as a bad habit. Yet a few scholars, most commonly ethnographers, have spent enough time in Yemeni qat chewing sessions to realize that there are social benefits that help explain the continued use of qat, whether in the sense of conviviality observed by R. B. Serjeant or as a cultural identity marker, as I argued almost two decades ago (Varisco 1986).

There is a substantial literature on the properties of qat and its use in specific cultural contexts, but little analysis has been done on the debate about the legitimacy of qat within Islamic law and science; nor has there been much attention paid to recent arguments by Yemenis against qat use from a development perspective. I provide here a brief overview of the nature of qat and its historical use within Yemen as background to the Yemeni discussion about the benefits and the detriments of this mild stimulant. Due to its ability to stimulate creative thought and smooth conversation, qat chewing has sometimes been poeticized by Yemeni poets as the elixer of life, but there are also detractors. Yemen is the only Arab country outside of Africa where *Catha edulis* took root and found a following.[1] Nearby Saudi Arabia and most of the Gulf States banned its use, perhaps all the moreso because it was a quintessentially Yemeni custom. Tracing the overall contour of the Yemeni debate about qat use provides a specific example of how a relatively mild stimulant, surely far closer to coffee than opium, became a diabolical drug in the eyes of some but a falsely maligned gift of nature for others.

THE STIMULANT *CATHA EDULIS*

The Western world first learned of qat through the pioneering work of the Swedish botanist Pehr Forsskål. As a member of the ill-fated royal Danish expedition to Arabia in 1763, Forsskål collected samples, described the plant and called it *Catha edulis* (Hepper and Friis 1994:100). The '*Catha*' here was his original coinage of the Arabic term into nomenclatural Latin; '*edulis*' signified that the leaves were consumed. While Forsskål died in Yemen after only six months of collecting in the country, his scientific work was eventually published by a colleague on the expedition. Today *Catha* refers to one of about forty genera in the celastraceae family. It appears to have evolved from *Catha spinosa*, a wild diploid variety in Ethiopia that is propagated naturally from seeds. *Catha edulis* is a triploid which is cultivated from shoots rather than seed. Depending on elevation, rainfall and the probability of frost, the plant can grow from shrub range of a meter to as tall as ten meters. It has a narrow and straight trunk with whitish bark and produces small white flowers. The primary use by Yemenis is for the leaves, especially the new growth and tender shoots.

The consumption of qat is historically linked to its cultivation and distribution within Yemen. Both rain fed and irrigated varieties were traditionally grown in Yemen, with the most suitable areas for dry farming in the southern and central highlands. Before the 1962 revolution in North Yemen most irrigation came from natural springs, limited perennial flow in wadis and hand-dug wells (Varisco 1996). Given the food needs of the population, production of qat trees was rather limited in the past even though it was an important cash crop in some areas. By the end of the 1970s unchecked drilling of tube wells and widespread use of diesel pumps greatly increased the amount of irrigated land, often leading to rapid drawdown rates of limited aquifers. Geographers and ethnographers who worked in North Yemen during the late 1970s and early 1980s report dramatic increases in qat production, primarily because of the unchecked construction of wells.

Scientific study of the pharmacological qualities of *Catha edulis* stems back more than a century.[2] Until the 1880s it was commonly thought that qat was like coffee in containing caffeine. A study in 1887 by two South African scientists identified the first active ingredient, now called 'cathine', which is an alkaloid known today as d-norpseudoephedrine. Although the stimulant effect of qat was similar to that of some ephedra plants, researchers eventually found a wider range of active ingredients. The most important of these was indicated by isolation of a substance called 'cathinone', which is similar to d-amphetamine in its stimulation of the central nervous system, blood pressure and heart rates. Cathinone is the primary factor in the stimulant effect from chewing fresh leaves, the way in which Yemenis currently consume qat.

Is *qat* a narcotic or dangerous drug? The most relevant research project in Yemen was conducted by John G. Kennedy (1987:176) who argues that the stimulant effect of qat, like that of the amphetamines, has the opposite impact from 'drowsiness-producing' narcotics. Conclusions of earlier international commissions on the potential danger of qat did not identify it as a dangerous narcotic (Halbach 1972). An advisory committee of the League of Nations reported in 1936 that there was no proof one way or the other of its specific negative effects; this uncertainty was echoed by the 1956 UN Commission on Narcotic Drugs. However, for political reasons emerging from the French colonial control in the Horn of Africa, in 1957 the government of France banned the import and use of qat in France itself. Up until the early 1990s the U.S. government considered qat only a controlled substance, because cathine is not classifiable as a narcotic. However, in 1992 the DEA listed the other major active ingredient cathinone as a Schedule I controlled substance in the same category as heroin, LSD and ecstasy (DEA 2002). The concern here is with a powerful lab-based derivative called methcathinone, which had become part of a major drug abuse problem in Russia. Clinical trials suggest that this qat derivative, unknown in Yemen, may be more potent than cocaine. The intake of cathinone in fresh leaves is not of the same order, but this has not stopped U.S. authorities from raiding American Yemenis who sell qat leaves (Hayes 2000).

Concern over qat use in Yemen, as is also the case in African countries where it is used, has focused to a large extent on health impact. The medical aspects of qat, whether therapeutic or damaging, have been a central focus of the debate over qat use since its introduction into Yemen several centuries ago. Modern studies of individuals in Yemen and elsewhere have been conducted primarily by physicians, often in clinics, rather than through systematic social surveys. The obvious effects on the body are stimulative, causing people to put off or avoid sleep, and literally felt in the stomach. One of the functions of qat chewing is to retard the appetite. Although there is no major nutritive value in consumption of the juices (the leafy mass is usually expectorated), an argument was made a half century ago that qat could be an important source of vitamin C (Mustard 1952).

Is qat a medical problem in Yemen? In a review of the available literature, Kennedy (1987:231) concluded that 'the argument that qat is responsible for the health problems of Yemen is exaggerated, but it also shows that they are not without foundation'.[3] Among the claims made by Western physicians and travellers for bodily harm are cancer of the mouth and stomach, loss of teeth, gastrointestinal problems, heart attacks, high blood pressure, constipation and impotence. Clinical studies suggest some evidence for minor health issues and potential psychological disorders, but the fact remains that the major health problems facing adult Yemenis are chronic diseases such as hepatitis, tuberculosis, schistosomiasis and malaria. A notable exception is the impact on pregnant women due to reduced placental blood flow and the unknown consequences of cathine transmission to babies in mother's milk (Kristiansson et al. (1987). A number of studies claiming negative impact on Yemeni health have appeared recently in the Annals of Saudi Medicine, but these are invariably negative about qat use.[4] Given that official Saudi policy bans qat use in its own country, it is not surprising that the focus in this journal is on negative health impact.[5]

Traditional Yemeni attitudes towards qat do not consider its use a major health problem. Probably the most common complaint is constipation, with an additional problem at times resulting from insomnia.[6] Prior to the modern period Yemeni physicians incorporated qat into the humoral system that infuses their understanding of health and disease. Qat was considered cold and dry, which explains why the recommended preparation for chewing is eating a meal of 'hot' food like sorghum porridge or meat.[7] One Yemeni writer, quoted by Serjeant (1983:174) recommended concoctions with qat leaves for reducing swellings, healing wounds, stopping nose bleeds, removing nausea and curing epilepsy.[8] In addition, it was said to mitigate depression and remove anxiety when taken in modest amounts. There are differences of opinion about its impact on libido and sexual performance. Jurists remarked favourably on the alleged effect of decreased sexual desire and physicians warned of possible dysfunction or impotence when qat was taken in excessive amounts. Kennedy (1987:129) found that 'desire was usually enhanced and length of performance increased', while noting that this may result from a combination of factors including the amount and kind of qat chewed.

Is qat addictive? Most medical experts have concluded that it is not, at least not in the sense of opium or even nicotine in tobacco. Yemeni workers who go to Saudi Arabia, where qat is banned, do not appear to suffer major withdrawal symptoms. In a thorough review of the issue, Kennedy (1987:210) argues that the widespread consumption of qat in Yemeni society is due to a kind of 'cultural drug dependence' or 'drug-facilitated sociability dependence' that must be considered alongside the physiological impact. Since Yemenis primarily chew in social gatherings, the earlier analogy to beer drinking of the British working class is apt. However, as will be described below, the qat-chewing session has served a vital social function in Yemeni society as a whole.

Kennedy's cautionary note is valuable, because it is almost impossible to separate the health effects of qat from other items consumed before, during or after the qat. For example, Yemeni men often smoke the water pipe, and increasingly use cheap, locally produced cigarettes while chewing. In the past several decades the insomnia of qat chewing has been resolved by Yemeni men through drinking large amounts of whiskey or other forms of alcohol. Although forbidden officially in this Islamic country, it was relatively easy to find this liquid contraband, although foreigners are often shocked to discover that bootleg beer usually sells for about the same price per unit as whiskey, since the transport risk is a main part of the value for the end user or abuser.

HISTORY OF QAT IN YEMAN

The exact introduction of qat into Yemen is unknown, although it shares a similar proto-history with coffee. Both plants are native to highland Ethiopia and it seems fairly certain that they were brought to Yemen by Sufi Muslim mystics. The ritual significance of qat for the Muslim has been pragmatic rather than dogmatic. The stimulant property in qat leaves allows an individual to stay awake for prayers, recite God's name in all-night ceremonies, and enhances the Ramadan fast.[9] Qat may have arrived to Yemen as early as the first part of the 14th century, although references are limited until Islamic legal opinions that appear in the 16th century. The earliest reference in a historical text mentions the arrival of qat during the reign of the Rasulid sultan al-Mu'ayyad Dawud, who died in 1321 CE. (al-'Umari 1920:1, 11–12).[10] A number of new exotic plants first appeared in Yemen during the Rasulid era, but it is odd that no mention is made of qat in the well-known travel guides of Ibn Battuta or Ibn al-Mujawir, who visited the court of Dawud. Nor is there any mention of the plant in the extensive corpus of Rasulid agricultural treatises and almanacs, even in the comprehensive work of the later sultan al-Malik al-Afdal al-'Abbas. There is a much later reference to qat as being introduced to Yemen in the mid-16th century during the reign of the Zaydi Imam Yahya Sharaf al-Din, but this refers more to a problem that had arisen with its use rather than the initial entry of the plant. Until further research comes up with a more definitive dating, it is prudent to assume that qat came via Sufi travellers and was probably introduced gradually into southern Yemen during the latter part of the 14th century or early 15th century.

Yemeni writers uniformly attribute the origin of qat, as well as coffee, to Ethiopia. The legendary trope most commonly heard in Yemen is that a man once noticed that his goat was hyperactive after eating the leaves of a certain tree. Upon trying the leaves himself, this man discovered its properties and spread the word. The choice of goat in this legend is not arbitrary, because this is one of the few local animals which may on occasion eat leaves off the qat shrub.[11]

The assumption that the species *Catha edulis* originated in Ethiopia has been challenged by Raman Revri (1983:4), who suggests on cytogenetic grounds that the qat plant might have evolved from a wild variety of *Catha spinosa* found in Yemen. This theory would suggest that the Abyssinians who controlled Yemen in the 6th century took the Yemeni plant back to Ethiopia, where it developed as a stimulant and eventually was reintroduced into Yemen. There is no historical evidence for such a shift, nor is it clear why Abyssinian soldiers in a foreign context would have recognized a pharmacological value apparently not known to the Yemenis themselves.

By the mid 16th century mention of qat is well established in religious and legal texts. An account by the author al-Jaziri links the appearance of coffee among the Sufis in Yemen to the master 'Ali ibn 'Umar al-Shadhili, who is also said to have made a drink from the qat leaves (Hattox 1985:18, 24). Concern about the legitimacy of coffee had been raised as early as 1511 CE, when a conference was held in Mecca to decide its theological and scientific place. The most important legal opinion on qat use was provided by Ibn Hajar al-Haytami around the middle of the 16th century. This author relates stories about qat use to several earlier authorities and also to the reign of a Tahirid Yemeni sultan at the end of the 15th century. By the 17th century qat figures prominently in popular Yemeni poetry, at times in metaphorical dialogue with coffee. Even Yemenite Jewish literature builds on the debate between qat and coffee (Klein-Franke 1987:280–297; Schopen 1978:201–205).

In recent years qat has become a major Yemeni cash crop, one that is entirely marketed and consumed locally. Little is known about the economic history of qat until the last century. The lack of any reference to qat in the surviving Rasulid tax records of the 13th and 14th centuries suggests that it was not being cultivated in marketable quantities, at least not in the southern highlands where it later became prominent. The opinion of Ibn Hajar al-Haytami indicates that qat had become an important crop in the southern town of Ta'izz by the start of the 16th century. Qat was observed by Carsten Niebuhr during his mid 18th century journey through Yemen, and by 1837, and certainly before, qat was recognized as the most important crop at Jabal Sabr above Ta'izz by the French botanist Paul Botta. By the 1930s in Aden taxes on qat were generating considerable government revenue, even though it was strictly controlled (Britton 1939:122).[12] By 1957 due to heavy imports it was banned in Aden Protectorate, a ban continued by the socialist government that took over in the late 1960s. With Yemen's unification in 1990 the ban, regionally limited all along, on qat was lifted in the south.

THE *QAT* CHEW

'This is our sovereign habit, O philosophe, and it is one of the bounties of Allah. We chew it, and through it we recover our strength. We obtain a little *keif* too – not the keif that wine affords but a keif of the spirit, a bodily repose, spiritual satisfaction, which otherwise we do not feel, except, of course, through religion ... If you are drooping, like a plant athirst, a little of the ghat will refresh you and brace you and bring back your energy. It also keeps you awake if you have to travel or perform long religious exercises at night. The virtues of al-ghat are many, O dear philosopher, and we would have you try it.' Ameen Rihani (1929:878)

Whether or not qat use started for a religious purpose among Sufis who wanted to stay awake, the predominant mode of chewing qat leaves in

Yemen today is part of an afternoon social gathering usually attended between the mid-afternoon *('asr)* and dusk *(maghrib)* prayers. In some parts of Yemen chewing may continue far into the evening. Anecdotal evidence and several localized surveys suggest that far more men chew than women. The most extensive survey of qat use, compiled by Italian doctors on some 27,000 patients treated at Yemeni clinics between 1955 and 1967, found that 91% of men and 59% of women chewed qat to some extent (Mancioli and Parrinello 1967). Estimates of qat consumption are highly variable, depending on the location of the survey, since some areas of Yemen had very little qat available in the past.[13] Thus, it is dangerous to read back from more recent statistics, many of which reflect increased cultivation in the past three decades. Western travel accounts over the past two centuries lead one to believe that much of the qat consumption was concentrated in the southern part of Yemen, including the port of Aden, and was often associated with specific classes. In the central highland valley of Ahjur, where I conducted research in the late 1970s, qat cultivation was just taking off on a commercial scale; older informants noted that most residents only chewed on rare occasions in the past.

Most people bring their own qat to a chewing session, unless a prominent host is providing for a special occasion or to build up clients. Farmers will pick from their own trees earlier in the day, while many people must buy qat from the local market. Since the leaves must be fresh, the turn-around time from plot to market is usually less than twenty-four hours. In the market qat is sold either by the bundle *(rubta)* or as choice leaves wrapped in a banana leaf. Yemenis recognize many varieties of qat, over 2000 according to Schopen (1978:66), based on geographical origin and qualities of taste and effect. Newer leaves and soft stems are preferred. The amount consumed in a given chewing session is about 100 grams, although it varies according to the desired effect and type of qat. When purchased on the branch, not all the leaves will be used and the middle of the room will sometimes fill up with the scattered rejects.

The term 'chewing' is somewhat of a misnomer, since the qat leaves are rarely swallowed. The Yemeni verb for the process is *khazana*, which literally means to store the leaves. The idea is to work the leaves into a corner of the cheek and gradually build up a wad. First-time chewers soon realize this is an acquired skill. Leaves are cleaned individually and inserted by hand for much of the chewing session. As the bitter juice descends into the stomach, a heightened sense of mental alertness begins within a quarter hour.[14] The result is a stimulus to conceptualization and conversation, which can become animated or remain at a minimum, depending on the individuals present and the news of the day. After two hours a more reflective mood sets in, a state of euphoria or well being that is sometimes called *kayf*. In his survey of qat users, Kennedy (1987:112–113) found that the main qualities of informant experience were 'increases in alertness, ability to concentrate, the flow of ideas, contentment, confidence and friendliness'. Even individuals who are normally shy around others feel less inhibitions. Poets praise qat as an aid to their muse, while some students consider it a necessary aid for university study.

If qat is chewed too fast or over too long a time, it can feel like being 'drugged'. This may lead to distorted speech, mild mental confusion, mood swings or even hallucinations. But ethnographic observation suggests that such an extreme is relatively rare. Most chewers regulate their own intake and are aware of potential social stigma if a confused state is reached. Unlike the ingestion of drugs, the influence depends on a slow process of intake through the stomach. In other words, an individual would have to work hard to reach such a state. It is important to note that aggressive behaviour is rarely found in qat chews, nor is qat thought locally in Yemen to induce a fighting spirit. People will sit next to each other, at times closely packed, without evident signs of irritation.[15] Passive reflexivity, a mood of introspection, is the ultimate outcome of normal chewing.

Yemenis chew qat in a variety of physical contexts, including while working, but by far the preferred location is a closed sitting room with no draft and a scenic view. In houses this may be a *mafraj* on the top floor. Chewing is usually done while sitting comfortably on mattresses with pillows behind and sometimes beside as arm rests. The middle of the room is reserved for the water pipe (*mada'a*), which is popular among the wealthier. Thermoses or small bottles of water are usually available and most Yemenis drink small amounts of cold water throughout the session. No hot drinks or food are consumed while chewing. The afternoon qat session follows the main noon meal by two or three hours and the main effect of chewing is to retard appetite in the evening. Some Yemenis reduce the alert mental state by drinking whiskey at the end of the evening; this can lead to loss of motor behaviour and worse in combination with the effect of the qat's active ingredients.

Although a few individuals chew in the morning or in isolation, the qat session must be approached as primarily a social phenomenon. Because the custom is so widespread, there will be multiple qat sessions in almost any community. Most are on the small side, less than a dozen people and only rarely would there be occasions for large numbers of individuals, *e.g.*, over a hundred. Since chewing is a daily phenomenon nationwide, there need not be any special occasion. Yemeni men and women traditionally conclude the main work of the day by mid-afternoon and thus the qat session often serves as a convenient social gathering for visiting, fulfilling social obligations, informal conduct of business or afternoon entertainment. Special occasions and societal rites of passage, such as celebration of a birth, circumcision, marriage and funerals, often feature a catered qat chew. During the fasting month of Ramadan the chew must be postponed until after the breaking of the fast. Conversations at qat sessions reflect the interests of those attending, including theological discussions.

Frequency of chewing varies as does the amount of qat chewed in a given setting. On a regular basis some men chew daily, especially in major qat-producing areas, but others prefer to chew on Thursday afternoons, the functional equivalent to Friday night in the West. Most sessions are gender segregated, although this is relaxed in small rural communities where a man and wife may chew together. Surveys and ethnographic observation indicate that men are more likely to chew than women. In the central highland valley of Ahjur, for example, women complain that they are too busy to take time off to chew. Since many will visit other women during the time for qat sessions, the tendency for women not to chew may be due in part to limited access in the past. Children start chewing around the age of puberty, when they are old enough to be regular participants in an adult setting.

Why do Yemenis chew qat? Enough research has been done to note that there is no single dominant reason. Functional explanations relate both to individual needs, such as relaxing after work, creative stimulus, release of inhibitions, achieving a euphoric mood, and group dynamics. In a Durkheimian sense, the social function of the chew is an increased solidarity through opportunity to express concerns, share a communally enjoyable experience and follow up on personal or business issues in a less formal manner. In this sense, to chew is to belong. Anthropologist Shelagh Weir (1985:156–167) argues that the most important role of the qat session is as an expression of conspicuous consumption, displaying wealth and acquiring prestige. While her own ethnographic research in Jabal Razih would seem to support such an idea, it would be difficult to apply it to both males and females and across Yemen regionally. In many areas of Yemen, such as my own fieldwork site in Ahjur, the qat chew is a decidedly egalitarian social context. Rich and poor often sit side by side and qat gifts may be exchanged; there is rarely indication of prestige according to wealth. Traditionally, respect in rural Yemen is given according to tribal or individual values rather than by wealth. In the 1970s the out-migration of Yemeni males and consequent remittance wealth sent back to Yemen served to break down traditional cultural categories. But Qat became an affordable commodity across classes in the 1970s, suggesting that it would ill serve as a widespread vehicle for prestige.[16]

While no single explanation, social or psychological, can sum up why qat chewing caught on and evolved in Yemeni culture, it may be possible to isolate probable reasons for the relatively recent increase in chewing. [17] Outside observers and Yemenis themselves point to the 1970s as a decade in which qat production and consumption skyrocketed. By the start of the 1970s two political events had fundamentally changed the lives of all Yemenis. The 1962 Republican revolution against the Zaydi imam in the North resulted in the opening up of Yemen to foreign advisors and investment and allowed ordinary Yemeni men to migrate for temporary work abroad. The British withdrawal from the Aden Protectorate in 1967 and subsequent

Marxist takeover sent many educated South Yemenis into exile in the north and Saudi Arabia. Uncertain political change was coupled with unparalleled economic investment in the North as basic infrastructure was established and imports flooded the local market. Yemeni men, in particular, were exposed to prejudice against their 'backward' Yemeni culture in Saudi Arabia and the Gulf. The spread of national television in the 1970s brought an awareness of how far Yemen seemingly lagged behind other Arab countries and the superpowers.

The emergence of a national Yemeni identity, first in the North after 1962 and then in an expanded sense after unification of north and south in 1990, has necessitated an ongoing redefining of traditional status and tribal categories. I argue that the chewing of qat has served as a powerful identity marker both to affirm the value of Yemen's rich cultural heritage and individual self-worth in a climate where Yemen was continually being disparaged by Westerners and fellow Arabs alike. Here was a custom which was in a sense only Yemeni, at least in the Arab world. Qat held a positive value within Yemeni tradition, even among religious scholars. As a commodity, qat was about the only commodity that was local and at the same time capable of being a cash crop that generated income for farmers at all levels and for local government through market taxes. Everything about qat, from its cultivation to its poetic adulation, was thoroughly Yemeni. Since the primary use was for social gatherings, chewing qat facilitated networks for channelling the ideas and needs in local development, whether in rural or urban areas. The meaning of chewing over the past three decades is precisely that it has given the chewer meaning in a world that threatens his and her identity.

THE LEGITIMACY OF QAT

'Believers, do not approach your prayers when you are drunk, but wait till you can grasp the meaning of your words; nor when you are polluted – unless you are travelling the road – until you have washed yourselves.'

The Quran, The Women, 4 (Dawood 1968:361)

'Do not falsely declare: 'This is lawful, and this forbidden.' In order to invent a falsehood about Allah. Those who invent falsehoods about Allah shall never prosper. Brief is their enjoyment of this life, and grievous the punishment that awaits them.'

The Quran, The Bee, 116–117 (Dawood 1968:305)

The legitimacy of consuming qat in Islamic teaching revolves around the extent to which it can be considered an intoxicant. While the Quran is at times ambiguous about the use of wine, later legal arguments articulated a stand against the use of any substance which caused intoxication, not just for the saying of prayers.[18] This was bolstered by a saying (*hadith*) attributed to the Prophet Muhammad that every intoxicant is forbidden (*kull muskir haram*). As the faith spread, new forms of drinks and drugs were encountered, but many of these were not specifically mentioned in either the Quran or statements by the prophet. Legal scholars thus operated on the basis of analogy (*qiyas*), inferring that a substance with intoxicating properties similar to those in wine or that altered the mind would be forbidden as well. The question of whether or not qat should be classified as a forbidden intoxicant surfaced about the same time as similar arguments about coffee and tobacco, all of which were relatively recent introductions and had become increasingly popular.

One of the earliest theological cases against qat was given by the Zaydi imam Yahya ibn Sharaf al-Din, who died in 1558 C.E.[19] This religious and political leader compared qat to the harmful effects of marijuana (*hashish* in Arabic) and opium, concluding that all of these were forbidden intoxicants in Islam. His text begins with a definition of intoxication as a state of inebriation and confusion of the mind. The evidence provided for this association, which other Islamic scholars would come to dispute, is the anecdotal case of a certain son of another imam who once chewed while setting out on a trip and became so confused that he went by his destination. When he finally came to his senses, he noticed some of the qat still in his hand and realized that must have been the cause of his confusion. The imam admitted that there might be natural pharmacological properties in the plant, but that it was problematic in a religious sense.

The opinion of Imam Sharaf al-Din, somewhat limited in evidence, is contradicted by the Yemeni scholar Yahya ibn al-Husayn, who wrote about a century later.[20] Ibn al-Husayn argues that the information given to Imam Sharaf al-Din was politically motivated by members of his court in order to denounce certain enemies. But the damage was done, since the imam had ordered the destruction of qat trees. Only later did he realize his mistake and reverse the ban. Ibn al-Husayn drew on the major legal opinion provided by Ibn Hajar al-Haytami around the middle of the 16th century. Ibn Hajar was familiar with Imam Sharaf-al-Din's prohibition, but took a more cautious point of view. The main reasons cited for prohibiting qat had been several obnoxious properties (*madarr*) attributed to chewing the leaves. These included yellowing the face, reducing libido and leading to an overproduction of semen and eventual incontinence. The last effect, if true, would represent a religious problem, since it would make the individual ritually impure and impair his ability to pray. Ibn Hajar did not find conclusive evidence that qat caused intoxication, just as there seemed to be none for banning coffee. His recommendation was that no formal prohibition be made until the medical evidence was available on this new substance.

The argument of Ibn al-Husayn expands on the caution of Ibn Hajar by suggesting that a number of Yemeni religious scholars found no religious reason to prohibit qat. The exception would be if it had a known health impact on a given individual, but it was noted that even a praised food such as honey could occasionally create an allergic reaction in some individuals. While it was well-known that wine, hashish and opium had been determined to be intoxicants by medical scholars, the case of qat was still open. Taking a liberal stand, Ibn al-Husayn reminded his readers of a statement of the Prophet that what is forbidden is clear and what is allowed is clear, but in between were things that were vague and liminal. Since there was insufficient evidence to condemn the use of qat outright, Ibn al-Husayn quoted the Quran to say that no man had a right to prohibit what God allows.

Interestingly, Ibn al-Husayn turns an alleged harmful effect of qat – decreased sexual desire and capability – into a rhetorical plus. Why should something that curbs sexual passion be seen as religiously objectionable?[21] The impact of qat chewing on sex is widely debated in Yemen, more often than not and quite literally in this case – tongue in cheek. Ibn Hajar recorded an account of a 16th century Tahirid sultan who forbade qat in the southern town of Ta'izz after the women of this town complained bitterly that it made their husbands unable to perform sexually. Lacking a viable viagra at the time, the sultan issued his ban. But the resulting economic blow was so severe that he later reversed it, suggesting that women's sexual dissatisfaction must have seemed far less of an evil than economic turmoil. Ibn al-Husayn's point is that loss of libido hardly makes qat an intoxicant. The possibility that some people may be adversely affected healthwise – even lessening the ability to have children – is not sufficient grounds to unilaterally condemn qat, since the same may be said medically about such common foods as honey and barley.

IS CHEWING VIABLE IN MODERN YEMEN?

'Examination of drug-use patterns in a country where millions of people are users on a regular basis, and where there has been familiarity with the drug for several hundred years, offers an opportunity to achieve perspectives not possible in countries with different attitudes and without such histories.'

(Kennedy 1987:1)

Foreign interest in the phenomenon of qat, whether ethnocentric censure or academic fascination, must be tempered with the variety of Yemeni views on the viability of qat in their contemporary society. Viability in a pragmatic sense covers the economic potential of qat cultivation and marketing, the physiological and psychological health impact and the cultural value of qat as a marker of Yemeni identity versus a symbolic obstacle to development. The economic reality of qat says it all. The estimated crop value was almost a third of the entire pre-oil-producing North Yemeni GDP in 1980. It is important to note that qat brought in substantial government revenues both through the traditional *zakat* production tax and through local and regional market taxes. Development planners over the past three decades in Yemen have almost always viewed qat as an obstacle to the introduction of cash crops with market value outside Yemen. Indeed, the upsurge in qat cultivation in the 1970s was directly blamed for decline in coffee production. By the early 1980s, according to Revri (1983:84), the gross profit margin of qat was sixteen times that of coffee.[22] This was hardly a problem for the bulk of Yemeni farmers, who could grow qat on small or large holdings with minimal capital investment. Yemen's share of the international coffee market had been delimited two centuries before; there was little chance non-plantation Mocha coffee would ever compete with the world coffee market.[23]

The outside expert disdain of qat was not shared by Yemeni farmers for practical reasons. First, they already knew how to grow qat and had little worry about pests or diseases. Attempts to introduce new cash crops like orange trees often failed for precisely these reasons. Second, there was an increasing demand for qat. This demand was year-round rather than seasonal, which meant there were few times when the market would be flooded with fresh bundles of leaves. Third, the high profit margin allowed farmers to reinvest in improvements to their land and local infrastructure and created the opportunity to experiment with other cash crops. Although much of the new tube – well irrigated land was given over to qat, it was a crop with minimal water needs. Since many Yemenis no longer needed to grow their own food, even though subsistence production continued, the cash from qat production allowed farmers to increase their household budget and enjoy a positively valued pastime.

In the case of qat one man's cash bonanza could be seen as another man's poison. Demand for qat, for the most part, defied the outside expert's law of supply and demand since there was never a need to over supply leaves which could effectively remain on the tree. As a result of increasing demand, stimulated in part by rapid population growth, the market price of qat has remained high despite increased production. Several studies from the early 1980s indicate a range of prices according to the quality and prestige of the qat. Shelagh Weir (1985:101) estimates that most qat chewers, who did not grow the plant themselves, spent between $30–$80 per week in 1979–1980. The upper limit would have been equal to the daily unskilled wage, suggesting that qat consumption might have left little else for family expenditures. But as Weir (1985:99) immediately points out, most Yemenis 'do not pay as little as they can, but as much as they can afford'. There were a number of ways in which qat could be obtained from relatives or by gifts in visiting certain prominent chewing sessions. There is little evidence that families faced starvation because men were throwing all their money away on qat.

As is evident in the quote of Fred Halliday at the beginning of this chapter, the litany of Western observers has often been that the qat habit ruins the work ethic, health and family life. Visitors to Yemen at times have brought with them a brand of prohibition-era preaching against the evils of drink to dismiss this Yemeni custom. The Arab poet Ameen Rihani (1929:883) lets his imagination carry him away in comparing the qat chew to a hashish den. But stereotyping in Western accounts often works against itself. In remembering his own servants while American consul in Aden, Charles Moser (1917:174) praised qat as the antidote to native lethargy: 'Without khat your Arab, labourer or gentleman, is evasive, apathetic, dull; with it he performs prodigies of strength and energy.' Nevertheless, Moser found the use of qat irrational, claiming that 2/3 of the labourer's daily 30 cents wage was spent on qat and only a third reserved for his family. The key element in all these comments is that Yemeni use of qat is backward and a hindrance to development into a civilized society. As Moser (1917:186) notes in an aside, 'No one in the world would desire to introduce the khat habit into civilized communities, where there are too many similar habits already . . .'

Attempts to limit qat consumption were promoted by the governments of both North and South Yemen before unification, but with little popular support in the north and not much reach beyond Aden in the socialist past. The Yemeni author Hamud Mansur, for example, published a short Arabic book in 1988 on The Harmful Effects of Qat in the Yemen Arab Republic (Adrar al-qat fi al-jumhuriyya al-'arabiyya al-yamaniyya).[24] After a brief nod to the widely assumed benefits of chewing, Mansur provides a list of what others have said are harmful effects on health, the individual psyche, sexual drive, society and the economy. In the end Mansur (1988:49) concludes that there is no unified Yemeni view on qat and calls for the establishment of an authority to investigate further the history of qat and determine the merits and problems of its probable use in the future.

In a sense Mansur's wish has been fulfilled in an informal way. Government committees and university professors in Yemen continually address the issue of the role of qat in Yemeni society. Mansur is right to point out that no one view predominates on what should be done with qat. Cultivation and consumption continue apace, although the evolving views of more conservative religious groups may be turning the tide against qat in a way that the country's intellectuals have not been able to achieve. The future viability of qat will depend on how its current role as a social and symbolic mainstay in the society plays out in a rapidly changing society. In 1999 President Ali Abdullah Salih of Yemen announced that he was personally giving up qat and would use the time to learn computers. Yet it appears that most Yemenis are more wired to their old habits than the internet. One thing is fairly certain, there is probably little chance for the hope of Abbas Faroughy (1947:18), more than half a century ago, that one day chewing gum would supplant the chewing of qat.

1 Recommended studies on the use of qat include Cassanelli (1986) for Somalia, Getahun and Krikorian (1973) for Ethiopia and Goldsmith (1988) for Kenya.

2 My description here is based on the survey in Kennedy (1987:180–187). For other detailed accounts of the properties of the leaves, see Halbach (1972), Mancioli and Parrinello (1967), Al-Motarreb A. *et al.* (2002), and Schopen (1978).

3 Kennedy's survey has an extensive bibliography. Relevant information is also accessible on the internet; see especially Yemen Gateway's Qat Page at <http://www.al-bab.com/yemen/soc/qat.htm> and the Kat Information Page at http://www.togdheer.com/khat/index.shtml.

4 For example, Hassan *et al.* (2002:34) concludes: 'This study confirms that Qat chewing induces anorexia, weak stream of micturition, post–chewing urethral discharge and insomnia (delayed bedtime), which result in late wake-up next morning and low work performance the next day. These effects are believed to be caused by the central and peripheral actions of cathinone and cathine in the Qat leaves.' The ethnocentric assumption that qat use is unproductive because it keeps people from working is implicit in this finding.

5 In 1956 the Saudi Mufti issued a fatwa condemning the cultivation, import and use of qat in Saudi Arabia, adding a year later that the penalty for users would be forty strokes of the lash (Al-Thani 1983:185).

6 Constipation was one of the few negative health side effects noted by the 1958 Qat Commission of Inquiry in Aden (Serjeant 1983:172). For discussion of Yemeni views on health and qat, see Weir (1985:42–45).

7 The diet and exercise of Yemenis prior to afternoon chewing are discussed by Kennedy (1987:81–82).

8 Based on information received in 1763, Niebuhr (1792:2, 351) wrote: 'To their kaad they ascribe the virtues of assisting digestion, and of fortifying the constitution against infectious distempers.'

9 This rationale was commonly given to me by Yemenis I lived with during ethnographic fieldwork in the central highland community of al-Ahjur during 1978–79. The same reason is given by Muslims in Ethiopia (Brooke 1960:53).

10 The author died 1349 CE. It is conceivable that the reference to qat is a later emendation.

11 Brooke (1960:53) observes for Ethiopia that hyena dung is sometimes placed around the base of the trees to keep goats from grazing.

12 Britton notes that the qat plant had been introduced from Yemen into France and the United States, presumably by African rather than Yemeni immigrants.

13 For information on the percentage of Yemeni chewers in various regions, see Varisco (1986:4) and Weir (1985:83–91).

14 Some women in Ahjur counteract the bitter taste of qat by eating fenugreek (*hilba*) and hot pepper (*bisbas*) in the earlier meal.

15 Kennedy (1987:115) thinks this may be due in part to a physiological cause: the qat acts to constrict the muscles and inhibit the need to urinate or defecate.

16 Other examples of conspicuous consumption are evident in Yemen as remittance cash entered the rural society, including a rapid inflation of bridewealth (Varisco and Adra 1984:141–142).

17 My points here are developed in more detail in Varisco (1986).

18 Kueny (2001) provides an excellent summary of the Quranic references to wine

and other intoxicants. It is important to remember that wine was used at times as a metaphor for life in paradise.

19 The Arabic text has been edited by 'Abd Allah al-Hibshi (1986:7–18).

20 The Arabic text is edited by al-Hibshi (1986:51–103). This treatise examines the legitimacy of coffee, qat and tobacco by reviewing previous legal opinions and arguing for caution in condemnation.

21 The traveler Hans Helfritz (1958:84) was told that the anaphrodisiacal quality of qat chewing strengthened fidelity for a man separated from his wife.

22 He records $48,000 as the gross profit on a hectare of qat and $3000 per hectare on coffee. Weir (1985) observes that the market value of three harvests of qat per year per hectare reached $130,000 in the late 1970s.

23 Gerholm (1977:55) pointed out that qat was a democratic crop, easily grown and marketed by small farmers, while coffee was far more demanding and required outside middlemen contacts.

24 Mansur emphasizes written statements by other Yemenis. For the translated dialogue of a commentary on qat by a Yemeni man from Jiblah, in the southern highlands, see Jastrow (1986).

REFERENCES

Britton, E. B. (1939). 'The Use of Qat', Geographical Journal 93:121–122.

Brooke, Clarke. (1960). 'Khat (Catha edulis): Its production and trade in the Middle East'. Geographical Journal 126:52–59.

Bury, G. Wyman. (1915). Arabia Infelix, or the Turks of Yemen. London: Macmillan.

Cassanelli, Lee V. (1986). 'Qat: Changes in the production and consumption of a quasilegal commodity in northeast Africa,. In Arjun Appadurai, editor, The Social Life of Things, 236–257. Cambridge: Cambridge University Press.

Dawood, N. J., (translator). (1968). The Koran. Baltimore: Penguin Books.

DEA (Drug Enforcement Administration). (2002). (June) 'Drug Intelligence Brief: Khat'. Electronic document. http://www.usdoj.gov/dea/pubs/intel/02032/02032. html. Accessed August, 2003.

Faroughy, Abbas. (1947). Introducing Yemen. New York: Orientalia.

Gerholm, Tomas. (1977). Market, Mosque and Mafraj: Social Inequality in a Yemeni Town. Stockholm: University of Stockholm.

Getahun, Amare and A. D. Krikorian. (1973). 'Chat: Coffee's rival from Harar, Ethiopia. I. Botany, cultivation and use.' Economic Botany 27:353–377.

Goldsmith, Paul. (1988). 'The production and marketing of miraa in Kenya.' In R. Cohen, editor, Satisfying Africa's Food Needs: food production and commercialization in African agriculture, 121–152. Boulder: L. Rienner Publications.

Halbach, H. (1972). 'Medical aspects of the chewing of khat leaves.' Bulletin of the World Health Organisation 47:21–29.

Halliday, Fred. (1974). Arabia Without Sultans. Baltimore: Penguin.

Hassan, Najeeb A. G. M. et al. (2000). The Subjective Effects of Chewing Leaves in Human Volunteers. Annals of Saudi Medicine 22:1–2, 34–37.

Hattox, Ralph S. (1985). Coffee and Coffeehouses: The Origins of a Social Beverage in the Medieval Near East. Seattle: University of Washington Press.

Hayes, Tom. (2000). 'Khat comes to America, prompting crackdown.' Electronic document. http://www.cognitiveliberty.org/dll/khatindex.htm. Accessed August, 2003.

Helfritz, Hans. (1958). The Yemen. A Secret Journey. London: Allen and Unwin.

Hepper, F. Nigel and I. Friis. (1994). The Plants of Pehr Forsskål's 'Flora Aegyptiaco-Arabica.' Kew: The Royal Botanic Gardens.

Al-Hibshi, 'Abd Allah, editor. (1986). Thalath rasa'il fi al-qat. Beirut: Dar al-Tan-wir.

Jastrow, Otto. (1986). 'Alles über Qât. Ein Text im arabischen Dialekt von Jiblih (Nordjemen).' Zeitschrift der Deutschen Morgenländischen Gesellschaft 136:23–55.

Kennedy, John G. (1987). The Flower of Paradise: The Institutionalized Use of the Drug Qat in North Yemen. Dordrecht: D. Reidel Publishing Company.

Klein-Franke, Aviva. (1987). 'The Jews of Yemen.' In Werner Daum, editor, Yemen: 3000 Years of Art and Civilisation in Arabia Felix, 265–299. Innsbruck: Pin-guin.

Kristiansson, Bengt et al. (1987). 'Use of khat in lactating women: A pilot study on breast-milk secretion.' Journal of Pharmacology 21:85–90.

Kueny, Kathryn. (2001). The Rhetoric of Sobriety: Wine in Early Islam. Albany: State University of New York Press.

Mancioli, Massimo and Antonino Parrinello. (1967). 'Il gat (Catha edulis).' La Clin-ica Terapeutica 43:2, 103–172.

Mansur, Hamud. (1988). Adrar al-qat fi al-jumhuriyya al-'arabiyya al-yamaniyya. Beirut: Dar al-Fikr al-Ma'asar.

Al-Maqalih, 'Abd al-'Aziz. (1983). 'Ishkal al-qat min manzur al-karama al-wataniyya.' Al-Thawra #4756, August 30, p. 8.

Moser, Charles. (1917). 'The Flower of Paradise – The part which khat plays in the life of the Yemen Arab.' The National Geographic Magazine 32(2):173–186.

Al-Motarreb A. et al. (2002). 'Khat: Pharmacological and medical aspects and its social use in Yemen.' Phytotherapy 16(5): 403–413.

Mustard, M. (1952). 'Ascorbic acid content of some miscellaneous tropical and sub-tropical plants and plant products.' Food Research 17:31–35.

Niebuhr, Carsten. (1792). Travels through Arabia. Translated by Robert Heron. Edinburgh: R. Morison and Son.

Revri, Raman. (1983). Catha Edulis Forsk. Geographical Dispersal, Botanical, Eco-logical and Agronomical Aspects with Special Reference to Yemen Arab Repub-lik. Göttingen.

Rihani, Ameen. (1929). 'Under the roofs of Sanaa.' Asia 29:878–883, 918–920.

Schopen, Armin. (1978). Das Qât. Geschichte und Gebrauch des Genussmittels Catha Edulis Forsk. In der Arabischen Republik Jemen. Wiesbaden: Franz Steiner.

Serjeant, R. B. (1983). 'Qât.' In R. B. Serjeant and Ronald Lewcock, editors, San'â': An Arabian Islamic City, 171–175. London: World of Islam Festival Trust.

Al-Thani, Ibrahim. (1983). 'Development: The Saudi Solution for the Problem of Khat.' In B. Shahandeh, et al., editors, International Conference on Khat, 181–194. Lausanne: E. Ruckstuhl.

Al-'Umari, Ibn Fadl Allah. (1920). Al-Mu'assassat al-masammat wa-masalik al-absar. Cairo.

Varisco, Daniel Martin. (1986). 'On the Meaning of Chewing: The Significance of Qât (Catha edulis) in the Yemen Arab Republic.' International Journal of Mid-dle East Studies 18:1–13.

——1996. 'Water Sources and Traditional Irrigation in Yemen.' New Arabian Stud-ies 3:238–257.

Varisco, Daniel Martin and Najwa Adra. (1984). 'Affluence and the Concept of the Tribe in the Central Highlands of the Yemen Arab Republic.' In Richard F. Sal-isbury and Elisabeth Tooker, editors, Affluence and Cultural Survival, 134–149. Washington, D.C.: American Ethnological Society.

Weir, Shelagh (1985) Qat in Yemen: Consumption and Social Change. London: British Museum Publications.

Chapter Seven

CAMBA (Bolivia) DRINKING PATTERNS: CHANGES IN ALCOHOL USE, ANTHROPOLOGY AND RESEARCH PERSPECTIVES

Dwight B. Heath

It is rare that a scientist is invited to write again about something that he published half a century earlier. Evidently the editors of this volume, like many others in drug and alcohol studies, consider the Camba to be an important case study, and this paper will try to explain why this is so. At the same time, it will provide an ethnographic and historical perspective on the Camba's exceptional and unproblematic uses of alcohol.

The original article (Heath, 1958) was among the earliest reports that provided fairly rich details about the drinking patterns of a non-Western people. By 'drinking patterns', I refer simply to such basic issues as who drinks beverages containing alcohol, what they drink, how, when, where, with whom, while doing what else, as well as how they and others feel about all these things, and why they say that such is the case. (Needless to say, it is incumbent on the conscientious ethnographer also to collect and report negative data – who does not drink; where, when, why, and how one should not drink, and so forth, as well as how people feel about all of those, and why.)

CAMBA DRINKING PATTERNS IN THE 1950S

During the past half-century, the Camba emerged from ethnographic obscurity to dubious fame as the people who drank more than anyone of the highest-proof beverage in customary usage, so that most adults were falling-down drunk at least five days each month. Even more importantly, they did all of that without experiencing any of the various so-called alco-

119

hol-related problems that are so often attributed to heavy drinkers. It is this combination of extremely heavy drinking and virtual freedom from negative consequences that makes the Camba case so interesting in drug and alcohol studies. There is an additional advantage in that I have enjoyed being able to chronicle this anomaly, together with several economic and cultural changes, for most of the last 50 years.

In the 1950s, the Camba were a population whose physical and cultural traits reflected the mix of indigenes with a few sixteenth-century Spanish settlers at the headwaters of the Amazon (in what is now the northern Santa Cruz region of eastern Bolivia). Although there is no shared sense of communal ancestry, the Camba appear first to have been identified as a population around 1850 (Heath, 1964) and have virtually disappeared 150 years later. Many individuals who called themselves Camba in the 1950s had spent their childhood in various neighbouring societies, speaking non-Western languages such as Itatín, Guarayo, Guaraní, Sirion and others. In those days, such populations were commonly referred to as 'tribal' or 'primitive', but we have learned from history and anthropology that both such labels are misleading. Because the people who still consider themselves to be members of those populations generally participate minimally with global media, trade, or languages, they are more often referred to as 'Indian', 'indigenous', or, in the terminology of political correctness, 'first nations'.

As peasant farmers in a region where dense tropical forest meets flat open grassland, the Camba in the 1950s were a sparse population living scattered on quasi-feudal haciendas, isolated homesteads or in a few small villages. Their language (Castellano Camba) was a simple form of rustic sixteenth-century Castillian, retaining several archaic words, rhythms and pronunciations, with random admixtures from several local Indian languages. Although dependent on hacienda-owners for food, housing and token wages, those who were tenant farmers had little sense of community and often moved from one settlement to another. Homesteaders were proudly independent although also poor and highly mobile. The web of kinship that often binds individuals in traditional rural communities had little meaning and few among the Camba even knew their grandparents.

The Camba differed from all of their neighbours in that they alone did not routinely drink a fermented homebrew as either a dietary staple or intoxicant. Some of the nearby Indians used manioc, others banana or plantain, maize, or various palm nuts as a basis for low-alcoholic beers (about 3 to 5 per cent ethanol by volume). The Camba, by contrast, drank an unfermented chicha made from maize, but nothing stronger during most of the week.

They more than made up the difference, however, when they did drink beverage alcohol. Virtually the only occasions when they drank were fiestas or formal parties, but there were quite enough of those. Every local or national holiday (of which there were many) as well as every weekend, was marked by one or more fiestas where neighbours were generally welcome.

Most such parties lasted at least a day and two nights; others stretched much longer.

Their principal celebratory beverage can be thought of as exceptionally strong rum, although it is more like the un-aged neutral spirits such as are used as tissue fixative in biological laboratories. Containing 89 per cent ethanol by volume, it is called simply *alcohol* (the same Arabic-derived word as in English, but with only two syllables).

Such a strong beverage was never easy to produce, and the Camba did not make it themselves. Since the 1930s, it has been a by-product of four or five technologically complex sugar refineries scattered around the area, owned and managed mostly by European expatriates and filled with expensive and sophisticated heavy machinery. In bright pink-washed metal cans, such *alcohol* is still shipped throughout the Andes, ostensibly to serve as primer for small stoves and lanterns fuelled by kerosene (or paraffin) under pressure. Diluted with an equal amount of water, it served as the ritual and celebratory beverage (*aguardiente*) among Quechua and Aymara Indians in the highlands, but the Camba proudly drank it neat.

Colourless and flavourless, *alcohol* was irritating to the mouth and throat, even among older drinkers who had had considerable experience. No one ever commented on bouquet, flavour, or even enjoyment in connection with the act of drinking. What they did happily proclaim to enjoy was the positive value of taking part in a fiesta, especially when it resulted in their becoming utterly intoxicated.

One of the most striking aspects of Camba drinking was the highly stylized manner in which people drank at those fiestas. It was a pattern so standardized as to constitute a ritual in the sense in which that term is used by social scientists: not sacred but secular, and not self-consciously formal but highly repetitive and regularly patterned. Anywhere from eight to 35 members of a group stood, sat or squatted in an approximate circle, usually in a courtyard of bare earth. A single bottle (used, 0.7 litre) and a single glass tumbler rested on a small table or tree stump. The person who contributed that first bottle was remembered but not signalled as 'sponsor' of the party. After pouring a glassful (about 300cc), he would walk to any member of the group – and there was literally no pattern that I could discern in hundreds of instances, with respect to age, sex, kinship, or other criterion. That person would smile and nod; the sponsor would smile and nod while saying '*Salud*' (Health) or '*A su salud*' (To your health), and drink half of the glassful in a quick draught. A would then hand the glass to B, who returned the toast and finished the glass. B would then refill the glass, and repeat the ritual with C. And so the drinking would proceed, with each member of the group getting roughly equal opportunities to ingest about 600 cc (at about 89 per cent ethanol by volume, or roughly 178 American proof). There were no rules about whom one should toast, but one was obliged always to accept such a toast.

Virtually all Camba adults (except the few Protestants) drank in those contexts, and most men were quite drunk (with blood-alcohol over .35 percent) at least twice a month. Women were usually integral to those small groups in which drinking took place, but they tended often to spit out a portion of their drinks surreptitiously and generally to exhibit less gross inebriation than men. Participants ranged from 12 years, the approximate age of maturity, to over 90. Although never explicitly stated, there appeared to be an implicit principle of reciprocity with respect to attending fiestas and providing alcohol although individual contributions were not signalled as such.

The Camba, who were generally somewhat reserved and laconic, became more relaxed, sociable, and talkative while drinking. There was usually a low undercurrent of small talk about crops, weather, reminiscences, or recent local happenings. Rarely there would be music (guitar or flute, sometimes with drum), to which some couples would dance in a desultory manner while the drinking ritual continued around them. As a bottle was emptied, a bystander (often a child) would replace it with a full one from a store that members of the group had assembled.

After the first couple of hours, the cycle of toasting would slow from a minute to as much as eight or ten minutes (without any comment). With that, the overall pace of a fiesta would slacken and intervals of silence would lengthen. By the fourth hour, many participants would stare dumbly at the ground except when toasted, and others who fell asleep or passed out were left where they fell. As some regained consciousness, the party gained new rhythm, so that a five, six, or seven hour cycle would be repeated, day and night, until the alcohol was exhausted or the call to work was sounded.

Just as a social rhythm could be discerned, so could a rhythm of change in most individuals. Normally quiet people would talk a little more while drinking; generalized indifference gave way to greater self-confidence including even some voicing of opinions.

In view of the high concentration of ethanol, a single toast would often mark the shift from exhilaration to oblivion for drinkers who were generally small and lean. Drunkenness was considered the inevitable and welcome consequence of drinking, and the Camba had no conception of moderate drinking, drinking to feel good or different stages of intoxication. The drinking group was both cohesive and permissive, so no guilt was associated with drinking or drunkenness.

Drunken behaviour, similarly, did not evoke any special comment because it differed so little from sober behaviour. It was extremely rare that any Camba, drunk or sober, should show any aggression, whether verbal, physical, sexually suggestive, threatening or of any other sort. Similarly, drunk or sober, no Camba would act like a clown or weep in a demonstration of maudlin sentimentality. No one acted particularly daring after drinking nor did they become unusually amicable or boisterous. None of the stereotypes that are often applied to heavy drinkers was salient for the simple reason that behaviour while drinking was so little different from normal behaviour during the long intervals between drinking.

Although a fiesta was ritualistic in its behavioural formality, it was by no means a solemn occasion. A fiesta might begin as early as Friday evening and not break up until Monday morning. A few newcomers might join occasionally, but only rarely did someone leave such a group. Eating consisted of infrequent handfuls of *masaco*, a thick mash of equal parts of lard and ground yuca (*Manihot esculenta*, known in some other regions as manioc or cassava), and bodily functions were casually performed nearby. A small coterie of young people stood around as bystanders, occasionally replenishing the fire, caring for infants, or finding more alcohol (for which they were later reimbursed).

The only legitimate reasons for ending a fiesta were exhaustion of the alcohol supply or the obligation to return to work. Generally, it was the independent homesteaders who ran out of drink whereas tenant farmers were kept to a weekly schedule by the landlords.

The blood-alcohol concentration of some individuals was so high that their sweat would sting their eyes at work after a fiesta, and one could smell the alcohol on them. Nevertheless, not only did no one complain of a hangover; the very concept was incomprehensible to them.

No one ever drank alone or could imagine anyone doing so. No one ever argued, fought, or acted aggressively while drinking. No one tried to be humorous, or to show off in any way, nor did anyone express maudlin sadness in such a context. No one claimed to enjoy drinking as such, but they did relish drunkenness – both before and after.

There were no magical properties attributed to *alcohol*, nor was drinking thought to signal manliness or aplomb. Although a bottle of *alcohol* cost the equivalent of three days' wages for a peasant, the long-term reciprocity of communal drinking meant that no household was economically deprived; they were poor by most standards, but it was not drinking that made them so, and no one went hungry. The fact that this outsider joined in the festivities was appreciated as a gesture of acceptance and friendship. An unexpected health benefit that many Camba cited was that *alcohol* was said to kill some intestinal parasites; few biomedical practitioners share that belief.

No one among the Camba used any other psychoactive drugs, with the mild exception of caffeine in coffee, although much of the local flora and some of the fauna are sources of hallucinogens and psychedelics that were used by other neighbouring populations.

After a lifetime of such drinking (more than 70 years for some individuals), there was no indication of dependence, abuse, tremors, liver disease (beyond that which was endemic among abstinent youths and Protestants as well as among drinkers), or other signs of damage. Drunken accidents

123

were virtually unknown, as were homicides, suicides, expressions of aggression, or interference with work or social relations.

There was little pressure on anyone to stop drinking or to drink less or in a different way. An exception to that generalization were the Protestant missionaries (generally foreigners who paid much more attention to their own small congregations than to the vast majority who were at least nominally Roman Catholic). Protestant converts were expected to abstain, and they did so, often boasting proudly of how that provided them with a small economic advantage. The Catholic clergy were also predominantly missionaries from Europe and the United States, but they tended to say little about local customs positively or negatively. Once in a while a priest would lament that Camba peasants were poor and that they were so often drunk, but (appropriately) without suggesting any causal link.

There were no official programs of social service or public health (except for the Rockefeller Foundation's ongoing anti-malaria campaign), and no health practitioner ever mentioned alcohol or drinking as a problem or a source of problems. What little attention was paid to policing had nothing to say on the subject, and the Catholic priests rarely made mention of it. Inasmuch as no individual was dependent on alcohol or drank other than in the prescribed context of a party, the question of abstaining for other than religious reasons never arose.

A TENTATIVE INTERPRETATION

Inasmuch as drinking in almost all societies is essentially a social activity, and because there was so little individual variation it seemed incumbent to look for functions in social terms. Because the outstanding feature of Camba drinking was the elaborately patterned behaviour that always accompanied it, that ritual appeared to be important. The single glass suggested a kind of communion and equality. Those features were generally lacking in the atomistic social organization, where there was little sense of identification with community, kin, co-workers, or others. Living and working pretty much alone for most of the week, they found in drinking parties a limited kind of sociability that was otherwise lacking. Without having realized it at the time, I was following Simmel (1949) in stressing the inherent value of socializing, which tends cross-culturally to be a major aspect of most drinking. The combined relaxing and stimulating physiological responses to drinking can be construed as having served to lower defences and to facilitate rapport among individuals who were more often isolated and introverted. Analogies can be drawn to other atomistic populations such as cowboys, seafarers, lumberjacks, or urban homeless persons, all of whom stereotypically enjoy episodic heavy drinking.

The suggestion that a fiesta constituted an in-group implied that there should also have been an identifiable out-group. Protestants were one such, scorned more for their unusual behaviours than for ideological reasons. Highland Indians, who dilute *alcohol* by half and called it *aguardiente*, were thought to be dirty, uncouth, and timid about drinking. By contrast, the anthropologist who joined them was called 'very much a Camba', ostensibly because he followed their drinking patterns.

In ethnography, one often looks to exceptions as well as predominant patterns for clues to the motives of individuals and the functions of institutions. The few exceptions to the episodic heavy drinking pattern among the Camba were Protestants and rare occasions such as wakes and the major national war commemoration.

The only abstaining adults were converts to ascetic Protestant sects (Baptist, Free Brothers, and Assembly of God), for whom abstention was an article of faith. Furthermore, those small congregations met at various times throughout the week; prayer meetings and volleyball engaged them together; members called each other 'Brother' and 'Sister'. In short, church affiliation served as a relatively stable primary reference group of a sort that was lacking in the lives of most of their Catholic neighbours.

The social ritual sequence of the fiesta was the only way in which the Camba drank, except at wakes. Then a similarly strict pattern involved a single bottle and a single (smaller) glass, with a hostess wordlessly offering a drink only to each male attendee. He could decline by shaking his head or accept with a nod. Then he would look around, nodding slightly to all present, drink in a single draught, and return the glass. Women were not offered drink because, in Camba terms, 'they always have so much sadness they don't need it'.

Commemoration of the disastrous Chaco War (with Paraguay, 1932–35) differed from every other national holiday in being fairly solemn and with few drinking parties. Hardships on the part of both veterans and others were very much alive in the memory of the Camba, many of who suffered greatly throughout that time. Although Bolivian nationality played little role in their daily lives, people not only remembered personal hardships but also were acutely aware that the Chaco War was only the most recent instance in which their country had been defeated by each of its neighbours, losing half of it territory. In fact, the sombre quality of the commemoration of the Chaco War marked it off as distinctly different from all other holidays. In a sense, it was very like a wake, and the Camba often spoke of it as such. It has been posited that the sharing of grief, like the sharing of food or drink, serves to a remarkable extent to simulate (and to stimulate) unity among individuals who otherwise have little in common; it is in keeping with the idea of drinking parties as surrogate occasions for sociability that both wakes and a grievous anniversary might be exceptions to the general pattern of drinking fiestas when people came together.

125

THIS STUDY AMONG ALCOHOL STUDIES

In light of the importance that has subsequently been given to the original study of Camba drinking patterns, it deserves mention that it was not a focus of my research but a serendipitous by-product. During the year when I first studied the Camba, it never occurred to me to think much about why they drank in such a way. As a postgraduate student, my aim in going to the tropical lowlands of Bolivia had been to compile the first thorough ethnographic account of the Camba. It became my doctoral dissertation in anthropology, with special emphasis on land tenure and social organization.

To be sure, during the original fieldwork my companion and I took part in frequent drinking bouts and I described them in considerable detail in my field notes, hoping eventually to learn more about social organization and attitudes. But it was not until we had returned to the United States and I was writing my dissertation that I learned about the emerging multidisciplinary field of *alcohol studies* and the fact that some other scholars were interested in drinking patterns as such. It was winter in New England, so our tanned faces were conspicuous. As a break from the tedium of writing, Ann and I had gone for a walk among the architecturally interesting old houses the university had converted to offices. In one such, two little old men looked up and abruptly asked, 'Where did you get those tans?' We began to explain, but as soon as we mentioned Bolivia, one of them interrupted, literally grabbing my lapels and asking 'How do they drink there? I don't know anyone who's been to Bolivia'.

As we recounted our experiences, they introduced themselves (Mark Keller and E. M. Jellinek, of the Yale Center of Alcohol Studies) and tried to impress upon me the importance of familiarizing myself with what had been written about drinking elsewhere. They were both struck by the colourful role that alcohol played in the lives of the Camba and by the fact that their drinking patterns were so extreme in cross-cultural perspective (Heath, 1991a:138–139). When Mark abruptly asked, 'Can you write an article for 'my' journal?' I was flattered but cautious and warned him that I would have to check my field notes to see whether I had enough data.

A few hours' review, and his assurance that there wasn't much theoretical literature that I would have to master in order to set my data into meaningful context, were all the encouragement I needed. With their help, I was quickly able to read virtually all that had been written about drinking from anthropological and sociological perspectives, and resolved that my paper should incorporate every issue that had been discussed in that context.

Such an audacious venture would hardly be feasible today, but at mid-century there were many fewer scholars so that some of us enjoyed what I have come to call 'expertise by default'. Fortunately, my adherence to the traditional ideal of paying attention to 'everything' in the lives of the population that I was studying (stemming from training at both Harvard and

Yale Universities) meant that I had built up sufficiently detailed fieldnotes even on that tangential subject. It was also an advantage that the world-wide descriptive and analytic literature on alcohol in social and cultural context was sufficiently sparse at the time that I was able to master it in a few weeks, and to link my findings to issues and approaches of which I had not even been aware during the field research.

One early outcome of the Camba study occurred even before it was published. The Yale Center of Alcohol Studies was a small and collegial group, so biochemist Leon Greenberg was interested when Keller happened to mention my work. He was surprised and delighted when he found further that I had bothered to bring back a sample of *alcohol*. After he had analyzed it in some detail, we were all surprised at the high concentration of ethanol, and Greenberg ventured to suggest that, as interesting and colourful as my yarns may have been, the Camba and I simply could not have drunk that way, 'because there would be an involuntary muscular closure of the oesophagus'. He had undoubtedly guessed that I would feel sufficiently challenged to agree to conduct an experiment by drinking what was left of the sample under controlled conditions in his laboratory, and with periodic measurements of my blood-alcohol concentration. Without digressing into irrelevant details, suffice it to say that I proved him wrong and we quietly wrote a new footnote in the physiology of alcohol that weekend by setting some sort of new record. It later became evident that paid human subjects had simply never been challenged to swallow such stuff.

There was another happy accident – more serendipity – in that some author failed to meet his or her deadline and Mark substituted my paper so that there was virtually no prepublication lag, even though Yale's *Quarterly Journal of Studies on Alcohol* was the major international and multidisciplinary outlet on the subject. That initial report about Camba drinking patterns was widely distributed and attracted considerable attention. It was quite evident that other scholars were interested by the quasi-ceremonial quality of Camba drinking and by the absence of alcohol-related problems, especially in light of the large quantities and frequencies involved.

As a beginning anthropologist, I had been careful in that original paper to include as many details as I thought might be useful to a broad range of readers. It was gratifying that so many colleagues chose the Camba as a salient case-study and interpreted the data in alternative ways to fit different theories and conceptual schemes.

First, the original paper was translated and published in both the National Sociological Journal in Bolivia, and in the general journal of the University of Santa Cruz, the huge political jurisdiction in which most of the Camba then lived. Like a few other social scientists, I viewed this as an important way of demonstrating my gratitude to the community who had been so generous in sharing their lives with me.

When Mandelbaum (1965) wrote the first major review-article on alcohol and culture, he chose the Camba case-study to illustrate the interplay of culture and personality. He accurately summarized the overall patterns and my emphasis on the atomistic social structure, but went slightly astray by interjecting a vaguely Freudian element, incorrectly positing 'fear and distrust of others' as a trait common among them.

More to the point was heavy reliance on the Camba by MacAndrew and Edgerton (1969) as the first example (among various ethnographic and historical cases) in which the evidence clearly contradicted what was then the dominant scientific model. This held that ethanol had the invariant pharmacological impact of encouraging aggressive and other antisocial behaviour, presumably by interfering with certain loci of control in the human brain. A careful review of cross-cultural evidence disproved those presumptions. That clear and concise book did much to discredit a number of simplistic biological and medical determinisms in alcohol studies at the time, and to establish the importance of social and cultural factors as significant variables when one attempts to interpret alcohol use and its outcomes.

A more colourful but less valid use of the Camba case occurred when Room (1984) used it as one of the more egregious examples of what he then called 'problem deflation'. Concerned that ethnographers often emphasized real and perceived benefits of drinking, unlike other social scientists who almost invariably stressed risks, dangers and harm, he offered several interpretations about why anthropologists were so obtuse, including a functionalist philosophical bias, qualitative research methods, membership in a 'wet generation', and failure to recognize that diseases differ from one culture to another. Nearly all of the 16 designated discussants of that paper rejected many of his assertions as having been based on gross misunderstandings of how ethnographers worked. His broad implication that there was a major breach and controversy in the field had the paradoxical advantage of focussing some attention on social science approaches at a time when other researchers were only beginning to give lip-service to the complexity of alcohol as requiring a combined 'biopsychosocial' approach.

At a time when cultural differences were very little appreciated in Western biomedicine, the Camba were often cited to illustrate behaviours that first appeared quaint and curious, but that became both logical and more understandable within the sociocultural context. In analyzing the linkages between sociability and alcohol, Partanen (1991) relied heavily on the Camba case as well as on other ethnographic accounts. Others have, from time to time, cited the extreme frequency of drunkenness of the Camba, their virtual lack of alcohol-related problems, or the fact that changing drinking patterns reflected changing social conditions. My own work as it tended over the years to focus more on cross-cultural comparisons and on governmental policies, consistently emphasized the importance of describing and analyzing drinking patterns (rather than relying almost exclusively on numerical measures of quantity and frequency of alcohol consumption). This took on added importance when a series of statements by World Health Organizations and others asserted that alcohol-related problems occurred in a constant and direct proportion to the amount of ethanol ingested (Edwards et al, 1994). It reached the point where some colleagues may have been alienated by my persistence in pointing out the frequent instances when their own data contradicted their presumption, which was phrased more as an axiom than as a hypothesis (Heath 1998, 1995, 2000).

During the same period, alcohol studies were beginning to be carried out internationally and cross-culturally. Growing from a base in marketing studies, the survey/questionnaire approach was adopted, adapted, and progressively refined in ways that emphasized quantification, enumeration, and graphic and statistical manipulation of the data. Qualitative studies tended to be rare, dealing with relatively small 'special populations' and to be both wordy and frustratingly qualified in their conclusions. An inappropriate bifurcation between quantitative and qualitative approaches deepened, until a few ambitious investigators effectively combined them again. Too often qualitative studies were summarily dismissed as being interesting but anecdotal, 'soft science', of little use because they did not allow for easy presentation in the standard formats of 'hard science' such as tabulation, statistical manipulation, or graphing. The term 'drinking patterns' itself was redolent of those supposed shortcomings, so that a rapidly accumulating body of anthropological evidence was appreciated almost exclusively by colleagues within the discipline and had diminishing impact on others in alcohol studies; only recently is that beginning to change (Rehm et al. 1996; Rehn et al, 2001).

For more than four decades, I was consistent in all scientific and professional contexts in stressing both the importance of drinking patterns and the fact that heavy drinking is not necessarily risky or harmful. As I subsequently reported in some detail about changes in the social situation of the Camba and about changes in their drinking patterns, some of the more simplistic theories about historical trends came into question (Heath 1995a). As I gained familiarity with and confidence in discussing national and international policies about alcohol and drugs, the inefficacy and counterproductive quality of many of them became apparent (Heath 1988, 1995, 2000). In addition, mounting scientific evidence has subsequently supported the view that alcohol is neither an unalloyed good nor inevitably bad, but – as most populations have recognized throughout the human experience – ambivalent, with results significantly affected by attitudes, values and expectancies.

CHANGES IN CAMBA DRINKING

Another respect in which the Camba as an ethnographic case-study differs from most other studies of alcohol use and its outcomes is that we have diachronic data rather than simply a 'snapshot' that represents a supposedly static ethnographic-present. Several times in the 1960s, 70s, and 80s, I was able to return to the Camba and each time I paid some attention to drink, drinking, and associated meanings, values and attitudes (Heath 1971, 1991b, 1995, 2002). It was a gratifying surprise that such a slice of history tended to support my original structural interpretation, while providing fresh insights into alternative adaptations, both spontaneous and imposed.

Unlike the many frequent so-called revolutions that had marked Bolivia's history, that in 1952 represented a real break, which unseated the traditional landowning oligarchy, and sowed the seeds of participant democracy (Heath, Gasmus and Beuchler, 1969). The combination of land reform (breaking up vast quasi-feudal holdings and giving title to small-scale farmers), universal suffrage (after more than a century in which the illiterate majority had no voice or vote), and educational reform (providing schooling to the rural poor, including Indians, as well as to wealthy and middle-class 'Whites'), all promised to result in pervasive societal upheaval if they were to be effectively implemented. In that fluid context, many of the Camba who had been tenant farmers became small-scale independent freeholders, and formerly landless peasants became homesteaders. Much remains to be done, but advances on all of those fronts have been greater and more rapid than anyone expected at the middle of the twentieth century.

Among the things that had originally attracted me to the tropical lowlands of Bolivia was the expectation of impending rapid social and economic change. During the 1960s and 70s, that former frontier enclave became linked with the rest of the world in various ways. A new highway across the Andes connected with another highway that serviced the highlands in the western part of the country, where fully two-thirds of the population and virtually all of the commercial and administrative activity were located. Two railroads arrived, connecting the Camba region with Brazil to the east and Argentina to the south. A tide of immigrants flowed in: conservative Mennonites from eastern Europe by way of Paraguay, Japanese and Okinawans from Asia and predominantly Quechua and Aymara-speaking Indians from the valleys and high plateau of the Andes.

The Bolivian government became a more influential presence. Land reform affected the traditional agricultural system. Foreign aid and petroleum exploration significantly impacted the economy. In addition, the beginnings of large-scale international trade in cocaine occurred. All of those together provided a very different ambience, although most such changes had little immediate impact on the rhythms of Camba life.

The Camba rapidly gained familiarity with the cumbersome procedures of claiming vacant land (beyond the frontier of deeds, even if occupied or used by indigenous tribal people) or ownership of plots on extensive haciendas where they had served as sharecroppers. Instead of filing claims individually, it was often cheaper and more efficient to create a *sindicato* (or peasant league) as a corporate plaintiff in appeals for expropriation or reallocation (Heath 1972). Each *sindicato* came to jointly represent a group with share interests and served as a strong and meaningful reference group such as had been missing in Camba culture beforehand. Together with the appeal for land came increasing political socialization, some agricultural extension services and grassroots decision making on topics such as local public works, schooling, and such. At meetings, there was ample discussion including women as well as men, aiming toward unanimity rather than simple majority rule.

During those tumultuous decades, I returned frequently to Bolivia for different kinds of research and consultation, but always made it a point to revisit my Camba friends and to keep abreast of their drinking patterns. It was gratifying to see that the changes I noted in Camba drinking fit well with the interpretation that I had originally given to those customs, beliefs, and practices. As will be noted in more detail below, a tightening of the social organization was reflected in a major diminution of drinking for a while, and, similarly, subsequent loosening of those social bonds was accompanied by a return to the earlier pattern of heavy drinking.

With the proliferation of *sindicatos* came political awareness and socialization. The newly incumbent Nationalist Revolutionary Movement (MNR) used *sindicatos* as a channel for arming the peasants (with weapons stripped from the discredited army), enlisting their support (in demonstrations as well as voting), and reminding them of the beneficence of the party. Not only did the *sindicatos* bring Camba together as nothing had before; they had frequent meetings in which populist aspirations were discussed. Members referred to each other as 'Compañero' (Comrade), signaling a new kind of class-consciousness. With the growing sense of social interrelatedness there was a marked diminution of drinking parties, which occurred less often, and tended to be shorter when they did occur.

With no exception, those individuals who were active in *sindicato* affairs said that they no longer took part in frequent drinking parties, and this included general members as well as those who held any office (such as director, secretary, or educational secretary, all of which were temporary and unpaid). Similarly, and again with no exception, those who said that they still participated in periodic drinking parties during that period were not involved in any way with the *sindicato* movement. These facts combined seem to support the earlier suggestion that the drinking party constituted an important social occasion for people who had no others – and, by implication, that those who enjoyed other kinds of social occasions might not depend on drinking parties for sociability.

During the late 1970s and 80s runaway inflation hurt all levels of Bolivian society, until a long period of economic stabilization and foreign investment created a local boom in Camba territory that had been a backwater of quasi-feudal subsistence farming. The forests were decimated, partly for sale as lumber, partly to fuel big new sugar refineries, and partly to make way for large-scale cotton and cattle raising. The rush of immigrants to the region increased, and most of the newcomers were more entrepreneurial and assertive than the Camba. Slow to adjust to the strikingly different ambience, many Camba lost their land and their sense of security. In the wake of a military coup, *sindicatos* were not only outlawed but actively harassed, and the brief experiment in participatory democracy was stifled. A sequence of drought, floods, pests and plant diseases upset the agricultural base of the people and the region. That economy was soon displaced by the illegal trade in coca and cocaine paste, which benefited a few newcomers but not the Camba.

It is sad to listen to my Camba friends reminisce nostalgically about the jungle which they used to take for granted as a bountiful larder where they would hunt for food, gather wild honey, collect fruits, nuts, herbal medicines, firewood, timbers for their houses and palm leaves for thatched roofs and walls or to make baskets. Erosion, flooding and pollution had become new and commonplace problems on the rivers where they used to fish. Virtually all of what outsiders saw as recent benefits had been deleterious for them: in the markets, there may have been more available but not what they wanted nor at prices they could afford. Motorized transport passed them by if they were lucky, and often hurt them and their little property. Even bare-bulb electric lighting cost more than their old fires or crude oil lamps, were too hot, and attracted annoying insects.

A younger generation have almost entirely moved to the cities where there were jobs or at least prospects for work, and where they were quick to drop their identity as Camba. A few older Camba men and women continued to get together on local saints' days and on major holidays to drink in a way that in 1989, looked very much like what I had encountered in 1956, although such groups were smaller and more widely scattered.

Those drinking parties again featured the single bottle and the single glass, with the same formulaic toasting and quick gulping of *alcohol*, the drink that still made them wince. A gentle undercurrent of talk tended to be more about the past than about the present, and the pace had slowed to a degree that is discernible only in that no one passed out, although most nodded at least briefly in the late hours. There was every indication, more than 40 years later, that those drinking parties were again important efforts at enhancing sociability in a society that provided few other occasions for it.

SOME CONCLUSIONS AND IMPLICATIONS

It may surprise some readers to learn that I consider it an advantage having originally come to the field of alcohol studies on the basis of an unusual corpus of observational data and without any grounding in the definitions, models, and theories that prevailed at the time. Although I did not fully realize it then, Camba drinking patterns as an exceptional case impressed upon me a healthy scepticism concerning many of the easy generalizations that scholars were making about alcohol. It is ironic that even the specialists had been relying heavily on samples of the population that were far from being representative; largely homeless single men in urban settings, college students in the United States, or long-term heavy drinkers who were dependent on alcohol and complaining of a variety of physiological, psychological and social problems. Little attention had been paid to any non-Western drinkers, and unrecognized ethnocentrism permeated the field. Having been ignorant of any presuppositions about drinking and its consequences, I was able to observe and report the behaviour, attitudes, values and outcomes with relative objectivity and in a frame of normalcy rather than pathology.

Beyond the descriptions, I also enjoyed the advantage of working from an academic base, firmly grounded in a department of anthropology. Although I paid attention to what others were saying and doing about treatment, and even lectured and otherwise participated in occasional programs, my income and job security were never dependent on my dealing with alcohol abusers and dependent people on any sustained basis. Similarly, although I kept abreast of work and writings on prevention and other policies, whether phrased in terms of public health or social welfare, there was no expectation that I should please the politically oriented constituencies that tend to dominate in those fields. Perhaps of crucial importance is the fact that the kinds of research that I did were small-scale, based on my own skills, and requiring no hiring of interviewers, assistants to code and transcribe data, others to 'clean up the data', and people to manipulate those statistics expertly and imaginatively in a way that would appear to justify large-scale funding. Although I have enjoyed pleasant, fruitful and sometimes even warmly cordial relations with many colleagues who are recognized around the world as experts in the field of alcohol and drug studies, my own primary affiliation, career and reputation, have all been squarely within the discipline of anthropology. There has never been any implication from any funding agencies that results or comments that might by interpreted as favourable to drink and drinking would be any less (or more) welcome than those unfavourable. That unusual combination of supportive circumstances has encouraged me to speak plainly on the subject, even when my views were not widely shared by fellow professionals or popular with the lay public (Heath in press).

Another advantage is the fact that the Camba case so dramatically contrasted with widespread presumptions about quantity, frequency and results of drinking, prompting me early to pay close attention to drinking patterns in other parts of the world and throughout history. That global perspective strongly reinforced my conviction that the social and cultural context of drinking was a crucial factor, although it had tended generally to be ignored or only vaguely implied as an undifferentiated part of 'the environment'. It appears as if the diachronic studies of Camba drinking served well to impress upon many colleagues the fact that qualitative data are not merely interesting anecdotes, but that they serve to differentiate times, changes in social structures and in the functions of institutions, the roles of motives and values in affecting human behaviour and even changes throughout scientific conceptions about the nature of social problems.

Other colleagues whose interests came to include alcohol and drugs have striven to incorporate quantitative with qualitative data and methods, and to collaborate closely with individuals and teams representing other disciplines. It was at least partly through contributions to the study of alcohol and drugs that anthropology and anthropologists gained recognition and acceptance in the broad field of public health. Beyond that, outspoken criticism of proposed laws, systems of taxation, and other policies that had already proven faulty resulted in some people paying attention to the persistent gap between recommendations and outcomes.

It is on that basis that I deign to offer a few conclusions and implications that stem not only from the initial study of Camba drinking patterns but also from a long career of paying close attention to changes in those drinking patterns, as well as changes in the fields of alcohol studies and anthropology. Beyond the first two or three such comments, sequence should not be construed as implying relative importance.

• Alcohol abuse and alcohol dependence, as tragic and important as they may be to some individuals and to some communities, are by no means inevitable consequences of drinking, even long-term drinking frequently resulting in inebriation.

• Although episodic heavy drinking is generally risky and tends to be dangerous, it is not always so. Just as poison is more in the dose than in the substance, a specific supportive context can permit heavy drinking to recur without deleterious consequences.

• The wide range of physical, psychological, social, and other pathologies that are generally referred to as alcohol-related problems is socially constructed. This is evidenced by the fact that such problems vary from time to time within a community as well as varying from one community to another.

• Insofar as they occur at all, such alcohol-related problems occur with different frequencies and sometimes with very different meanings in communities with various sociocultural systems.

• Even some problems that may appear to be based on neurophysiological or biochemical processes (such as hangover or blackout) are both absent and incomprehensible in some intellectual contexts.

• The quantity and frequency of drinking as routinely measured in social surveys fails accurately to represent the meanings or effects of drinking. By numerically equating moderate but regular drinkers with infrequent drinkers, they tend to make unproblematic drinking appear risky and trivialize our need to learn more about heavy drinking.

• Within limits, it matters less *how much* one drinks than *how* one drinks. Attitudes, values and expectations all play important roles in relation to alcohol use and its outcomes. Greater attention to drinking patterns would help to identify salient variables that intervene between sheer quantity of alcohol ingestion and behavioural and other outcomes.

• Although the deductive method of research has unquestioned power in evaluating a limited number of dependent or independent variables in rigidly controlled scientific experiments, the inductive method has special strength in leaving the investigator open to recognizing patterns and variables that might otherwise be overlooked. This is especially the case in complex social contexts.

• The quantity and frequency of drinking as routinely measured in social surveys fails accurately to represent the meanings or effects of drinking. By numerically equating moderate but regular drinkers with infrequent heavy drinkers, they tend to make variables that intervene between sheer quantity of alcohol ingestion and behavioural and other outcomes.

REFERENCES

Edwards, G., P.Edwards, T.F. Babor, S. Casswell, R. Ferrence, N. Giesbrecht, C. Godfrey, H.D. Holder, P. Lemmens, K. Makela, L.T.Midanik, T. Norstrom, E. Osterberg, A. Romelsjo, R. Room, J. Simpura dnd O-J. Skog .(1994). *Alcohol Policy and the Public Good* (Oxford: Oxford University Press).
Heath, D. B. (1958) 'Drinking Patterns of the Bolivian Camba', *Quarterly Journal of Studies on Alcohol*, 19:491–508.
——(1964) 'Ethnogenesis and Ethnohistory: Sociocultural Emergence in the Bolivian Oriente', in *Actas y Memorias del XXXV Congreso Internacional de Americanistas,* (México: Congreso Internacional de Americanistas).

135

——(1971) 'Peasants, Revolution, and Drinking: Interethnic Drinking Patterns in Two Bolivian Communities', *Human Organization*, 30:179–86.

——(1988) 'Alcohol Control Policies and Drinking Patterns: An International Game of Politics against Science', *Journal of Substance Abuse*, 1:109–25.

——(1991a) 'The Mutual Relevance of Anthropological and Sociological Perspectives on Alcohol Study', in P. M. Roman (ed.), *Alcohol: The Development of Sociological Perspectives on Use and Abuse* (New Brunswick, NJ: Rutgers Center of Alcohol Studies).

——(1991b) 'Continuity and Change in Drinking Patterns of the Bolivian Camba', in D.J.Pittman and H.R. White (eds.), *Society, Culture, and Drinking Patterns Reexamined*(New Brunswick, NJ: Rutgers Center of Alcohol Studies).

——(1995B) *International Handbook on Alcohol and Culture* (Westport, CT: Greenwood).

——(2000) *Drinking Occasions: Comparative Perspectives on Alcohol and Culture* (Baltimore, MD: Brunner/Mazell).

——(2002) 'Changes in Drinking Patterns in Five Bolivian Cultures: A Cautionary Tale about Historical Approaches', in D. B. Heath (ed.), *Contemporary Cultures and Societies of Latin America* (3rd ed.) (Prospect Heights, IL: Waveland Press).

——(In press) 'Anthropology, Alcohol, and a Parallel Career: Serendipity Compounded', *Social History of Alcohol Review* (expected 2003).

C.J.Erasmus and H.C.Buechler. (1969) *Land Reform and Social Revolution in Bolivia* (New York: Praeger).

MacAndrew,D., and R.E.Edgerton. (1969) *Drunken Comportment: A Social Explanation* (Chicago: Aldine) (new edition, 2003).

Mandelbaum, D.G.(1965) 'Alcohol and Culture' [with comments by six authors], *Current Anthropology*, 6:281–94.

Partanen,J. (1991) *Sociability and Intoxication: Alcohol and Drinking in Kenya, Africa, and the Modern World* (Finnish Foundation for Alcohol Studies, vol. 39) (Helsinki: Finnish Foundation for Alcohol Studies).

Rehm, J., M.J. Ashley, R. Room, E. Single, S. Bondy, R. Ferrence and N. Giesbrecht. (1996) 'On the Emerging Paradigm of Drinking Patterns and their Social and Health Consequences', *Addiction*, 91:1615–22.

Rehn,M., R.Room and G. Edwards. (2001) *Alcohol in the European Region: Consumption, Harm and Policies* [(Copenhagen: World Health Organization Regional Office for Europe)].

Room,R. (1984) 'Alcohol and Ethnography: A Case of Problem Deflation?' [(with comments by 15 authors)], *Current Anthropology*, 25:169–91.

Simmel,G. (1949) 'The Sociology of Sociability', *American Journal of Sociology*, 55:254–61; (original in German, 1911).

Chapter Eight

THE DIS-EASE OVER NATIVE NORTH AMERICAN DRINKING: EXPERIENCES OF THE INNU OF NORTHERN LABRADOR

Colin Samson

THE UNSETTLING NATURE OF NATIVE AMERICAN DRINKING

We all jumped in the huge red Dodge pick-up to drive along the bumpy spruce-lined highway between Sheshatshiu and Goose Bay. As my friend Bob drove, his wife, and daughter were wedged between us in the front. Another daughter and boyfriend were in the back. I had asked to speak to Bob about his schooling, as part of a research project I was carrying out for the Band Council. He was one of the people in the village whose experiences I wanted to hear about. Bob was a long time activist for the rights of his people, a hunter, a believer in the Innu way of life, and also a philosopher. He could quote Frantz Fanon, the Bible and talk philosophy, but he had been raised in the country in the interior of Labrador, the land the Innu call *Nitassinan*. Only as a teenager did he settle in Sheshatshiu, the village built by the Canadian government in an effort to assimilate the Innu and prevent them from practicing nomadic hunting. [1]

Bob had told me he would talk about his school days when we took a ride up to Goose Bay, the settler community, some 33 kilometres away. We dropped the women off at Bingo, and then us men went to a bar. Bob ordered a Labatt's Blue and I did too. We played several games of pool, and other Innu men joined in. As the night proceeded, I noticed that Bob was getting through quite a few bottles, but his steady hand on the pool cue never veered. After a couple of hours, it was time to collect the women from the Bingo hall. Bob tossed me the keys, while he proceeded with another round of pool. When I returned with the women, Bob was sitting at the bar. I ordered another beer and we talked. His mood had changed. He became more taciturn. Everything I said was disputed. Sometimes, not only was it disputed, but my motives were questioned. At the time, I had been reading of the Scottish fur trader Donald Smith, later Lord Strathcona, who had dealings with Bob's ancestors. I quoted Smith's uncharitable views of the Innu as a joke. Bob knew it was a joke, but told me I was being patronising. The agony of counter-claims, accusations and interrogation persisted for some time while Bob's wife played slot machines. Eventually she persuaded him to go, and we all piled in the truck, now augmented by several young Innu men.

Again, I was the driver. Instead of heading back to Sheshatshiu, we turned in the opposite direction towards the only liquor store still open in Goose Bay. There several of the young men got out, purchased six packs, but only one returned to the truck with beer for everyone. The journey back was now a lot longer. Our progress along the road was halted every few minutes, by someone shouting for me to stop so they could relieve themselves. Finally we reached Bob's house. His wife went straight to bed, but Bob kneeled in the dirt outside the front door to urinate. He could barely walk into the house, and affectionately told me that I had never seen him like this. From here on we sat at the table smoking cigarettes and I listened to eloquent, but often disconnected ruminations on dreams, assimilation, the Innu way of life and the Bible. Eventually, I made my way back to the house in which I was staying about an hour before I was due to get up for a trip to go into a hunting camp in the interior.

In the short film, *The History of the Luiseño People, La Jolla Reservation – Christmas Day 1990*, performance artist James Luna draws the viewer into his Christmas Day on the reservation. It begins with a visit to the convenience store in his pick up. At the store Luna buys a case of beer, gets into his truck, and starts drinking while driving home. When he arrives home, he switches on the TV which is showing 1950s American dance shows featuring Bob Hope and Bing Crosby. As the saccharine enthusiasm radiates from the TV screen, Luna slumps down in the chair, and continues drinking and chain smoking. The sparsely furnished room features a Christmas tree, sporting only a beer can for decoration. Luna wears dark shades, although almost no light penetrates into the room. Most of the performance involves Luna making a series of phone calls to friends and family. These conversations, to friends and family members, are almost always unresolved. Remarks to his children about their Christmas presents reveal that Luna has sent them nothing, making only vague promises to make amends by seeing them later. In answer to a question from his mother, he tells her that he is not drinking, taking another muffled swig and stifling a burp as he does so. The most acrimonious exchange is with his, presumably white, ex-wife who reminds him of his alimony payments. After receiving some verbal abuse, she is reminded that 'we are different'. In a more reflective moment, Luna tells her, 'I think that way, but I don't feel that way'. Meanwhile pop-tops release gas from can after can of beer, cigarettes are lit and smoked, and the jaunty television soundtrack reminds us that this is Christmas Day.

The Innu and the Luiseño are separated by the continent itself. *Nitassi-nan* is in Labrador, in the far corner of Northeast North America. The La Jolla reservation is near San Diego just north of the US-Mexico border. While the two peoples differ substantially in that European colonization had its effects on their societies in different centuries, what is common to both these stories is a certain dis-ease on the part of the non-native observer at being drawn in to Native American drinking. At the bar, in the truck and in the house, I was immersed in Bob's drinking. I could think of no inoffensive way to extricate myself, despite the discomfort, and as the night wore on, the more uncomfortable it all became. Similarly, the viewer of James Luna's performance feels as though they have been drawn into the room with him. As the drinking and smoking and incessant phone calls become increasingly compulsive, one feels trapped in a world of dark brooding, broken promises, and acrimony that the Christmas entertainment on the TV only seems to amplify.

Why this dis-ease towards American Indian drinking? In her book on Navajo cosmology, Maureen Trudelle Schwarz (2001:154–55) notes that although numerous anthropologists must have come across problem drinking in their work with Native Americans, very few mention it in their final reports. In this chapter, I will explore some of the reasons for and ramifications of the widespread silences and dis-ease over Native American drinking. Using several examples, but drawing on my own work with the Innu of Northern Labrador, I will look at various historical contexts for indigenous peoples consumption of alcohol, medical and lay attitudes towards Indian drinking, interpretations of such drinking, and the personal and cultural consequences of it.

DRINKING AND DISPOSSESSION

I would like to delve further into why American Indian drinking is unsettling to the non-indigenous person, and why many indigenous peoples are so frank and open about this side of their lives. Perhaps this frankness is because American Indians, despite centuries of Christian missionary activity, do not internalise the connections between drunkenness and sin, and hence, the attribution of individual fault, in the same way as Europeans. Rather, alcohol is expressive of their histories and experiences in interaction with whites. Indeed, if one considers how dispossession and assimilation, almost always involving some sort of violence, might affect a group of people, it is natural to assume alcohol could be used as a means of dealing with the assaults on the self. Evidence from a range of Native American societies indicate that problems related to drinking, rather than alcohol *per se* coincided with acts of dispossession. For the Anishenaabeg of Minnesota:

> ... the evidence suggests that dispossession during that period [early twentieth century], particularly at the White Earth and Leech Lake reservations, increased alcohol-related problems. (Abbott, 1999:28)

For their Ojibwa relatives further north in Ontario, much later:

> ... the widespread and pathological use of alcohol in the community began in the mid 1960s, after the people were moved to the new reserve and connected to the town of Kenora by road (Shkilnyk, 1985: 18).

Shortly after a move away from their homelands, the Sayisi Dene of Northern Manitoba:

> Unable to hunt or trap, scorned by the townsfolk of Churchill, living in grinding poverty, and filled with a sense of powerlessness and loss, most of the adults at Camp-10 became addicted to alcohol. Within a couple of years, their community collapsed into disorder and despair (Bussidor and Bilgen-Reinart, 1997:71).

Non-indigenous people affected by much less stressful and less permanent sources of adversity certainly take to the bottle, as we know from almost daily newspaper stories about sports heroes, celebrities and politicians, who have experienced, often only minor, setbacks or embarrassment. The difference, though, is that *Europeans* dismantled Native American societies – or at least aggressively attempted to do so – whereas the rich and famous are seen to have brought about their own downfall, often from excess, ambition or narcissism. Even if Europeans or those of European descent in North America do not admit to this, and many, if not most, do not do so readily, a lingering sense of wrongdoing cannot be escaped. In this context, the nervous reactions of the sociologist ostensibly documenting the history of Innu education, the viewer drawn into Luna's performances, and the uncanny absences in the published works of anthropologists, are more intelligible.

An uneasiness over the legacy of dispossession is reflected in the US and Canadian government apologies for a wide range of injustices perpetrated against indigenous peoples. These apologies have come as evidence has mounted that Native North Americans are disproportionately poor, unhealthy, living in substandard dwellings and dying prematurely. In Canada, Minister of Indian Affairs Jane Stewart (1998) listed a whole host of current conditions of Aboriginal communities that her government admitted was a legacy of centuries of injustice and abuse in boarding schools. Interestingly, while appalling rates of infant mortality, youth suicide, unemployment, illiteracy and poverty were all mentioned, alcohol was not alluded to in Stewart's statement. The vast bulk of the initiatives unveiled were highly visible and symbolic gestures involving 'infrastructure', 'partnership', and 'governance' which do not alter the fundamental colonial relationship between Canada and Aboriginal peoples. Considering the gravity of the issues, it was significant that the apology came not from the Prime Minister, but the lower ranking Minister of Indian Affairs (Petruzellis, 2000:3).

But, even these apologies distance us from the experience of Native American drinking. In some ways, they function as acts of redemption, clearing the way for what one author (Rasmussen, 2000) terms reconciliation-to-forget. It is important, and even psychically necessary, for the governments of Canada and the US (and we could add similarly established states such as Australia and New Zealand) and their settler populations to brush aside many of the historical events that helped establish a 'dominant society'. The notion that self-perceived thriving post-industrial democracies are founded on dispossession and injustice is a hard pill to swallow. This is why, I believe, Federal officials in Canada, for example, have been so quick to deny allegations that Aboriginal peoples suffer *continuing* injustice, land appropriation, racism and colonisation.

When National Chief Matthew Coon-Come of the Assembly of First Nations (AFN) addressed the World Conference against Racism in Durban in 2001, he delivered a withering (and impeccably substantiated) attack on Canada for its ongoing maltreatment of Aboriginal peoples. However, his protests received vehement denials and ultimately the sanction of massive funding cuts to the AFN (Orkin, 2003:15), strategically directed at the ultimately successful removal of Coon-Come as the National Chief (Orkin, 2004). Such defensiveness also helps explain why aboriginal peoples register in the Canadian national identity as '. . . absent as a contemporary active citizen; the Indian is remembered as a romanticized figure in history, but forgotten as the colonised victim of an ongoing genocide' (Petruzellis, 2000:5).

Guilt must be factored among the driving forces explaining these vigorous and often ill tempered denials of the links between drinking (as well as other social problems) and white-native relations. The problem is, what do we do with guilt? How can members of the dominant society rid themselves of these feelings of uneasiness, now increasingly brought on by reminders from activists such as Coon Come, artists such as Luna, and the uncannily alcohol-free field reports of social researchers ?

DRINKING AS A MEDICAL PROBLEM

One technique is to address the symptoms of Native American problem drinking by constituting it as a disease and appropriating funds for social service and medical interventions. Here, the ravages of alcohol are approached by funding alcohol treatment facilities, social work intervention, pan-native healing therapies, and medical treatment for some of the worst effects of prolonged alcohol abuse, including Fetal Alcohol Syndrome. These programmes, along with government research funding for social science and medical research, have huge benefits for the state and the settler population, in that they are visible emblems of actions aiming 'to do something about the problem'. In Sheshatshiu, one of the Innu villages where I have worked intermittently since 1994, *most* of the public buildings house institutions aimed at social pathology remediation. There is a new treatment centre for drug using and solvent abusing adolescents, a new clinic to deal with the rampant proliferation of new diseases such as diabetes and obesity, a group home for errant youth, a women's shelter for the victims of domestic violence, and the Innu Uauatshitun or Alcohol Centre which provides alcohol counselling and sponsors frequent sweat lodges.[2] The other Innu village in Labrador, Natuashish, has a roughly similar set-up. In addition there are occasional mobile treatment units, set up in areas of the interior important to the Innu hunting life and more professionalised care in specialised facilities in other parts of Canada. Ultimately the government funds all such efforts.

While it is undeniable that these programmes have benefited some Innu drinkers, and similar programmes in other parts of North America have done the same, the problem of alcohol abuse continues to be a source of Native American ill health, social instability, and death. This proliferation of the problem gives support to what some find a more palatable explanation; that alcoholism is actually something to which Native Americans have a genetic predisposition. Here, inevitably genetics must rely on a concept of race. That is, that Native Americans, perhaps even all indigenous peoples, share certain configurations of genes that 'predispose' to alcoholism. Vizenor (1984:119) calls this 'a racist response to a serious national problem'. It is racist, not only in that it ignores the genetic variability among peoples grouped together as a homogenous biological unit, but because it ultimately inferiorizes and stereotypes Native Americans. The fact that many white male sports fans, to use but one of many possible examples, tend to engage in group oriented problem drinking has not, to my knowledge, led to any research or theorising on the genetic origins of Caucasian sports fan alcoholism. Genetic explanations, as Duster (1984) has observed, tend to be invoked in relation to those occupying the lower positions of the social stratification ladder.

Such explanations suffer from numerous methodological and philosophical problems. How can there be a biological explanation for a condition known as 'alcoholism' which can only be socially defined? Even if it were defined as such, what possible biological pathways exist between the hypothesized genetic configurations and the scenes enacted on the La Jolla Reservation on Christmas Day? How is it that historical, social, political, experiential, and psychological factors can be marginalised, as they must, in order to establish genetic cause or 'predisposition'? Fortunately, while such accounts are still common in the non-indigenous popular imagination, 'so far as clinicians and medical researchers can tell, [Native Americans] are no more susceptible physiologically to abusing alcohol than other Americans' (Mancall, 2000:194). May (1999:229) puts it in even stronger terms, stating that 'the most persistent myth about Indians is that they have particular biophysiological reasons for not being able to hold their alcohol'. Then, after reviewing the literature showing no significant differences between the rates at which Indians and non-Indians metabolize alcohol, May concludes, 'therefore no basis at all for this myth is found in scientific literature, and it should not be a consideration in current prevention and intervention programs'. Inevitably, the myth feeds off stereotypes, dating back to the seventeenth century, of the craven, alcoholic Indian totally dependent on trade, gifts, welfare or some other artifact of their interactions with Europeans (Berkhofer, 1978:30, Duran, 1996:113–114, Murray, 2000:28)

INDIAN DRUNKENNESS AS A SQUANDERING OF WHITE GENEROSITY

While many popular and even liberal responses to Native American drinking have invoked scientific causes, a deeper and more hostile reaction is held by many of the non-indigenous North American population. Instead of seeing 'alcoholism', over which the individual has little control, the victim is seen as having brought about their own misfortunes through acts of free will. Here, uneasiness is channeled into a narrative inversion in which an irony is presented; these troubled native people are those who have actually benefited from their contacts with whites, not only in terms of cultural elevation, but as a result of the economic support provided by governments. For example, visitors to Sheshatshiu often first see the Innu through the eyes of taxi drivers who make runs in their old American sedans along the ice-scoured, bumpy road from Goose Bay airport. It does not take many trips to establish that taxi drivers are rarely fans of the Innu. To them, the Innu are enemies of progress. The economic livelihood of Happy Valley-Goose Bay, on the whole, depends on the military presence at the air base, and the organised Innu protest campaign against low-level flying which attracted international criticism of Canada (Wadden, 1991) was not well received by taxi drivers or virtually anyone else in the settler communities. What riles taxi drivers and other settlers is that the Innu actually want to participate in deciding on what happens to all of the land of Labrador, including that upon which they are living. 'They have no right to any of the land', a driver once told me, 'as far as I am concerned, they are totally dependent on the government for welfare, they neglect their children, and I can't understand how they afford booze and bingo'.

In the views of settlers like taxi drivers, the degraded, alcohol-ridden and dependent state of the Innu disqualifies them from land or any other claims. Their inability to function in the most fundamental spheres of life makes them ill-suited to claim any rights, and it is always assumed that it is the Innu who 'claim' from Canada and not the reverse. How can people who do not know how to raise children, stay sober and work, claim anything? Another taxi driver, like many others a keen observer of Innu manners, called them racists. The Innu 'just sit around and take government money, but they won't live under the laws of all Canadians. They want their cake and to eat it too'. Nevertheless, there is a sense in which the taxi drivers are themselves bound to, even parasitic upon, this distasteful world they describe. A considerable amount of their trade involves ferrying residents of Sheshatshiu back and forth to Goose Bay. A return trip can bring in $80, and sometimes such a trip will be made simply to buy beer, much of which is consumed on the return journey. Taxi drivers are among the prime beneficiaries of the welfare handouts they so abhor. The general view in the neighbouring settler communities of Goose Bay and North West River, and even among many professionals working with the Innu, is that alcohol abuse is something that Innu drinkers are to be personally blamed for. What exacerbates the perception of blame in this way is the notion that the drinking is senseless in the context of government or white generosity. This was well documented in the Innu villages on the North Shore. Silberstein (1998:69) provides a vivid evocation of such sentiments:

> Your Indians told you that we took their land? Is that it? But the real content of history, that I am sure they didn't tell you. The truth is we built their houses, their roads. Today, they travel by motor boats and snowmobiles; they have airplanes and live off welfare. They don't pay federal taxes, and they are never happy. [translation by Sarah Crowe]

For these settlers, the disturbing knowledge of Innu prior occupation of, and deep connections to the land, is also sometimes channeled into a discourse on the Innu as unworthy of land rights on account of drinking. The tables are turned and the indigenous peoples are now something akin to celebrities who foolishly squander the goodwill of the public towards them. But, again there is a difference. Celebrities who take to the bottle are rarely resented; Native Americans often are. Perhaps one explanation for these attitudes is that the Innu – and many other indigenous North Americans – display their inebriation in very public ways. Although some non-indigenous drinking is certainly in public – one need only think of sports fans again – there are nearly always time and place boundaries on such drinking. Anyone familiar with Native American drinking will know that the time and place limitations are few. As Brody (1975:109) has observed in his remarks on Northern White attitudes towards Inuit drinking, 'Whites who criticize drunken Inuit are very often themselves heavy drinkers, but they restrict the evidence of their drinking and do it privately. Even those Whites who idealize the traditional Inuit approve of the Inuk who exhibits middle-class behaviour.'

That many indigenous peoples conceptually disconnect drinking from the conduct that often follows from it, merely confirms the white perception of Indian culpability. To many Innu, for example, the person is not necessarily seen as responsible for their actions across all contexts, since a web of circumstances is always crucial to understanding why someone did something. In the case of misadventure, accidents or even violence, it is the alcohol not the individual that is seen as principally responsible. An illustration of this occurred in a court case I witnessed in North West River involving Sheshatshiu Innu. A witness to a violent assault that involved his friends was questioned about a statement he made on the night of the incident. He continually proclaimed that he could not remember it because he was drunk at the time. After the questioning, he then asked the judge why statements are taken from Innu when they are drunk. While the question was simply brushed aside, it touched on a key difference between Innu and Euro-Canadian perceptions of the self. For this witness, his drunkenness explained why he made a statement against his friend. Had he been sober, he may well have chosen to keep silent. Hence, it was his belief that such a statement should not be binding (Samson, 2003:315).[3] The uneasiness about Native American drinking therefore originates from incomprehension at the public, and seemingly irresponsible, display of insobriety. What clearer evidence of native ingratitude? Yet, what clearer evidence of a refusal to be gratified by what the European has brought them and brought upon them?

PROTEST DRINKING

Elsewhere (Samson, 2001, Samson, 2003:284–292) I have described encounters with Innu drinkers. These have been as invariably uncomfortable as those at the Goose Bay bar with which I introduced this essay. Although I never felt unsafe, the drinkers became judge and jury to me, my motivations and intelligence were questioned, and I was put in positions of having to answer for myself. It struck me that this was a way of turning the tables – not simply upon me as a social researcher – but upon the Euro-Canadian authorities that ultimately control the lives of the Innu. Drinking was an escape, at least temporarily, from domination and most immediately from the torpor that sedentary life has created. While inebriated, drinkers are neither accountable to authorities nor to any responsibilities they may have.

Beyond their family, an Innu person's responsibilities are almost all geared towards complying with the requirements of various externally imposed institutions. Children must be sent to a school that principally operates the Newfoundland curriculum; the Social Services department regulates welfare payments and child protection; the police and courts enforce and uphold Canadian laws. Even the Innu Nation and the Band Councils are bound to uphold certain externally imposed rules upon the Innu themselves. Unlike hunting, there are few activities in the villages that create any sense of collective well-being or social cohesion.

This imposed order is becoming more entrenched. With time, the orientation to the distinctly Innu hunting world in the interior of the Labrador-Quebec peninsula has diminished. This is particularly true in the village of Sheshatshiu, where the Outpost Program, a Band Council administered operation to transport families to the country has virtually ground to a halt. Despite the recommendations of a 1993 Canadian Human Rights Commission report to provide continuous funding for the Outpost Program, many fewer families now go to the country than at the time I started working with the Innu in 1994, as a result of the government failure to fund the program (Backhouse and McRae, 2002:25). Funds for an 'Alternative School' (*Innu Tshiskutamashun*) to teach Innu youth in the country were terminated despite many documented successes and widespread public support. At the same time, a model of development based on creating Innu entrepreneurs and joint ventures with resource extraction and other industries has introduced a more nakedly commercial form of social organisation. The problem with this capitalistic ethos is that it promotes highly unequal distribution of benefits and becomes a further basis for emphasizing individual rather than collective well-being. As more emphasis is placed upon entrepreneurship, joint ventures and shareholding as the way forward for the Innu (Dyson, 2003), the attachments Innu have by virtue of 'being Innu' will further attenuate. At the same time, Innu land has continually been appropriated for resource extraction, including mega-projects such as the Lower Churchill River hydro-electric generating plant and the Voisey's Bay mining operation (Samson, 2003:96–111).

Contemporary Innu social life takes place in separation from their land and way of life. While this separation has occurred, an imposed authoritative order has established itself in villages, and these social units themselves effectively act as compounds for a once nomadic people, since the money economy demands a more fixed existence. Not only do permanent settlements violate the more open sense of space customary for the Innu and necessary for successful hunting, but the village itself is predicated upon re-orienting the Innu towards activities and ways of conceiving of the world that are Euro-Canadian. Even in the last nine years, since my first association with the Innu, this process has accelerated enormously. It is in this context of continuous change that drinking occurs. The *Tshenut* ('older people') that I have spoken to are almost unanimous in drawing a connection between this separation from the land, imposed laws and living arrangements and alcohol. For example, the late Matthew Penashue told me in 1999:

> The Innu are burdened with change ... All this change was imposed upon the Innu. The Innu are not happy as they once were because these changes are focused more on the white way of life. This in turn brings social problems such as the abuse of alcohol, sexual abuse and marital break-ups.

The open display of inebriation, of course, is a graphic illustration of a refusal to accommodate to the imposed authoritative and disciplinary order. While under the influence of alcohol, an Innu can manage to forget that almost all of his or her activities are in some ways regulated and controlled by an external power. Drinking provides momentary freedom and levity, even a way out of what many Innu describe as the prison-like conditions of village life. George Rich (2003) has described the conditions in the new village of Natuashish, completed in 2003 for the Mushuau Innu of Davis Inlet, as like being 'jailed for life'. Hunters frequently speak of the burden of 'having to stay in one place', as Jean-Pierre Ashini of Sheshatshiu told me some years ago. This feeling of incarceration is common among other indigenous peoples who have been similarly consigned to villages or reserves in Canada. Ojibwa of the Grassy Narrows Reserve spoke of being in cages, concentration camps and corrals (Shkilnyk 1985:174).

However, while losing cognizance of this sense of incarceration, the drinker not only fails to conform to the expected behaviour of a Euro-Canadian sedentary village or town dweller, which is what invites so much settler wrath, but they may also violate legal codes of order which will lead to criminal proceedings. Ironically, the drinker's quest to escape one form of caging results in another form. Even here, however, if a court case results from alcohol related conduct, the widely held Innu view that alcohol changes the nature of the person and is not to be considered a binding characteristic, is almost always brushed aside in favour of the European notion of personhood as a continuous narrative self (Samson, 2003: 315–316).

It is hard to avoid the impression that drinking among the Innu and other similarly situated people is, in some ways, a method of finding a 'way out' of what is experienced as oppressive confinement and external regulation.

Alcohol does provide this, albeit temporarily and often with dire consequences. It does this not only literally through the altered sense of reality achieved by inebriation, but symbolically by demonstrating that as a drinker, the individual will be a hard nut to crack as a candidate for assimilation. In this sense, drinking can be seen as a reaction to being frustrated in efforts to maintain indigenous identity, while also 'at the same time borrowing freely from the material aspects of white culture' (Lurie, 1971:315). Hence, it is not that indigenous people drink because they haven't received the 'good life' that the state has so frequently promised and failed to deliver. This may, of course, be a factor, but in the process of delivering this 'good life', indigenous institutions and social organisation have been pushed aside or, in many cases, rendered impotent. For the Innu, for example, the valued statuses of the hunter who provides food, the shaman that communicates with the animals, the older persons who are the teachers, and the craftsperson who can make a canoe, snowshoes or a salmon spear, are all made redundant by imposed authority in the villages. As Lurie (1971:317) put it in her paper on Indian drinking as protest, '... Indian people are more likely to get drunk when they feel thwarted in achieving Indian rather than white goals or when their success as Indians or simply individuals apart from Indian-white comparisons is interpreted as achieving status as whites'.

THE ALCOHOL TRADE

One further aspect of the situation needs to be brought into the picture: indigenous peoples drinking is good for business. The Goose Bay taxi drivers are simply at the end of a trail that leads back to liquor stores, manufacturers and the Canadian government itself which taxes these products. Like other indigenous communities, the Innu political bodies have attempted to control the situation by periodic roadblocks in Sheshatshiu and an outright ban in Davis Inlet, and now Natuashish. Despite these actions, alcohol has seeped into the villages and even a thriving bootlegging trade has been known to operate, bringing in booze to Natuashish and selling it at vastly marked up prices. In the absence of this, home-brewed spruce beer is sometimes consumed but this is reckoned to be a poor substitute for manufactured alcoholic drinks. Lucrative licit and illicit economies ensure motives to supply alcohol to the Innu and other indigenous peoples remain. In many areas of North America, liquor stores and bars are strategically located within easy proximity of native communities. In fact a small convenience store which is always well stocked with beer is one of the first businesses one encounters driving into Goose Bay from Sheshatshiu.

Although alcohol was known to some indigenous North Americans prior to European contact, this was chiefly among agriculturists rather than Northern hunters. While the initial contacts with native peoples show wide variations in native reactions to alcohol, there was no 'all-consuming craving nor an epic of drunken mayhem and debauchery . . .' (MacAndrew and Edgerton, 1969:114). The beginning of sustained and deleterious alcohol use in much of North America can be traced back to the fur trade. As Lurie (1971: 324) states, 'the initial and continuing encounters and interactions between whites and Indians were intimately associated with alcohol'. In many parts of North America, the traders' practice of supplying Indians with alcohol was reported by fur traders, missionaries, travellers and explorers as having calamitous effects (MacAndrew and Edgerton, 1969: 100–07). Depravity, violence, disease and death were all witnessed around trading posts and fill countless pages of frontier diaries. As Saum (1965: 211) pointed out, 'liquor did so much to abase the Indian in the trader's eyes because it deprived him of the only virtues with which he had been credited. In drinking sessions, the modicum of serenity and aloofness of native life gave way to ugly familiarity . . .'

In alcohol, the image of the Native American as a virtuous and noble savage became strained. Both alcohol and the noble savage, however, were products of the European colonisation of North America. The fact is that alcohol was absolutely essential to the fur trade.[4] 'Trading, thus helped by alcohol, led to more trading', Brody (1981:250) points out that in relation to twentieth century Northern Athapaskans, 'rival trading companies used alcohol to make a visit to their particular posts more attractive'. Similarly, for some centuries earlier in New England, Murray (2000:26–27) concludes that 'the heart of the role of alcohol . . . [is that] it acts not just as an unfortunate addition to rational trade but as its dark alter ego, in the way that it reveals the need for excessive rather than rational behaviour in the consumer'. The problem with generating 'excessive behaviour' however, is that it often led to the deaths of 'consumers'.

As early as the 17th century, the Jesuit missionaries encamped on the North Shore of the Gulf of St. Lawrence blamed alcohol for vast population declines among the Innu, dispersal from their lands and even some evidence of extinction of the more Southerly groups who had the most sustained contact with the *coureurs de bois* (Bailey, 1976:66–67). Further West in the 19th century, the fur trade among the Sioux led to 'drunken homicide [becoming] commonplace in the Indian camps. Other Sioux simply passed out on the way home and froze to death on the prairie tundra' (Lazarus, 1991:12). Although alcohol introduced by the traders undoubtedly led to untimely American Indian deaths, this might well have been considered a necessary price to pay. Only through binding Indians into producing furs for trade instead of hunting to live could the fur trade operate. The shift from native self-reliance to dependence on trade was a *sine qua non* of the business itself.

Nonetheless, both the fur trade and alcohol affected indigenous peoples differently and came into play at different times in the cycle of colonisation. The Innu inhabiting the Northerly Ungava territories are recorded as being less than enthusiastic traders. This is partly due to the necessity of hunting big game animals such as caribou in the Subarctic tundra (Davies, 1963:247). While some unruliness was recorded when fur traders supplied the Innu with 'grog' at the trading posts, it did not seem to imperil their hunting activities and, as long as they maintained their hunting life, they were certainly free of the worst of the self-destructive effects of alcohol. For example, the Hudson's Bay Company factor John M'Lean who was stationed at Fort Chimo and North West River in the early 19th century rarely mentioned alcohol among the 'Nascopie', although he did display his disdain for drinking among other natives.[5] Even later, by the mid nineteenth century, as the fur trade progressed there is not much evidence of any widespread drinking among the Innu in the Labrador area. According to Brother Elsner of the Moravian mission at Hopedale on the Labrador coast, 'they are very fond of rum, but get it only in small quantities as *presents*. The *sale* of spirits to Indians is contrary to the law' (quoted in MacDonald, 1996:94). Around this time, the trading companies operating in Labrador ceased supplying alcohol to the native peoples and there were fines imposed on anyone who did. Reports of 'outbursts of ferocity', as well as intoxicated Innu becoming subject to 'the vices of slaves, liars, cheats and drunkards' (Harper, 1964: 46) were more common on the North Shore of the St. Lawrence where trading was more active and settler populations more numerous. But even here, it was not alcohol that took the heaviest toll on the Innu. 'We are often told rum kills the Indian; I think not', the American naturalist Audubon reported from his visit to the Natashquan area, 'it is oftener the want of food, the loss of hope as he loses sight of all that was once abundant, before the white man intruded on his land and killed off the wild quadrupeds and birds with which he has fed and clothed himself', (quoted by Harper, 1964:45).

For most Innu currently living in Labrador, neither the fur trade nor white intrusion succeeded in changing their way of life. They were able to continue nomadic hunting and, as some ethnographers have pointed out, integrate alcohol into their religious lives. In the diaries of his 1927–8 ethnographic visit, American anthropologist William Duncan Strong (Leacock and Rothschild, 1994) observed that the Mushuau Innu drank spruce beer and home brew to celebrate a big kill. He records no particular adverse effects other than mild chaos. Speck (1977:92) observed that after particular dreams, hunters would drink whisky to give their soul-spirits a libation to pay for the revelation of a caribou by a river and to induce its fulfillment. Similarly, Georg Henriksen (1993), an anthropologist who has worked with the Innu since the mid-1960s, argued that Innu used alcohol not only to celebrate but, along with drumming, singing and dancing, to communicate with the Animal Gods.

The adverse effects of drinking, including mass inebriation, social disorganisation, marital disharmony, child neglect and untimely deaths, coincide with drinking patterns since sedentarisation in the 1960s and 1970s. Sedentarisation put a final end to permanent nomadic hunting as a way of life. It brought dependency on the Canadian government and other white intermediaries and occasioned a profound loss of meaning. In the early sedentarisation phase, alcohol, along with Innu religious activities and shamanism were suppressed by the church, and as Henriksen (1993:8–9) puts it, '[t]he people were thereby deprived of some of their crucial means to obtain spiritual power'. This same sense of spiritual dispossession is still advanced today as a reason for Innu drinking. When challenged in 2003 that non-native Canadians see alcohol as the problem to the troubles of the Innu, Simeon Tshakapesh, Chief of Natuashish responded, 'Our values are damaged when our drum is broken. Our belief system is out of balance. We're all confused. Elders were told that they were worshipping the Devil, so they wore big crosses to get away from the Devil'.

Along with this heavy handed intrusion of missionaries came the painful separation from the land. Instead of days being filled with purposeful activity, life at the new villages was relatively meaningless. Food came in cans from the government-run store, money came from welfare or in some cases, seasonal wage labour that bore little resemblance to the manifold activities of the hunting life, and houses, being stationary, did not require the same kind of attention as tents. Hence, as the priest overseeing the movement to Davis Inlet in the late 1960s recorded, with a lot of 'leisure time, they automatically turned to a natural tranquillizer and that is homebrew' (Peters, 1972:21–22). This was also fuelled by a shift in gender roles, as the male hunters' roles as providers were usurped by white authorities. Women's roles in hunting and in the extended family groups diminished substantially and were replaced by their intended replacement as homemakers in the village. Both sexes carried reduced responsibilities in the village, but Peters (1972:23) believed that the men were particularly affected. As he put it, 'the proud and skilful hunter-provider loses partially his role, which has deep psychological effects on the men, making them lose all self esteem and from pure frustration they try to drown their feelings in the abuse of homebrew' (Peters, 1972:23).

With sedentarisation, the Innu made fermented homebrew. This was a purposeful act. Alcohol was not some mere convenience that they could purchase at the store. They actively produced alcohol themselves in order to deal with the profound loss of a way of life. In 2003 when I visited Natuashish, the Chief told me that he thought up to eighty percent of the population was heavily drinking. He, along with a few other families, vacated the village in order to avoid the inevitable chaos of the weekends after people had received their welfare or employment cheques. The scale of drinking in Natuashish appeared greater than I had ever witnessed in the old village of Davis Inlet. Now, although there may be a few people who still produce homebrew, nearly all of the alcohol is Canadian manufactured beers, wines and spirits. It is brought in by bootleggers, who are enriched from the trade. The bootleggers in Natuashish and the liquor stores in Goose Bay have been able to profit in ways unimaginable to the fur traders.

ALCOHOL AND SUFFERING

Heavy alcohol consumption is a serious problem for indigenous peoples in the US and Canada.[6] Although it is difficult to ascertain the extent of problem drinking among the Innu in Sheshatshiu and Natuashish, it is fairly common knowledge that at least half of the adult population of the villages drink heavily, especially on weekends. In 1977, just a decade after the Mushuau Innu people had been settled in villages, physician Peter Sarsfield (1977:83) was dispatched by the Naskapi-Montagnais Innu Association to comment on the health conditions in Northern Labrador. 'There is no evidence of community strength and much evidence of individual breakdown', he observed, 'as alcohol abuse is commonplace and increasing in severity'. He continued, 'alcohol abuse is destroying lives in Davis Inlet and altering the quality of life for everyone who lives in the town' (ibid., 85). For Sheshatshiu, Sarsfield (ibid., 97) pointed out, 'the major health problems ... are alcohol abuse and associated trauma, respiratory infections, malnutrition, skin and ear infections'. In the same year, another survey estimated that 53% of the adults in Davis Inlet had alcohol problems (cited in Scott and Conn, 1987:1650). By 1990, in Davis Inlet, 'the estimated rate of alcoholism was estimated ... to be a rate of 80–85% of the population over fifteen years of age. Fifty percent of these people are intoxicated on a daily basis' (McTimoney and Associates, 1990:6). Between 1973 and 1992 sixty people died in Davis Inlet. Of these deaths, forty-seven or 71% were alcohol related (Innu Nation and Mushuau Innu Band Council, 1995:187).

Since these records were taken, significant numbers of Innu have died in accidents when they have been drinking heavily. These include instances of starting house fires, falling through ice, being run over on the road or simply passing out and freezing to death. Drinking, of course, has a knock-on effect as it is deeply entwined with ubiquitous youth petrol-sniffing, suicide and family breakdown, as well as with diabetes and heart disease which are rife in indigenous communities. These tragic effects of alcohol among the Innu are mirrored in many other Aboriginal communities in Canada. Citing various research over the last twenty years, a recent Health Canada (2003:53) survey confirmed this, but spent only one of its eighty-seven pages on alcohol abuse. The most harrowing evidence, however, comes not from Health Canada, but from the testimonials of Aboriginal peoples themselves. The Innu have produced numerous accounts documenting this, particularly powerful is the short film *Ntapueu* and the oral history record,

Gathering Voices (Innu Nation and Mushuau Innu Band Council, 1995).

Although many variables are of course involved, what seems to be a major factor in the sites of very heavy drinking in Northern Canada is a process of very rapid cultural change brought on by colonization and continuous external pressure to transform. This often leads to rapid 'deculturation', in which people are losing their bearings in their own way of life, but – not being successfully assimilated into the colonising society – they have few ties in any established social order (Young, 1994:215, Kirmayer, 1994:30). As Elizabeth Penashue of Sheshatshiu said, ' some kids don't want to go to the country. They think they are not Innu. They feel ashamed to say they are Innu.' Nevertheless, it is not simply a rejection of what is Innu that really affects many of these children. It is a rejection of everything in the imposed village society that they have grown into. Many children, like those who are kept in the Group Home in Sheshatshiu, 'don't like school, the community or *nutshimit*', as the Innu assistant there once told me.

CONCLUSION

This brings us back to the uneasiness and disquiet over Native American drinking. As illustrated by this brief history of the Innu, alcohol is a key link between the gradual erosion of the indigenous way of life and the imposition of Euro-Canadian power. In fact alcohol was the 'tranquiliser' Innu reached for to cope with the radical breach with the land when they were first sedentarised. The lack of purpose symbolized by heavy drinking is one of the reasons why so many young Innu feel no attachment either to the life of the country – adults are too busy drinking to be concerned with it – or the community – it holds few joys when parents are on the bottle. To avoid acknowledging this loss, however, whites draw upon medical reasoning, and stereotypes of craven, dependent Indians squandering goodwill. Even when the pain of dispossession is acknowledged, as in official state apologies, its continuing effects and links with ongoing native self-destruction are largely ignored. Yet, in a contradictory sort of way, drinking can be a form of rebellion against this lack of purpose. It is an attempt to feel and experience emotions amid a numbing sense of torpor brought upon by a lack of control over one's destiny, as successive generations of Innu are now finding out as their children are dispatched to Newfoundland-controlled schools, their justice is appropriated by Canadian law, the land is gradually removed for mega-projects and their leaders are encouraged to become entrepreneurs. Alcohol may well be, as Lurie (1971) suggests, one of 'the world's oldest protest movements'. Yet, paradoxically, if Innu and other indigenous peoples continue to destroy themselves through alcohol at the current rate, there will soon be little left to protest over. The children who don't like the country or the community will grow up dissatisfied only with living conditions in the village. The state will continue its policy of visibly spending money to address this with institutional solutions, as it would with any other 'disadvantaged' population. There will be nothing beyond their ancestry that is particularly unique about being Innu. Meanwhile, the hard commercial realities tying alcohol to indignity – from the fur trade to the bootleggers – will guarantee business for these quasi-medical institutions. Meanwhile, if the problem persists, the settlers will find comfort in their racist views of squandering Indians, while in this light, the state can continue to appear generous and few will contest how its wealth is derived from aboriginal lands.

This may sound pessimistic but in many ways it should not be seen as an admission that nothing can be done. Rather, it is a call to recognize the intermeshing factors that have brought about the situation in the first place. Most Innu adults know that the 'good life' is on the land. Unlike many other Native Americans they are fortunate that their land, while encroached upon, is still there and that they still have the skills and abilities to keep connections with it. Cultural continuity, as shown in several other examples across North America, is one of the surest safeguards against rampant social pathology (Chandler and Lalonde, 1998; Dell et. al., 2002). Only through maintaining pride in being Innu can the worst effects of alcohol be vitiated. This can only be done through maintaining connections with the land, enabling all generations of Innu to engage in meaningful and purposeful activity, and hence to achieve Innu goals, rather than constantly being thwarted in achieving Euro-Canadian goals. This is obviously a long term enterprise, operating against the constant pressures to assimilate. But one factor is in favour of the Innu. Because of their relatively recent subjection to the dominant society, their land, language, hunting skills, and religion still survive.

ACKNOWLEDGEMENTS

Parts of the research for this paper have been made possible by the Research Institute for the Study of Man, the Canadian High Commission and the University of Essex. I would particularly like to thank my friends in Sheshatshiu and Natuashish – Basile Penashue, Napes Ashini, George Rich, and Anthony Jenkinson to name a few. I have also benefited from the support and advice of Jules Pretty, Nigel South, Jane Hindley, James Wilson, Ed Martin and Andy Orkin.

1   This 'sedentarisation' of the Innu in the 1950s and 1960s has been perhaps the single most important factor in the dramatic change of fortune experienced by them. Before this time they were relatively independent hunters, successfully negotiating one of the most demanding terrains on the planet.
2   The sweat lodge or metashan is carried out in a canvas tent made as airtight as possible. Inside, hot rocks are placed in a hole in the middle of the tent. Water

is then poured over the rocks creating hot steam which becomes trapped in the tent. The sweating participants usually speak of alcohol and other problems while others silently listen. The event is experienced by many Innu as cathartic.

3   The Jesuit records show that this attitude dates back to the earliest days of contact with native peoples along the St. Lawrence. In his report of 1632, Father Le Jeune quoted a native person called to account for fighting, thievery and violence while drunk, as responding, 'It is not we who did that, but thou who gavest us this drink' (Thwaites, 1896–1901, V: 49–51). In an intriguing analysis of the exculpatory properties of alcohol among Native Americans, MacAndrew and Edgerton (1969:136, 144) argue that Indians based their deportment while drinking on those who sold it to them. Since the traders often feigned drunkenness while sharing alcohol with Indians in order to cheat Indians out of their pelts, native people responded, so the argument goes, by learning to exculpate themselves in a more literal way with alcohol. MacAndrew and Edgerton (ibid., 163) add that some Indians believed that alcohol contained bad spirits which drove them to act in certain disastrous ways. Hence, they could not be held responsible. How this argument may hold over time and space is difficult to ascertain. My impression is that these arguments are tangential with regard to the Innu in the current context of sedentarisation. I explore this more fully in an analysis of the contextual nature of crime for the Innu (Samson, 2003: 296–325).

4   Alcohol was also necessary to colonial occupation of North America. In the seventeenth century, the English used alcohol as both a means of securing furs and as a way of disturbing the more amicable relations between native peoples and the French along the St. Lawrence. The French, more interested in colonisation through conversion than military force, strictly prohibited alcohol trading with Indians at this time (Trudel, 1973:182, 187). However, as rivalry between the British and French became more intense in the late seventeenth and through the eighteenth centuries, the traders often managed to avoid the prohibitions to the great dismay of missionaries (Bailey, 1969:74, Eccles, 1992:222–23).

5   On the Ottawa River, M'Lean (1968:23) records meetings with natives in which, '. . . scenes of a revolting nature were of frequent occurrence. Rum and brandy flowed in streams, and dollars were scattered about as if they had been of no greater value than pebbles on the beach'.

6   Although there are numerous methodological and conceptual problems with measuring the scale of the alcohol problem numerically (Young, 1994:200), comparisons almost always show that alcohol extracts a greater toll on indigenous North Americans than others. In 1999, 'the prevalence of primary alcohol abuse among American Indians and Alaska Native admissions was high for both males and females: 66 and 56 percent, respectively' (Drug and Alcohol Services Information Service, 2002). In the 1980s, it was found that about 27% of Native American deaths in the US were alcohol-related (May, 1999: 228). Nevertheless, there are variations across North America.

REFERENCES

Abbot, K . (1999) 'Alcohol and the Anishinaabeg of Minnesota in the Early Twentieth Century', *Western Historical Quarterly*, 30: 25–43.

Backhouse, C. and D. McCrae (2002) *Report to the Canadian Human Rights Commission on the Treatment of the Innu of Labrador by the Government of Canada,* University of Ottawa, Faculty of Law.

Bailey, A. G. (1976) *The Conflict of European and Eastern Algonkian Cultures 1504–1700: A Study in Canadian Civilization.* Second Edition. (Toronto: University of Toronto Press).

Berkhofer, R. (1978) *The White Man's Indian: Images of the American Indian from*

Columbus to the Present, (New York: Vintage).

Brody, H. (1975) *The People's Land: Inuit, Whites and the Eastern Arctic,* (Vancouver: Douglas and McIntyre).

Brody, H. (1981) *Maps and Dreams,* (New York: Pantheon).

Bussidor, I. and Bilgen-Reinart, Ü (1997) *Night Spirits: The Story of the Relocation of the Sayisi Dene,* (Winnipeg: University of Manitoba Press).

Chandler, M. and C. Lalonde, (1998) 'Cultural Continuity as a Hedge Against Suicide in Canada's First Nations', *Transcultural Psychiatry,* 35, (2): 191–219.

Davies, K.G. (Ed.), (1963) *Northern Quebec and Labrador Journals and Correspondence 1819–35,* (London: The Hudson's Bay Company Record Society).

Dell, D. , et. al., (2002) 'Resiliency and Holistic Inhalant Abuse Treatment', unpublished manuscript, Prince Albert, Saskatchewan: White Buffalo Youth Inhalant Treatment Centre.

Drug and Alcohol Services Information Service, (2002) *The DASIS Report,* accessed on-line at http://www.samhsa.gov/oas/facts.cfm.

Duran, B. (1996) 'Indigenous Versus Colonial Discourse: Alcohol and American Indian Identity', in S. E. Bird, (Ed.), *Dressing in Feathers: The Construction of the Indian in American Popular Culture,* (Boulder, CO: Westview Press), 111–128.

Duster, T. (1984) 'A Social Frame for Biological Knowledge', in Troy Duster and Karen Garrett, (Eds), *Cultural Perspectives on Biological Knowledge,* (Norwood, NJ: Ablex), 1–40.

Dyson, Janet, (2003) 'A Boost for Innu Business: Development Center gets $499,035 from ACOA', *The Labradorian,* June 30: A3.

Eccles, W.J., (1992) 'The Fur Trade and Eighteenth Century Imperialism', in Alan Karras and J.R. McNeill, (eds.), *Atlantic American Societies: From Columbus through Abolition, 1492–1882,* (London: Routledge), 212–241.

Harper, F. (1964) *The Friendly Montagnais and their Neighbors in the Ungava Peninsula,* (Lawrence, Kansas: the Allen Press).

Health Canada, (2003) *Statistical Profile on the Health of First Nations in Canada,* (Ottawa: Health Canada).

Henriksen, G. (1993) 'Life and Death Among the Mushuau Innu of Northern Labrador', ISER Research and Policy papers No. 17, (St. John's: Institute of Social and Economic Research Press).

Innu Nation and Mushuau Innu Band Council, (1995) *Gathering Voices: Finding Strength to Help Our Children,* (Vancouver: Douglas and McIntyre).

Kirmayer, L. (1994) 'Suicide Among Canadian Aboriginal Peoples', *Transcultural Psychiatric Research Review,* 31: 3–58.

Lazarus, E. (1991) *Black Hills, White Justice: The Sioux Nation versus the United States, 1775 to the Present,* (New York: HarperCollins).

Leacock, E. B. and N. Rothschild, (1994) *Labrador Winter: the Ethnographic Journals of William Duncan Strong,* (Washington, DC: Smithsonian Institution Press).

Lurie, N. O. (1971) 'The World's Oldest Protest Demonstration: North American Indian Drinking Patterns', *Pacific Historical Review,* XL, 3: 311–32.

MacAndrew, C. , and R. Edgerton, (1969) *Drunken Comportment: A Social Explanation,* (New York: Aldine).

MacDonald, D. (1996) *Lord Strathcona: A Biography of Donald Alexander Smith,* Toronto: Dundurn Press.

Mancall, P. (2000) 'The Bewitching Tyranny of Custom: The Social Costs of Indian Drinking in Colonial America', in P. Mancall and J. Merrell (Eds.), *American Encounters: Natives and Newcomers from European Contact to Indian Removal – 1500–1850,* (New York: Routledge), 194-215.

May, P. (1999) 'The Epidemiology of Alcohol Abuse among American Indians: The Mythical and Real properties', in D. Champagne, (Ed.), *Contemporary Native*

American Cultural Issues, (Walnut Creek, CA: Alta Mira Press), 227–244.

McTimoney, D. C. and Associates, (1990) *Davis Inlet Assessment*, prepared for Medical Services Branch, Health and Welfare Canada, Halifax.

Murray, D. (2000) *Indian Giving: Economies of Power in Indian-White Exchanges*, (Amherst: University of Massachusetts Press).

Orkin, A. (2003) 'When the Law Breaks Down: Aboriginal Peoples in Canada and Governmental Defiance of the Rule of Law', *Osgoode Hall Law Journal*, 41, 2&3: 445–462 .

Orkin, A. (2004), Personal Communication.

Peters, F. (1972) 'Acculturation Process Among the Naskopi Indians of Davis Inlet under Influence of the North-American Society', Unpublished Manuscript, (Natuashish: Mushuau Innu Band Council).

Petruzellis, J. (2000) 'Genocide, Hockey and the National Psyche', presentation at the *British Association of Canadian Studies Conference*, Edinburgh, April 15.

Rasmussen, D. (2000) 'Reconciliation-to-forgive Versus Reconciliation-to-forget' paper presented at Cultural Survival forum on 'Justice before Reconciliation in Canada', Harvard University, October.

Rich, G. (2003) Statement to the Regional Meeting of Experts on Indigenous Rights in Canada and the Commonwealth Caribbean Region, 23–25 June, Georgetown, Guyana.

Sarsfield, P. (1977) *Report to the Naskapi Montagnais Innu Association and the Labrador Inuit Association Regarding the Health Care Delivery System in Northern Labrador*, (Sheshatshiu: Naskapi Montagnais Innu Association) .

Samson, C. (2001) 'Drinking and Healing: Reflections On The Lost Autonomy Of The Innu', *Indigenous Nations Studies Journal*, 2, (2): 37–56.

——(2003) *A Way of Life That Does Not Exist: Canada and the Extinguishment of the Innu*, (St. John's: ISER Books, and London: Verso Press) .

Saum, L. (1965) *The Fur Trader and the Indian*, (Seattle: University of Washington Press).

Schwarz, M. T. (2001) *Navajo Lifeways: Contemporary Issues, Ancient Knowledge*, (Norman: University of Oklahoma Press).

Scott, R. and S. Conn, (1987) 'The Failure of Scientific Medicine: Davis Inlet as an Example of Sociopolitical Morbidity', *Canadian Family Physician*, 33: 1649–1653.

Shkilnyk, A. (1985) *A Poison Stronger Than Love: The Destruction of an Ojibwa Community*, (New Haven: Yale University Press).

Silberstein, J . (1998) *Innu: A La Recontre des Montagnais du Quebec-Labrador*, (Paris: Albin-Michel).

Speck, F. (1977) *Naskapi: The Savage Hunters of the Labrador Peninsula*, Second Edition, (Norman : University of Oklahoma Press).

Stewart, J. (1998) 'Notes for an address by the Honourable Jane Stewart, Minister of Indian Affairs and Northern Development on the Occasion of the Unveiling of *Gathering Strength – Canada's Aboriginal Action Plan*', Ottawa, 7 January.

Thwaites, R. G. (1896–1901) *The Jesuit Relations and Allied Documents*, Volume V, (Cleveland: Burrows Brothers).

Trudel, M. (1973) *The Beginnings of New France 1524–1663*, translated by P. Claxton, (Toronto: McClelland and Stewart).

Vizenor, G. (1984) *The People Named the Chippewa: Narrative Histories*, (Minneapolis: University of Minnesota Press).

Wadden, M. (1991) *Nitassinan: The Innu Struggle to Reclaim their Homeland*, (Vancouver: Douglas and MacIntyre).

Young, T. K. (1994) *The Health of Native Americans*, (New York: Oxford University Press).

Chapter Nine

IN SEARCH OF THE DIVINE: WIXÁRIKA (Huichol) PEYOTE TRADITIONS IN MEXICO

Stacy B. Schaefer

'Wirikuta [the sacred peyote desert] is one of the most beautiful places I know. There all of our gods are reunited and they protect us. Many times my father has spoken to me about this place and when I listened I got the urge to go there ... We journeyed to Wirikuta in the same way that the gods traveled. We walked numerous days to the same places that they had passed. We try to see what our gods saw and learn their lessons; that's why we go to Wirikuta... Wirikuta is the place we want to go to. I feel happy to know that I will be able to return there on another occasion [pilgrimage]. When I go to Wirikuta I don't want to leave ... My name is Santiaga, and I am 9 years old.'

(Instituto Nacional Indigenista1992)[1]

INTRODUCTION

Every year Huichol Indians, or Wixáritari (Wixárika[2] -singular) as they prefer to call themselves, make the arduous pilgrimage 300 miles from their homelands in the Sierra Madre Occidental of Jalisco, Mexico to the desert of San Luis Potosí to collect the sacred peyote. Peyote (*Lophophora williamsii)* is a small, spineless cactus which inhabits the Chihuahua desert region of northern Mexico into the border area of the United States in the state of Texas. Despite its unassuming appearance, peyote is a remarkable plant; it produces more than 60 different alkaloids, the most abundant and notable one being the vision-producing chemical, mescaline (Trout 1999).

158

Indeed, peyote, and the pilgrimage to the peyote desert are extraordinary catalysts that Wixáritari have employed for centuries in order to bring meaning to their lives and to ensure the health and unification of their families and community. Their peyote traditions also enable them to have direct communication with the gods in order to advance their understanding of esoteric knowledge, enhance their creative abilities, and work towards balancing the forces of nature and the world surrounding them.

The cultural framework Wixáritari have constructed around this revered plant, including the ritual use of peyote and the synergistic quality of its pharmacological activity, can potentiate life-transforming experiences for its members. For some this may begin in childhood, as exemplified in the narrative from the young Wixárika girl quoted above. At whatever age an individual is introduced to peyote, the integration of this vision-producing plant into the core of Wixárika cultural traditions is, for many members, ever present throughout their lifetime.

In this chapter, the following questions are explored. How long has peyote held a prominent role in Wixárika culture? In what manner is it integrated into their worldview, their subsistence activities and the traditions of their religious beliefs? How does peyote use teach cultural values and reinforce them within Wixárika society? Finally, as we move into the 21st century, how has globalization, and its far-reaching impact on even the most remote areas in the world, affected the Wixárika and their ancient peyote traditions in terms of group solidarity and cultural identity, the ecological health of the natural peyote habitat, and their legal rights under Mexican laws and under United Nations conventions? Will peyote continue to hold a powerful place in Wixárika culture?

HISTORICAL RELATIONS BETWEEN PEYOTE AND INDIGENOUS CULTURES.

The earliest date for peyote use among indigenous peoples, comes from a rock shelter site in the south Texas area of the Chihuahua desert. Dried peyotes strung on a fibre cord, just as Wixáritari continue to do today, were radiocarbon dated, revealing that this peyote necklace was made around 5,000B.C. (Furst 1989). It is evident that bands of early hunter gatherer groups, as they traveled through the Chihuahua desert environment, sampled the local flora looking for edible plants and ones that had thirst-quenching properties. Upon consuming the bitter tasting peyote cactus, these peoples most likely discovered that it assuages hunger and thirst, provides endurance, and has medicinal qualities. Some of the many alkaloids within peyote are known to contain antibiotic properties and serve as an analgesic (Schultes1938, McCleary et.al. 1960, Anderson 1996, Schaefer 1996a). Wixáritari today consume small amounts of peyote for these same salutary qualities. The early hunter gatherers must have undoubtedly discovered that this spineless cactus, when eaten in sufficient quantity, can also induce visionary experiences. Some of the stylized themes found on rock art from this area may, as suggested by Boyd and Dering (1996), be visual depictions of mystical peyote experiences these indigenous people felt compelled to reproduce. Moreover, it is quite plausible that in this vast desert region a mutually beneficial relationship was formed between humans and peyote. The consumption of peyote contributed to the physical survival and spiritual development of hunter gatherers, while human intervention in the natural growth and reproductive cycle of peyote may have stimulated an increase in the range and density of peyote (Bauml, 2003 personal communication[3]). Even in contemporary times, Wixáritari are well attuned to the growth cycle of peyote and its reproduction. Peyote flowers and the seed-bearing pinkish-red fleshy fruit that follow are metaphors that are used interchangeably for the peyote plant, women and their sexual anatomy. Fertility is also a prominent theme in the origin myth of the pilgrimage.

At the time Spaniards arrived in North America, the ritual use of peyote had spread across a wide range of indigenous groups that inhabited the Chihuahua desert region and beyond. Spanish chroniclers disdainfully referred to peyote as the 'diabolical root'; the most well documented cases of its use are among the Aztecs and Chichimecs (Sahagun 1950–1960, Ruiz de Alarcón1984). Needless to say, the Spanish clergy worked fervently to abolish such practices for they associated them with heathenism and the devil. Paradoxically, the colonization of much of North America facilitated the diffusion of peyote and its ritual use to indigenous groups where colonists and missionaries were stationed, particularly among those communities residing where it grew. In the seventeenth century, during the Mexican Inquisition, interrogations as far north as Santa Fe, New Mexico, questioned the accused of whether they had used peyote, which was equated with witchcraft and was believed to be used in divination rituals (Stewart 1987:24, La Barre 1989:24).

The few published Spanish documents from the Wixárika sierra during the colonial period do not mention peyote use; however, they do describe the frustration Franciscan missionaries experienced at every turn, especially when they encountered clandestine shrines made by Wixariatri to venerate their gods (Santoscoy 1899). The Spaniards did not have the same impact on the Wixárika as they had on most other indigenous groups in Mexico; in fact, Spaniards did not make inroads into the sierra until 1720. They remained in Wixárika territory for less than one hundred years. The earliest description of Wixáritari and their peyote traditions was written at the end of the 19th century by the Norweigan explorer Carl Lumholtz. At this time peyote was an important element in the cultural traditions of other indigenous groups residing in the Sierra Madre mountain range, such as the Cora, Tepehuano, and farther north among the Tarahumara (Lumholtz

1902). Presently, the Wixárika are the only remaining group that continue to harvest peyote and have collectively maintained their peyote traditions.

The pilgrimage to the peyote desert, known as Wirikuta, is spoken of in many Wixárika myths that explain the origin of the world and its first people, the ancestor deities. One version of the creation myth tells of the brilliant star god Xurawe, who challenged the other gods to a deer hunt across the sierra landscape down to the desert where the mortally wounded deer transformed into a large cluster of peyote. Kauyumarie, the blue deer god who serves as the tutelary messenger of the shaman, is featured in another part of the myth. In the desert of Wirikuta he cuts open a large cactus (*Echinocactus*), inside of it he finds tamales which are actually peyote, and he shares them with his companions. There are also two goddesses ütuanaka and Wiri'üwi, who travel together to Wirikuta. The story of the pilgrimage tells that these women discovered the peyote and consumed it. They were awed by this transforming encounter with the sacred succulent and afterwards both of them discovered they were pregnant. Wiri'üwi stayed in Wirikuta to become the mother of peyote, ütuanaka, the earth goddess returned to the sierra to share the wonder of peyote and Wirikuta with her community. Another series of myths speak of a powerful shaman named Maxa Kwaxi who arrived in the Wixárika sierra from the desert, bringing peyote and other desert dwelling hunter gatherer traditions with him. This mythical figure, Maxa Kwaxi, may have actually been a real person from a tribe related to the Chichimecs that inhabited this desert area (Diguet 1899, 1907). It has also been proposed that in the Prehispanic past Wixárika may have also participated in a long-distance trade network with peyote being one of the precious commodities (Weigand 1975, 1981). Regardless of the origins of Wixárika peyote traditions, it is clear that peyote and the pilgrimage to Wirikuta are intrinsically linked to their sustenance, and hence, their cultural lifeways.

PEYOTE IN SUBSISTENCE ACTIVITIES AND RELIGIOUS CEREMONIES

For many Wixáritari, peyote is just as important for their survival as are deer and maize. Their subsistence activities revolve around this trinity; all are considered to be the same entity that can transform from one form to the other. In Wixárika thought, maize and deer provide nourishment for the body, while peyote brings sustenance for the soul. Peyote is ever-present throughout the annual ceremonial cycle, which is divided into the dry season from December to June and the rainy season from July to November. During the dry season animals are hunted and wild plants gathered, while they let their maize fields lie fallow. The dry season is also the time for making the peyote pilgrimage to Wirikuta. Temple groups and ranch groups of extended family (explained further below) travel to the sacred desert to fulfil ritual responsibilities in the temple for the next five years. Some pilgrims make the journey because they want to learn to become shamans, master musicians or master artisans. Others go on the pilgrimage because they have asked the gods to help them to better their lives and the lives of their family members, oftentimes in matters of health, abundant crops and livestock.

The transition between the end of the dry season and the beginning of the rainy season is marked by the temple ceremony Hikuri Neixa, Dance of the Peyote. At this time the intent of the temple members is to ask the gods to call upon the rain to make the earth fertile for planting. Fresh and ground peyote mixed with water into a frothy drink are consumed during the ceremony and for two days and nights the temple members dance with their companions, and often with members of other temples who have the same ritual responsibilities. Food and maize beer are shared followed by ploughing the communal plot of land for the temple group and sowing maize, bean and squash seeds. In the very centre of the field, offerings are placed in a hole that is the mouth of the earth goddess, encircled by peyotes that are planted in the soil. The rainy season brings a shift in the annual cycle of activities, it's a time when Wixáritari devote their energies to tending their crops and cattle.

With the rainy season nearing the end of its cycle comes the harvest ceremony, Tatei Neixa – Dance of our Mother. The first young ears of maize and squash are honoured in this ceremony as is the peyote pilgrimage. Children five years of age and younger gather around the fire in the ritual patio with their parents. The shaman, through his song, magically transforms the children into birds and together they metaphysically make the pilgrimage to the peyote desert (Furst and Anguiano 1976). For the first five years of life, Wixárika children are considered to be in a very delicate state; high infant mortality rates of over 50% substantiate such beliefs (López, et al. 1997). It is for this reason that young children participate in the ceremony to protect and strengthen their life force. Once they reach five years of age, children are believed to have a complete soul. They have also begun to develop a cognitive map of the peyote desert and the sacred places visited on the way.

The syncretic form of Catholicism that Wixáritari have adopted and integrated into their more traditional beliefs and practices include peyote in a most unique manner. During Holy Week, known as *Semana Santa*, Wixáritari not only recognize and ritually enact the Easter story, they also incorporate the peyote pilgrimage into the ceremonial activities. This is a time when the different temple groups gather with their leading shamans to sing and recount their most recent journey to Wirikuta. Peyote is consumed by the members during the Easter pageantry and offered in votive bowls to the Catholic saints and Christ figures.

The influence of peyote is also found in more intimate settings such as family ranches. Wixárika society is composed of numerous ranches made up of extended family members from three, four, up to five generations of kin. Peyote is consumed during ranch ceremonies to mark the planting season; it is also ingested during ceremonies to welcome back family members who have returned from the pilgrimage to Wirikuta. While the family members are on the journey, those who have remained at the ranch fast and pray for their safe return. Upon their arrival home, the pilgrims provide everyone, from as young as two years old to the most senior of the family, with peyote that they have collected especially for each kin member to ritually consume around the fire near the shrine of the family ancestors. Peyote is also consumed by family members outside of a ceremonial context for endurance in physically demanding work, such as ploughing and cultivating their fields. It is eaten to diminish hunger and thirst, especially if one is travelling far from home and carrying little food or water. Peyote is also taken to remain awake and alert, especially during all-night ceremonies. In these instances smaller amounts of peyote are eaten and usually do not induce strong visionary experiences.

PEYOTE AS AN ENCULTURATING FORCE

Peyote is ever present in Wixárika culture, from the pilgrimage and the ceremonies, to myths and songs, to the brilliantly colored designs seen under the influence of this potent plant that are duplicated onto their clothing, bags, offerings and art work.

Peyote, therefore, is an enculturating force, that provides a unique path for Wixáritari to actually communicate directly with the gods in their pantheon. In other words, Wixáritari are not just passive believers of the worldview they are taught when very young, rather, they actually interact with aspects of it and through these visionary experiences their cultural beliefs become very real and deeply etched into their lives (Eger 1978, Schaefer 1996a, 2002).

Wixárika children do not usually consume significant amounts of peyote to bring on visionary experiences until early adolescence. For a number of youth it is a life-transforming event. The peyote experience, related below in abbreviated form, is from a Wixárika man recounting his first pilgrimage and the intimate connection he experienced between deer and peyote. At eleven years of age, this stunningly vivid experience was not only enduringly memorable for him but also confirmation that the Wixárika religious beliefs he had been taught are, indeed, reflections of something very real.

I made some votive arrows for Kauyumarie, the deer god, to leave where there is peyote in Wirikuta. They were for Kauyumari

163

because he knows everything, he knows everything about the world
... When I arrived to Wirikuta I left one of the arrows ... the
other peyoteros [pilgrims] took out a large gourd bowl and filled
it with peyote. They told me that since this was my first trip to
Wirikuta I had to eat all of the peyote in the bowl. I wanted to
know about god, how the world began, how the sun first appeared,
how the fire, the maize, the earth and the god of rain first appeared
... I continued eating [peyote]. Then I finished.

One of the votive gourd bowls [on the ground] was decorated
inside with beads in the figure of a deer. In two or three hours I
looked at the votive bowl and the deer inside the bowl was really
large. How can that be? I continued eating more [peyote], and as
I was looking into the votive bowl the deer grew in size and jumped
out of the bowl. It was standing on the ground and moved in front
of us.

Then I found a large peyote, I was looking at it and there was a
little deer on top of the peyote where the white tufts of the plant
are. It was a tiny little deer – how can that be? I'm seeing deer
everywhere, why? I remembered hearing my grandfather ... say
that this is the way that you always begin to learn. And with the
peyote it is the same.

Well the peyote was really, really large ..., the deer passed very
close by me. I was in the middle of the peyote where the white tufts
are. I [must have] flown up there, I was seated in the middle of the
peyote and I flew higher up, to the mountain top of Cerro Que-
mado [an inactive volcano above Wirikuta where offerings are
left]. I was standing up there and I was looking at the whole world
– the ocean looked really small. I not only saw the ocean but all
the animals that live in the ocean, whales, snakes, mermaids ...
everything. [The deer told me] ... you should be calm ... then I
was back down below in Wirikuta ...

The age a person is first introduced to peyote ranges greatly. While many
Wixáritari consume peyote upon reaching adolescence, some may not ingest
this sacred plant until they are middle-aged, and some may never consume
peyote in their lifetime. At the other end of the age continuum, some
Wixárika children are introduced to peyote while in their mothers' wombs
as some women consume peyote at various stages of their pregnancies.

A number of Wixárika women are cautious about consuming peyote during the first trimester of pregnancy because it may induce a miscarriage. It
is not uncommon for a woman and her spouse to consult a shaman before

eating peyote. The shaman purifies the woman and the peyote by praying over them and ritually 'calming' the peyote so no harm comes to her or her unborn child. Reports from Wixárika women allege that the foetus can definitely feel the effects of the peyote; after a quiet period the foetus can become very active and move in the womb. Some women say that the baby is 'dancing inside'. Research conducted in the US during the 1960s and 1970s on laboratory animals that were injected with mescaline showed that mescaline could cross the placental barrier, as well as the partially-developed blood/brain barrier in the foetus. Although these animal experiments do not precisely replicate the dose/response of peyote consumption, nor its effects on a human mother and her foetus, these studies provide some indication of the kinds of interactions that might occur (Schaefer 1996c, Maickel and Snodgrass 1973, Shah et al 1973, Taska and Schoolar 1972).

Some Wixáritari that have spoken with the author on this topic believe that when a mother is pregnant and consumes peyote this can predispose the child to become a specially-gifted person in traditional occupations. One woman put it like this:

> I always like to eat peyote. It doesn't matter if I am pregnant . . . if I feel well I like to eat it. There in Wirikuta the people pray to the gods, and for some the gods give them the prize [a child] that has the design of a shaman . . . a clearer of fields . . . or a deer hunter . . . That's how they are born, I think that it happens like this because it is a custom that will never be lost.

Wixárika women may consume peyote when they are lactating and then mescaline and other alkaloids from the peyote are, in turn, passed on to the nursing child. Women have commented to me that they notice a difference in the behaviour of their babies after nursing them during a period when they have consumed peyote, a change also noted by the author. On one occasion the six-month-old baby seated on his mother's lap next to me became very engaged in grasping out at things in front of him; whatever he saw, however, was invisible to others present. Once when accompanying an extended family on the pilgrimage to Wirikuta, the youngest pilgrim on the journey, a four-month-old boy, was given a tiny piece of peyote to eat that had been blessed by his shaman grandmother; his mother nursed him so that it would be easier for him to swallow the cactus. The two-year old toddler of the mother demonstrated a real liking for the peyote and, despite its bitter taste, she took a few small harvested peyote from her parent's bags and ate them. Her family showed no concern over her actions. They explained to me that when a child shows an affinity for peyote that it is a good omen indicating that the child has the proclivity to become a powerful shaman.

Early on in their lives Wixáritari also learn through these peyote traditions the morals and values of their culture; one being the importance of remaining chaste and faithful to your spouse. This is reinforced during the peyote pilgrimage when before the journey all the pilgrims and their family members, regardless of whether they go to Wirikuta or not, must confess out loud in front of the leading shaman and the group the names of people with whom they have had sexual affairs. This includes sexual relations before marriage, or if married, with someone other than one's spouse. A knot is ritually tied onto a rope for every name uttered. When complete the rope is passed over the person's head and body and then thrown into the fire. It is a purification ritual in which everyone must participate because afterwards, as the pilgrims proceed on their journey, their souls are all united until their return. If a person does not truthfully confess any wrongdoings it could endanger the lives and health of all the pilgrims and their families, causing serious consequences. One young woman I knew from a family ranch experienced this first hand. Before she married, she had had several sexual affairs. Being newly married, she did not want to make these encounters known. When her parents returned from the pilgrimage and gave everyone at the ranch peyote to ingest, the young woman had a terrifying experience several hours later. Everyone could hear her moaning and thrashing around in the bamboo structure where she and her husband slept. The woman's mother explained to me that the peyote was punishing her. The next morning, the family shaman and the mother beseeched the woman to confess and be purified; doing so would also have beneficial effects on the well-being of the entire family. With great hesitation the woman complied by repeating the purification ritual.

The ritual manner in which peyote is consumed also reinforces Wixárika ideology and worldview. Taken in this context, peyote can be a tool that enables a person to explore the depths and reaches of the cosmos while at the same time gaining expertise in esoteric knowledge deemed especially important by members of the culture. Some Wixáritari refer to it as carrying out an intensely dedicated study to acquire a particular speciality, be it learning to be a shaman, a master artisan, a master violinist, etc. Those who choose to go through apprenticeships in this way are initiated into life-transforming experiences which bring special cultural knowledge. A master violin player described his first peyote experience as a young adolescent when he accompanied a temple group on the pilgrimage to Wirikuta with the aspiration of learning to play the violin.

> The first time I ate peyote I ate a small amount to see if it would bring me luck. I wanted to play the violin . . . Then I felt this way . . . some animals appeared, they were like dinosaurs, and a big snake; they were all huge, really big! I was surprised to see them . . . they asked me what I was thinking, what I was feeling.

Well, at that time I lost myself [travelling with the peyote]. I thought my companions no longer lived, not even my brother. Only the offerings we had left were there and these animals were alive. 'No', they told me, 'your companions have sinned but over there where the offerings are, are the things you have been thinking about'.

'Look, over there is a violin. It's yours but first you have to confess your wrongdoings' they told me. 'Look at the others who confessed, they are dirty, as if they had mucous all over them. We don't like the way they are. God doesn't want them to be dirty. So, we will clean [purify] you.' And they cleaned me with their tongues. Their tongues were enormous! They cleaned me all over. Then a light like a star appeared, it came from over there, where the sun rises. First they cleaned me, then the light fell all around me and cleaned me all over. Then I appeared like a bright light, a really beautiful light ... then they took me ... up to the sky.

Wixáritari also revere peyote for its mind-altering qualities to facilitate communication with the gods and to provide a means to tap into their own creativity. While inebriated with peyote, songs are spontaneously composed or heard sung to them by one of the gods who appears while in this altered state. In the latter case, a person who has received a song from a god may afterwards be asked by the shaman to sing the song and share it with the group because it is considered a gift from the gods. Divine communications may also appear in the form of brilliantly coloured geometric designs in constant kaleidoscope-like movement. Although most of these designs are entoptic patterns, meaning that they are inherently related to the physical geometry of the eye, and are typical of what anyone may see under the influence of peyote, Wixáritari have put cultural meaning onto these dazzling designs that splash across one's field of vision (Kluver 1966, Oster 1971). They are considered to be blessings from the gods and women duplicate these designs in their artwork, especially in their embroideries. Not reproducing these designs could anger the gods, causing the woman or a member of her family to fall ill, possibly with a life-threatening illness (Eger 1978, Schaefer 1996a, 2002).

The role of the shaman in Wixárika peyote traditions cannot be overstated. Wise from years of personal experience with the peyote, during which much of the knowledge he or she holds has been imparted, the shaman serves as botanist, healer, psychologist, and religious specialist. The shaman takes on the responsibility of a spiritual guide that teaches family and community members about peyote and advises them on all the rituals necessary to properly carry out a pilgrimage. Shamans help individuals select specific peyote and counsel them on the amount to ingest, then they bless and purify the peyote and the individuals before the selected plants are consumed. After the effects of peyote inebriation have waned, shamans interpret the visions individuals describe to them, placing them within a meaningful framework that helps the peyote seekers reach a deeper understanding of their lives and their place within the universe. On an individualistic level, the pilgrims learn from the shaman what future actions they need to take to overcome personal challenges, achieve specific goals, and to follow a divine path that will continue to bring such intimate encounters with their gods. On the level of family and community, the shamans instruct the peyote seekers on what forthcoming communal ritual activities must be completed to propitiate the gods and bring greater balance to the forces of nature. When properly carried out, these efforts benefit the community by infusing its members with a renewed sense of purpose, which in turn brings greater unification within the whole community.

PEYOTE IN THE ERA OF GLOBALIZATION

As we move into the 21st century, these ancient peyote traditions continue to hold a prominent place in Wixárika culture, despite the tremendous changes brought by increasing interactions with the dominant Western world. Every year, temple and family groups still make the pilgrimage to the peyote desert; shamans and others find that the teachings to be learned from the peyote and from the communication it facilitates with the gods remain powerful and meaningful in their lives. Even with acculturative pressures mounting, Wixárika peyote traditions continue to be an integrating force that tempers the ever more rapid changes brought about by globalization. Nowadays a majority of younger generations of Wixáritari attend schools with classes taught by bilingual Wixárika teachers. The school administrators' work to accommodate the schedules of children who join their parents on the pilgrimage, as well as the work schedule of bilingual teachers who, in fulfilling temple and ranch ritual roles, travel to Wirikuta as well.

Globalization has affected the Wixáritari and their peyote traditions in other ways. Now they are integrally tied to the national economy; within their communities the commercial economy is dominant over their more traditional reciprocal forms of exchange. To maintain a cash flow, many leave the sierra to earn money. Some find temporary work as field hands in tobacco and other commercial agricultural industries, some work in factories in larger cities, while others sell their artwork in tourist areas. Many of these migrant workers, upon returning to their communities, allocate a portion of their earnings to finance community and temple obligations, including peyote pilgrimages. This migration to find work elsewhere occurs primarily in the dry season and makes it increasingly difficult for temple and family members to coordinate their pilgrimage to Wirikuta. Another result of the emerging commercial economy and its impact on Wixárika culture is the manner in which pilgrims travel to Wirikuta. In the past Wixáritari made the pilgrimage on foot. Presently many cannot spare long periods of time away from their work schedule to complete these ritual activities. In the recent past Wixáritari arranged with mestizos (individuals of mixed Indian and Spanish ancestry who make up the vast majority of the Mexican populationi) to transport them to the peyote desert for what was often a prohibitively expensive fee. Currently, more Wixáritari are buying trucks and a number of these individuals contract out their services to take pilgrims to the peyote desert and back. This turn of events makes the journey more cost-effective for the pilgrims and has enabled Wixáritari to achieve greater agency in their lives to carry out their religious traditions.

In the current era of globalization, more and more outsiders from Europe, Canada, the United States, Japan, mestizos from Mexican cities and other places outside of Mexico are attracted to the Wixáritari and their 'colourful' peyote traditions. They arrive regularly at Wixárika communities; many are seeking peyote and the experiences it brings, while others hope to join Wixáritari on a pilgrimage to the peyote desert. Every couple of years or so it is common to see an international documentary film crew come to the sierra with plans to film the pilgrimage and other Wixárika traditions. Some Wixáritari welcome these foreigners, especially if they help pay the costs incurred to make the journey. Other Wixáritari oppose Westerners accompanying them. Their arguments against the inclusion of outsiders are concerned with both divine and more material realities. For example, how might the gods perceive this arrangement and what if they are displeased? What if the foreigners draw attention to the Wixárika pilgrims themselves and the peyote they transport back to the Sierra prompting state and federal authorities to arrest and prosecute them?

Mexican legislation on the use of peyote by indigenous people such as the Wixárika is ambiguous. The 1971 UN Convention on Psychotropic Substances was ratified in Mexico by President Echeverria. This far-sweeping drug policy treaty was based on the United States' Comprehensive Drug Abuse Prevention and Control Act of 1970 whereby under Part II of this Act, The Controlled Substance Act, peyote was classified as a schedule one drug along with other 'hallucinogens' and potentially addictive drugs such as heroin and morphine. The United States' 1970 Drug Act includes a clause that addresses the special rights of indigenous people in the United States who are members of the Native America Church to use peyote in their religious ceremonies.

The 1971 Convention on Psychoactive Substances that Mexico signed into law has no such clause specifically addressing the rights of indigenous peoples to use peyote. The wording of the treaty on this point is vague. It merely states that there are diverse indigenous groups that use wild plants, some of which may contain psychotropic substances (including mescaline). A further UN Convention ratified by the Mexican government and the International Labour Organization may be interpreted as allowing peyote use among indigenous people in its decree that the values and social, cultural, religious and spiritual practices of indigenous groups should be safeguarded and protected. An additional piece of legislation, Article 4 in the Mexican Constitution, states that the law protects and promotes the development of indigenous languages, cultures, customs, and so forth. Unclear as these bodies of legislation may be, other Mexican drug laws such as The Federal Penal Code and The General Law of Health, specifically state that peyote use is illegal in Mexico for everyone (Rajsbaum 1996, Schaefer 1998).

And if that were not challenging enough for Wixáritari and their efforts to continue to practice their peyote traditions, military check-points established throughout the nation by the federal government, 'stop and search' travellers along the roads that lead to the Wixárika sierra and roads that pilgrims take to the peyote desert. Few soldiers stationed at these military posts are familiar with Wixárika Indians, their culture or their peyote traditions, nor are they aware of these various bodies of laws and how they may be interpreted in regard to Wixáritari and the legal (albeit ambiguous) rights to use and transport peyote. In several instances in 1998, the entire group of pilgrims returning with peyote to their communities were incarcerated (women and children included) and charged by the authorities for transporting, and intent to sell, illegal drugs.

This happened to one temple group when the pilgrims, having passed through Zacatecas, were arrested on their return home from Wirikuta At this stage of the pilgrimage, all the members are considered to be in a very sacred space. One leading shaman from the group offered his thoughts to a journalist about their incarceration and how it was adversely affecting the sanctity of the peyote and the success of the pilgrimage.

> In respect to peyote, I do not consider that we are committing anything illegal, we do not want to sell it, only use it in religious ceremonies, and this has been going on for many years. It is a tradition that we have passed down from parents to children, but when the military realized that we had peyote they told us we were violating the law and that they were going to confiscate it and arrest us . . .
> . . . for the problem that we have I am very worried, the people from [our] community that stayed behind are waiting for us and remain fasting until we return with the sacred water and the peyote, and I am also worried by the fact that the peyote that we collected for the community has had to go back . . . to Zacatecas. This is not permitted and now I don't know if the peyote and the sacred water that the military confiscated will provide us with the same divine grace. Because of the way it has been treated it could bring misfortune or sickness to our community.
>
> (Arcos 1998:3).

170

Another phenomenon that has had a negative impact on Wixárika pilgrimages is the increasing number of outsiders who independently travel to Wirikuta to commune with the peyote in this remote desert environment. Some are drawn there because of New Age shamanic tours that avow that, through their experiences in this sacred place with the visionary plant sacrament, participants will acquire greater power and meaning in their lives. Those who don't come as a tour group, preferring to make the journey on their own, hire local mestizos from outlying pueblos to taxi them into the peyote habitat with their four-wheel drive vehicles. This has become a lucrative enterprise for some, especially since there are few economic opportunities available in the region. The effect this particular type of tourism has had on Wirikuta has been devastating. The four-wheel drive vehicles endanger this natural habitat, as do some foreigners and local mestizos who harvest large quantities of peyote, removing the plant in its entirety, tap root and all. In some instances, the peyote is taken to clandestine laboratories where the mescaline is extracted from the plant and formed into the shape of large beads that are painted and sent to Europe and elsewhere (Silviano Camberos, personal communication 1996, Furst and Schaefer 1996). Wixáritari, on the other hand, are well-attuned to this desert environment and to the most ecological methods for harvesting peyote which entails cutting the button-shaped top plant and leaving the tap root in place. This method allows the plant to regenerate with new growth where it had been harvested. Moreover, Wixáritari do not harvest excessively large quantities of peyote, only as much as they can carry in either several bags or a carrying basket. The alarming depletion of the peyote by others deeply troubles Wixáritari. They are equally dismayed by the graffiti some outsiders have painted on the rocks of their sacred places in this desert region.

The peyote in the Mexican desert have also attracted trans-national attention and been impacted upon by indigenous peoples from the US and Canada who are members of the Native American Church (NAC). Peyote is an essential element in this syncretic religion that blends pan-Indian traditions with Christianity. Membership in the Native American Church has grown exponentially since it was formally recognized in 1916 by the US government as a bona fide religion. Since its inception, the number of registered NAC members has increased to over 300,000 (Anderson 1996). The supply of peyote north of the Mexican border cannot meet the demand of NAC members. The peyote habitat on the US side of the international border runs along a small portion of South Texas. Ever since the North American Free Trade Agreement was ratified in 1994, this area has been targeted for growth and development. Farmers are paid subsidies as incentives to plow over the natural vegetation in this region using plows that rip peyote from the ground, tap root and all, and plant seed grass for cattle. The expanse of the peyote habitat is far greater on the Mexican side of the Chihuahua desert region, beginning south of the US/Mexico border, extending as far south as Wirikuta in the state of San Luis Potosí. Anecdotal evidence suggests that peyote from the Mexican side of the border is being harvested and transported to south Texas to be sold to Native American Church members. The US authorities apply the same laws to illegally transporting peyote across the border as they do for any schedule one drug. This does not deter some peyote runners from taking that risk.

Some members of the Native American Church go to Wirikuta or other parts of the Mexican desert to harvest peyote themselves. In a few cases, several NAC members unfamiliar with the legal status of peyote have been arrested by the Mexican police for harvesting these plants (Jerry Patchen, personal communication 1997). Representatives from the Navaho chapters of the NAC have unsuccessfully tried to arrange special trade relations with Mexico to obtain this sacramental plant. Legal authorities representing the Mexican government insist that the drug laws in Mexico are ambiguous enough with respect to their own indigenous peoples and difficult to interpret, particularly because of the clauses in the laws and conventions that address the rights of indigenous peoples to continue to practice their cultural and religious traditions. What is certain in this body of laws, however, is that there are no special treaties to include Native Americans who are not citizens of Mexico and who did not originally inhabit the lands within the contemporary national borders of the country.

In response to the severity of the ecological threats and potential destruction of Wirikuta, the governor of the state of San Luis Potosí in 1994 declared formal protection for 73,690 hectares of this peyote desert as a 'Place of Historic Cultural Patrimony and as an Ecological Zone of the Wixárika Ethnic Group' (Instituto de Ecología 1994). More recently, in 2000, the state administration formalized a new decree which increases the Wirikuta region under protection up to 141,000 hectares (Humberto Fernandez: personal communication, 2003).

The Mexican non-governmental organization Conservación Humana is working closely with Wixáritari on many levels to protect their cultural traditions and the ecology of Wirikuta. At the international level the organization has strived to have Wirikuta and the road to Wirikuta recognized and protected under the UNESCO World Heritage Convention. The UNESCO committee has shown great interest in the protection of Wirikuta; however, the Mexican government was the official entity that needed to propose it to the committee for consideration. In September, 2003, the Mexican government acted to promote the pilgrimage route and Wirikuta for inclusion in the World Heritage Convention and this proposal now awaits further review and approval before it can be admitted into the international agreement (Humberto Fernandez, personal communication, 2003). On the local level, Conservación Humana is working with mestizos to educate them about the importance of protecting Wirikuta and its flora and fauna. Staff from the organization are also working with the local inhabitants in the development of other economic opportunities that would enable these people to earn money without having to cater to the clandestine tourist trade that has arisen in the region (Conservación Humana 1996, 1997a, 1997b).

CONCLUSION

Indigenous peoples in North America have had a long, intimate relationship with peyote that goes far back in human history. The Wixárika are the last of the indigenous peoples to have maintained the core of their cultural distinctiveness, in large part due to the vitality their peyote traditions bring to their collective worldview. In the 21st Century peyote continues to be an integral element in the lives of many Wixáritari; through family and community life, peyote traditions continue to be passed down to the younger generations in a meaningful way. Despite modernization, globalization and associated acculturative pressures on the integrity of Wixárika culture, many have integrated these changes within the framework of Wixárika cultural beliefs and practices. While large numbers of Wixaritari seasonally migrate from their sierra homelands to mestizo communities to work as wage labourers or artisans, the money they earn will help sustain temple ceremonies and family expenses to make the pilgrimage to Wirikuta. Some of the wealthier Wixárika have become merchants in their communities and contract out their large trucks to take pilgrims to the peyote desert and back, facilitating the necessary travel. Wixáritari still face challenges along the Mexican highways as they transport their sacred peyote back to their homelands, and this problem will continue as long as the Mexican drug laws remain as they are today. The most fragile part of this cultural equation is the ecological health of the peyote and the land it inhabits. The decimation of peyote and the destruction of the unique environment that supports it means the termination of an ancient body of traditions that, in the face of Westernization and change, continues to bring purpose and meaning to the lives of many Wixáritari. If, or (as I hope) when, Wirikuta is included in the UNESCO Convention, it will create a more safe and secure future for this endangered desert land and its peyote populations, and will further guarantee for Wixárika the right, if they so choose, to continue to seek the divine through their sacred visionary plant.

1   This passage and all others quoted are translated into English from Spanish by the author.
2   The orthography followed for the Wixárika language conforms to the linguistic style used by José Luis Iturriozx Leza, Director of the Departamento de Lenguas Indígenas at the Universidad de Guadalajara, Mexico. The /x/ is pronounced as a retroflexed fricative like the / r/ in Czech 'Dvorak'. Hence, Wixárika is pronounced weezzaareeka with the accent on the middle 'a'.

3   I wish to thank my colleague and compañero Jim Bauml, Senior Biologist at the Los Angeles County Arboretum and Botanic Garden, for his expertise in ethnobotany and his collegiality in our ongoing research on peyote and peyote traditions in Mexico and the US. In our discussions on the mutually beneficial relationship that could have potentially developed between humans and peyote, he elaborated upon this in an e-mail dated September 16, 2003 'That is to say, although the short-term effects of harvesting the tops would be to reduce reproduction, the long-terms effects may have been quite the opposite with the stimulation of dormant axillary buds on the subterranean tap root producing more than one, sometimes many, new heads, ultimately improving overall flower and seed production.'

REFERENCES

Anderson, E. (1996) *Peyote: The Divine Cactus*, (Tuscon: University of Arizona Press).

Arcos, Angeles and Carlos Chavez (1998) 'Rompiendo la ruta sagrada del Hikuri', *Ojarasca*, April 1998, Mexico D.F. pp. 2–3.

Boyd, C.E. and J. P. Dering (1996) 'Medicinal and Halucinogenic Plants Identified in the Sediments and Pictographs of the Lower Pecos, Texas Archaic'. *Antiquity* 7(268):256–275.

Conservación Humana A.C. (1996) Real de Catorce-Virikuta, San Luis Potosí, México: Breve Panorama de la situación biológico, socioeconómico y cultural. (manuscipt)

——(1997a) 'Talleres de difusión y participación comunitaria para la conservación biológico y cultural de la región de Virikuta, San Luis Potosí.'(manuscript)

——(1997b) 'The Initiative for the Conservation of the Sacred Sites and the Protection of the Traditional Pilgrimage Routes of the Huichol Indians of México. (manuscript)

Diguet, L. (1899) La sierra de Nayarit et ses indigenes. Contributions a l'étude ethnographique des races primitives du Mexique. *Nouvelles Archives des Missions Scientifiques et Litteraires*, Paris 9:571–630.

——(1907) Le 'peyote' et son usage ritual chez les indiens de Nayarit. *Journal de la Societé des Americanistes de Paris* 4:21–29.

Eger, Susan (1978) 'Huichol Women's Art', in K. Berrin (ed.) *Art of the Huichol Indians*, New York: Fine Arts Museums of San Francisco/Harry N. Abrams, pp. 35–53.

Furst, P.T. (1972) 'To Find Our Life: The Peyote Hunt of the Huichol Indians of Mexico' in P.T. Furst (ed.) *Flesh of the Gods: The Ritual Use of Hallucinogens*. (New York: Praeger).

——(1989) 'Review of Peyote Religion: A History, by Omer Stewart', *American Ethnologist* 16(2):386–387.

——(1996) 'Myth as History, History as Myth: A New Look at Some Old Problems in Huichol Origins, in S. B. Schaefer and P. T. Furst (eds.), *People of the Peyote: Huichol Indian History, Religion and Survival*. (Albuquerque: University of New Mexico Press).

Furst, P. T. and M. Anguiano (1976) '"To Fly as Birds': Myth and Ritual as Agents of Enculturation among the Huichol Indians of Mexico', in J. Wilbert (ed.) *Enculturation in Latin America: An Anthology*, (L.A.: UCLA Latin American Center Publications), pp. 95–181.

Furst, P.T. and S. B. Schaefer (1996)'Peyote Pilgrims and Don Juan Seekers: Huichol Indians in a Multicultural World', , in S. B. Schaefer and P. T. Furst (eds.), *People of the Peyote: Huichol Indian History, Religion and Survival*. (Albuquerque: University of New Mexico Press) pp. 503–521.

Instituto Naciona de Ecología (1994) 'Norma Oficial Mexicana NOM-0590Ecol–1994, que determina la especies y subespecies de flora y fauna silvestrs, terrestres y acuáticas en el peligro de extinción amenazadas, raras y las sujectas a protección especial que establece especificaciones para su protección.' *Diario Oficial*, 16 de mayo de 1994, pp. 2–60.

Instituto Nacional Indigenísta (1992) *Lugares sagrados: Relato Wirrarika*. Mexico D.F.: Instituto Nacional Indigenísta.

Klüver, H. (1966) *Mescal and Mechanisms of Hallucinations*. Chicago, University of Chicago Press.

La Barre, W. (1989) *The Peyote Cult*, (Norman, Oklahoma and London: University of Oklahoma Press).

López, López, J.L., L.Salazar Montes, et al. (1997) *Aproximación a la salud en la zona huichol de Jalisco*. Guadalajara, Mexico: Universidad de Guadalakara/Fondo para la Salud de los Niños Indígenas UNICEF.

Lumholtz, C. (1902) *Unknown Mexico*, vol.2. New York: Scribner's and Sons.

Mandell, A. (1978) 'The Neurochemistry of Religions: Insight and Ecstasy', in K.Berrin (ed.) *Art of the Huichol Indians* (New York: The Fine Arts Museums of San Francisco/Harry N. Abrams), pp. 71–81.

Maickel, R. P. and W.R. Snodgrass (1973) 'Physiochemical factors in Maternal-fetal Distribution of Drugs', *Toxicology and Applied Pharmacology* 26:218–230.

McCleary, J. A., P. S. Syperd, and D.L. Walkington (1960) 'Antibiotic Activity of an Extract of Peyote (*Lophohora williamsii* (Lemaire) Coulter)', *Economic Botany* 14:247–249.

Myerhoff, B. G. (1974) *Peyote Hunt: The Sacred Journey of the Huichol Indians*, (Ithaca: Cornell University Press).

Oster, Gerald (1971) 'Phosphenes', *Scientific American* 222:83–87.

Rajsbaum, Ari (1996) 'El Uso Tradicional de Plantas y Animales Frente La Ley', *Ce-Acatl: Revista de la Cultura de Anáhuac* 82:38–82.

Ruiz de Alarcón, Hernando (1984) Treatise on the Heathen Superstitions That Today Live Among the Indians Native to This New Spain, 1629, J.R. Andrews and R. Hassig (trans.) (Norman, Oklahoma and London: University of Oklahoma Press.)

Sahagun, B. (1950–69) Florentine Codex: General History of New Spain (12 vols)., C. Dibble and A.J. Anderson (trans.) (Santa Fe, New Mexico, The School of American Research and The University of Utah Press).

Santoscoy, A. (1899) *Nayarit. Colección de documentos inéditos, hstóricos acerca de la sierra de ese nombre*. Guadalajara, Mexico: Tipo-Lit y Enc. de José María Yquiniz.

Schaefer, S. B. (1996a)'The Crossing of the Souls: Peyote, Perception, and Meaning among the Huichol Indians', in S. B. Schaefer and P.T. .Furst (eds.), *People of the Peyote: Huichol Indian History, Religion and Survival*. (Albuquerque: University of New Mexico Press). pp. 138–168.

——(1996b)'The Cosmos Contained: The Temple Where Sun and Moon Meet'. in S. B. Schaefer and P. T. Furst (eds.), People of the Peyote: Huichol Indian History, Religion and Survival. (Albuquerque: University of New Mexico Press), pp. 332–373.

——(1996c) 'Pregnancy and Peyote among the Huichol Indians of Mexico: A Preliminary Report.' *Yearbook for Ethnomedicine and the Study of Consciousness/ Jarbuch für Ethnomedizin und Bewufsteinsforschung* 5: 67–78. Berlin.

——(1998) 'Freedom of Expression: Huichol Indians – Their Peyote-Inspired Art and Mexican Drug Laws', *Yearbook for Ethnomedicine and the Study of Consciousness/ Jarbuch für Ethnomedizin und Bewufsteinsforschung* 7: 205–221. Berlin.

175

——(2000) 'The Peyote Religion and Mescalero Apache: An Ethnohistorical View from West Texas,, *Journal of Big Bend Studies* 12:51–70.

——(2002) *To Think With A Good Heart: Wixárika Women, Weavers, and Shamans*, (Salt Lake City: University of Utah Press).

Schultes, R.E. (1938) 'The Appeal of Peyote (*Lophophora williamsii*) As a Medicine', *American Anthropologist* 40:698–715.

Shah, N.S., A.E. Neely, K.R. Shah, et al. (1973) 'Placental Transfer and Fetal Distribution of Mescaline-14 in the Mouse', *The Journal of Pharmacology and Experimental Therapies*, 184(2) 489–493.

Stewwart, O.C. (1987) *Peyote Religion: A History.* Norman, Oklahoma and London: University of Oklahoma Press.

Taska, R.J. and J.C. Schoolar (1972) 'Placental Transfer and Fetal Distribution of Mescaline-14 in Monkeys', *The Journal of Pharmacology and Experimental Therapies*, 182(2) 427–432.

Trout and Friends (1999) 'Sacred Cacti: Botany, Chemistry, Cultivation & Utilization', *Trout Notes Volume #1 Revised Edition*. Austin, Texas: Better Days Publishers.

Weigand, P.C. (1975) 'Possible References to La Quemada in Huichol Mythology' *Ethnohistory* 22(1):15–20.

——(1981) 'Differential Acculturation among the Huichol Indians', in P. Weigand and T. Hinton (eds.) *Themes of Indigenous Acculturation in Northwest Mexico*, (Tuscon, University of Arizona Press), pp. 9–21.

Chapter Ten

GANJA AND THE ROAD TO DECRIMINALISATION IN JAMAICA

Barry Chevannes

INTRODUCTION

Ganja (*cannabis*) came to Jamaica with the Indians after Emancipation in 1838[1], although it was clearly known to many of the Africans from the region of the Koongo. Its use spread rapidly among the rural and urban working classes, into whose pharmacopoeia it was incorporated as a potent medicinal plant and stimulant, becoming culturally entrenched by the turn of the twentieth century. Its criminalisation, beginning in 1912 and lasting up to the present, has had no effect in curbing its proliferation or eradicating its entrenchment. To the contrary, its cultural legitimacy has deepened. After six decades of stiffer and stiffer sanctions, and a subsequent three of less punitive ones, state policy towards ganja has been a failure, requiring new approaches and changes to the extent that international law allows. This chapter reviews the historical and cultural contexts of the law against ganja and its escalation and amelioration, leading to present attempts by the State to decriminalise use.

BACKGROUND

No evidence has yet been found that prior to the coming of Indians to Jamaica *cannabis sativa,* by whatever name, was known, let alone used, by the slave or slaveholding populations. That it was known among Central Africans, large numbers of whom were held and enslaved, has been established by Warner-Lewis (2003). The Ovimbundu knew it variously as dagga

177

and kif. Perhaps due to the circumstances under which those Africans came, perhaps due also to the fact that unlike the ackee (*blighia sapida*) from West Africa it was never seen as a dietary supplement, cannabis does not seem to have reached Jamaica before the period of the Atlantic slave trade. Surely, if it had, it would have been at least mentioned in Sloane's comprehensive work of 1707? And had it, it is unlikely that *ganja*, a Hindi word, would have become the name by which it has been known throughout Jamaica since the nineteenth century.

Given an Indian origin, then, we can assume that diffusion throughout Jamaica took place by way of the sugar plantations, whose labour force the Indians were recruited to supplement, following the refusal of the now-free Africans to work for the wages being offered by the planters. If one is right about this, then it becomes clearer why Jamaican workers to this day use ganja as a stimulant. One of the beliefs most commonly-held by small cultivators, construction workers and those working on the estates is that ganja helps with hard work. Rubin and Comitas (1974:70) made an 'after-lunch' videotape study of small farmers and found that those who smoked expended higher outputs of energy than the control group but that this tapered off to comparatively lower levels by the end of the day. The output of the control group, remained fairly even throughout the day. However, facts like these meant and continue to mean nothing to the tens of thousands of manual workers on the docks, in the fields and on work sites, who often leave the trails of their presence in the small seedlings that spring up after they have gone.

Following its introduction, ganja also came to be regarded as a powerful medicinal plant, taking its place alongside other native herbs, plants and barks. According to Indian mythology it was a gift of Hanuman, the monkey-god, to humankind. There is no evidence of diffusion of this myth, although its sacralisation by the Rastafari in the 1950s as a gift of Jah (God) through King Solomon, on whose grave it first grew, could be regarded as a reinterpretation of the plant's divine origin. Importantly, by the time of Emancipation the Africans already had a highly developed pharmacopoeia (Campbell 1988) and system of healing, governing preparation, procedures, dosages and, in some instances, side-effects. In this system ganja came to figure as something of a panacea, a cure for a wide range of ailments, such as flu, colds, loss of appetite, asthma, and failing eyesight; a bath with the leaves inured new-born infants against colds and other ailments, while a regular administration of the tea has been believed to enhance intelligence (Rubin and Comitas 1974: 48). As a very handy medicine to have around the house, ganja is steeped in white over-proof rum, and left buried in the earth for nine days.

Working as a member of the Vera Rubin and Lambros Comitas team of researchers, who in 1970 and 1971 carried out a study of the effects of long-term use of ganja, I was told by an informant in his eighties that up to the time of the first World War, Indian men used it as a recreational substance in their yards in West Kingston and would compete with their African friends to see who could smoke the most. According to him, the Indians showed displeasure whenever, as sometimes happened, they were out-smoked by an African, because it was like being beaten at their own game. Such recreational use, but without the competition, has continued into the present. In my 1971 fieldwork in the Cockburn Gardens area of Kingston, where lived a heavy concentration of Indians, ganja smoking was an after-work recreational activity, pursued in conjunction with the heavy drinking of white rum and stout, and amidst the singing of Hindi songs to the music of the saranggi (violin), the manjira (bell), and the dolak (drum), the recounting of stories, or the racing of cardboard 'horses' in the gutter after a shower of rain. Then as dusk fell, participants would depart for home.

Ganja therefore has both medicinal and recreational uses of great significance, yet at the same time, it is well-known among folk that ganja produces bad effects for some people. Old informants used to speak of having visions of a 'little dancing green man' after they had smoked for the first time, though never in subsequent use. According to Rubin and Comitas, since expectations from cannabis are generally culturally determined, this hallucination is clearly one of them, as its occurrence elsewhere has never been reported (p. 139). But there are those who, after smoking or ingesting, undergo mood and behavioural changes, including paranoia and even psychosis. Knight (1976) has described this as *ganja psychosis* but an ethnoscientific term of very long usage would describe such bad reactions as having a *light head*. It is thus well recognised that, as beneficial as the plant may be, its use needs to be restricted to those who have the head for it. Obviously, there could be no way to diagnose who would and would not be susceptible to a bad reaction except through trial and error. This implies that users did not see a negative reaction as producing a permanent change of personality.

Another negative reaction that ganja was, at one time, thought to produce was a proneness to violence. This seemed to have been the reason for Jamaica including ganja in its ratification of the 1912 Hague Opium Convention signed by Great Britain[2], not on the basis of expert or scientific evidence but on the basis of unsubstantiated allegations. Forty years previously the Governor had mentioned in a report to the Colonial Office that it was believed that ganja had induced an Indian to murder his wife. Forty years later, allegation had become fact. But the colonial administration of 1912 did not suffer for want of expert opinion, since the India Hemp Commission Report, which had been available for nearly two decades, had found no basis for linking violence and other forms of social deviance to ganja. Moreover, a United Kingdom Royal Commission had as recently as 1901 concluded that cannabis was relatively harmless and not worth banning. No doubt encouraged by the fact that during the meetings of the Hague

Convention, a resolution had been passed to study the question of Indian hemp, the Jamaican Legislature signalled its intention to suppress it.

Such was the power of this ruling idea about ganja that twenty years later, Marcus Garvey could editorialise thus, in his August 13, 1932 edition of his *New Jamaican*:

Ganja is a dangerous weed. It has been pronounced so by responsible authorities.

> The smoking of it does a great deal of harm or injury to the smoker; we understand it has the same effect on the subject as opium has. Every day we hear of cases of ganja sellers being brought before the Court – fines, small and heavy, have been inflicted with the object of destroying the trade but yet it grows . . . That our people are being destroyed by the use of ganja there is absolutely no doubt. We have come in contact with young men and middle aged men who have become a menace to society through the smoking of ganja. Sometimes they perform in such a crazy manner as to frighten us. Aren't we playing with the danger by not more severely putting it down?
>
> Most of the people who smoke ganja do so as a means of getting themselves in such a state or condition as to forget their troubles and worries–troubles and worries brought on by the bad conditions that exist in the country (Quoted in Lewis 1998:152).

According to this influential view, ganja was as dangerous as opium, inducing people to escape from reality through its use and / or making people behave crazily enough to frighten others. Only the open confrontation with a group that was to make ganja its *cause celebre* would compel Jamaican society to alter its view. This was in the 1960s, and the group was the Rastafari. Since then ganja is no longer thought of as a stimulant to violent behaviour; instead the talk now is that it de-motivates those who smoke it. In sum, by the time it was proscribed by law, ganja had enjoyed widespread acceptance among the people. This continued after the first legal prohibitions were put in place. In the rest of this chapter, the staging posts on the road to criminalisation and then to prospects for decriminalisation are described.

THE DANGEROUS DRUGS ACT

First passed in 1924, the Dangerous Drugs Act brought into force prohibitions mandated by the Hague Convention, and included penalties for cultivation, trafficking and smoking of ganja. Strengthened by the first Geneva Convention of 1925, and by the second Geneva Convention of 1931, which called for limiting the manufacture of narcotics and regulating their distribution, the Act was amended in 1941 with increased penalties and the imposition for the first time of mandatory imprisonment for first conviction. The Act went through four subsequent amendments up to 1964, each in the general direction of stiffer penalties. By the time the provisions for mandatory sentencing were repealed in 1972, first conviction for possession and smoking could result in a sentence of between eighteen months and three years, and between three and five years for a second conviction. The law also gave the police powers of search without a magistrate's warrant

COLONIAL LAW VERSUS CULTURAL IDENTIFICATION: THE RASTAFARI

The better to understand the contexts for the sequence of legal amendments noted above, a brief introduction of the Rastafari is necessary. Formed in the months following the 1930 coronation of Tafari Makonnen as Emperor Haile Selassie I of Ethiopia, Rastafari came to believe in the divinity of this monarch, a descendant of King Solomon and Queen Candace of Sheba, as the ancient kingdom of Ethiopia was then known, on the authority of a prophecy of the Pan-Africanist and Back-to-Africa advocate, Marcus Garvey. The Rastafari advocated the repatriation of the descendants of Africans captured or sold into slavery, to correct the injustice of slavery, and throughout the 1930s and 1940s delivered a trenchant critique of the oppressive and racist nature of the colonial system. This they ritualised in a number of ways that the colonial order found upsetting: the preaching that God was black; the valorising of Africa and the racial characteristics of Africans; the denunciation of allegiance to the British monarchy and challenging of its authority; the violation of the social codes of self-presentation; and the sacralisation of the banned substance, ganja. It was these last two expressions of rejection of social and legal 'standards' introduced in the early 1930s that became signatures of identity for the fledgling religious movement.

In the 1930s, the hair culture of black men dictated a close, well-combed crop, which was generally covered outdoors in public and laid bare indoors. From about 1934, the Rastafari adopted the practice of sacralising head and facial hair. This they justified by reference to the Nazarite vow of Samson, the Jewish hero, whose exploits against the Philistines are recounted in the Bible (Book of Judges). The effect of this defiance of the social code was to inspire fear and a reputation as 'black heart men' who stole and kidnapped children. This fear was captured in a folk song of the 1940s, whose refrain was:

Run, man without beard,
Beardman back o' you!

181

Following the emergence, from around 1949, of the Kenyan anti-colonial movement led by the Mau-Mau, as a mark of identification with what they saw as a struggle against a common enemy, the Rastafari adopted the matted hair style of some of the Kenyan warriors. At that time in Jamaica such a hairstyle was a mark of derelicts and people of unsound mind. They thus carried the violation of the hair code a step further, by appearing in public uncombed and untonsured. Left entirely to itself, the hair grew into a tangled mat, which became known as dreadlocks, from the name Rastafari gave those defiant and aggressive members who initiated the innovation. With the adoption of the dreadlocks Rastafari dug itself deeper in the margins of society.

In 1954, the police raided (for the third and last time) the Rastafari community of Pinnacle, fifteen miles outside of Kingston, destroying it in the process. Pinnacle was an abandoned estate, which had been acquired by Leonard Howell, the acknowledged founder of the movement, and settled by his followers. Howell had been supporting himself and the community by supplying the markets in Kingston and Spanish Town with ganja. In the raid, the police seized eight tonnes of ganja and burned nine thousand plants, 'la plus grosse prise de l'histoire jamaicaine' (Lee 1999: 225). Such a large quantity clearly identified the Rastafari with ganja.

That identification was to become complete and final when, their existence already marginal, the Dreadlocks launched a challenge to the established order by ritualising their use of ganja (Chevannes 1991). Whereas other Rastafari groups instituted strict measures to deny the police a pretext for invading their meetings, the Dreadlocks embraced ganja use in theirs. Their argument was that given the benefits of the substance, state prosecution of ganja use by the people is nothing but another example of the oppression of black people, in this case denying them the enlightenment that comes from smoking it in their 'circles of reasoning'. Their ritualisation took the form of passing around the 'cup', as they called the huka, in a counter-clockwise direction, while engaging in the lofty discourse they came to refer to as 'reasoning'.

For the next decade or so this reform movement within the Rastafari spread rapidly and by the end of the decade of the 1960s had embraced virtually all who professed the doctrine. However, this was not before the movement as a whole was thrown headlong into real as opposed to symbolic confrontation with the wider society. In 1960 Claudius Henry, a Rastafari leader, along with some of his leading members, was charged with 'treason felony'[3], following the discovery of an arms cache on the premises of his church and a letter inviting the victorious revolutionary Cuban leader, Fidel Castro, to take over Jamaica as the Rastafari repatriated to Africa. As if this was not enough, two weeks later British troops launched a raid on a secret guerrilla camp operated by Henry's son, and suffered two casualties in the ensuing battle. The outrage that followed was turned against all Rastafari members, in particular the now visible Dreadlocks, who became fair game for the police. In their desperation the Rastafari appealed to the University of the West Indies to conduct a study of the movement in order to promote wider understanding of its beliefs and show that it did not espouse violence. The famous report by Smith, Augier and Nettleford (1960) was the result, and with its publication the tide against the movement began to turn.

The Government adopted the recommendation of the University scholars that it seriously consider migration to Africa. A nine-man Mission which included three Rastafari was tasked to visit and negotiate with six countries on the continent. Pleased with a successful first approach, the Government then sent a Technical Mission to work out details of agreements but this was aborted when a general election was called and the incumbent party lost power to the opposition.

The mood of the new Government, whose 1962 victory gave it the mandate to negotiate independence from Britain (achieved later that year) was at first less than responsive to the problems of the marginal group that the Rastafari represented. Their position hardened when in 1963 at Coral Gardens in Montego Bay, the tourism capital of the country, a Rastafari man chopped to death two persons at a petrol station, and was expressed in a 1964 amendment to the Dangerous Drugs Law which imposed the stiffest sanctions yet. Eight years later during a Parliamentary debate considering amelioration of the Dangerous Drugs Act, the former Minister of Education, Edwin Allen, explained that the intention of his Government in increasing the sanctions was to protect the fledgling tourism sector, on which the newly independent country was hoping to capitalise.

However, despite the University Report, the Government had seriously misread the significance of Coral Gardens. They saw in it the typical action of a marginal group that harboured violent criminals, instead of the action of one unstable individual, as the Rastafari insisted, and therefore failed until too late to notice the growing popularity of the Rastafari among the urban poor and dispossessed. In their 1960 University Report, Smith *et al.* (1960:30) had found that in some communities Rastafari was the prevailing doctrine and ideology. But it was the youth population of urban unemployed that was to provide the bedrock of support for the movement. This came principally through the newly discovered national music, ska, and its successive variations, rock steady and reggae. The music became for them a ready vehicle to express the anger and frustration, the hopes and visions, of a generation that had quickly lost confidence in the promise of Independence but was finding it instead in the philosophy of Rastafari. Themes of a distant land that was home, of Africa, of Ethiopia and His Imperial Majesty, of Marcus Garvey and black nationalism began to be heard in the popular rhythms, and these served to enhance the legitimacy of the Rastafari among the poor. So strong became the Rastafari stamp on the popular music that by 1970 the overwhelming majority of recording artistes were Dreadlocks.

Meanwhile, in 1966 aware of its declining popularity and hoping to improve its chances in the upcoming election, the Government invited Haile Selassie on a state visit. The enthusiastic reception the Emperor received from the people was unprecedented. On his arrival, the Rastafari broke onto the tarmac, surrounded the Imperial aircraft and in exultation lit up their 'chalices' with the holy herb, forcing the official welcome to be aborted. Recognising Mortimo Planno, the Dreadlocks member of the nine-man Mission that had visited Ethiopia, His Imperial Majesty sent him word to request the brethren to allow him to disembark, a gesture that elevated the Rastafari in the public's eye. For the duration of the Emperor's visit, the Rastafari were invited to state functions and accorded recognition and privileges never before realised, never since given. And everywhere he went across the island the crowds turned out in large numbers to see the man some said was God.

With a change of Government in 1972, and the obvious ineffectiveness of the law, the oppressive mandatory provisions in the Dangerous Drugs Act were repealed almost at once. At the same time, due to the rise in the export of ganja to the United States, the amendments sought to stiffen the penalties for exporting. Since that time, the Act has been amended twice, in 1987 and again in 1994, to curb the new threat from the importation and trafficking of cocaine, and to revise the fines in keeping with the depreciation of the Jamaican dollar.

As it now stands, as far as ganja is concerned, the relevant section of the Act makes four provisions. The first governs fines of not less than $500 for every ounce of ganja exported or imported or imprisonment of up to thirty-five years if convicted before a Circuit Court. Conviction before a Resident Magistrate fetches fines of between $300 and $500 for every ounce, up to half-million dollars, or imprisonment of up to three years. The second targets cultivators and traffickers, owners of premises where ganja is stored or sold, and of vehicles that convey the substance. Conviction before a Circuit Court fetches fines of not less than $200 per ounce, or imprisonment of up to thirty-five years, while summary conviction before a Resident Magistrate attracts fines of between $100 and $200 per ounce, but not exceeding $500,000, or imprisonment of no more than three years. For possession, according to the third section, the Circuit Court may impose a fine or imprisonment not exceeding five years. Where possession cases are tried before a Resident Magistrate, the Magistrate may impose a fine of not more than $100 per ounce, or imprisonment not exceeding three years. The fourth provision treats smoking as an offence to be tried before a Resident Magistrate, and embraces in its sanctions owners who allow their premises to be so used, smokers and those caught in possession of ganja pipes and other smoking utensils. Fines may not exceed $5,000, or imprisonments exceed twelve months, on first conviction. On second or subsequent convictions, however, these sanctions double to $10,000 and up to two years imprisonment. In all four provisions, the Court has discretion to impose both fine and imprisonment.

AMELIORATION

In spite of these changes, ganja use has not only continued, but seems to have been increasing among the youth sector. Stone (1990) found that the largest consumers of ganja were males thirty years old and younger, while, according to Dreher, Shapiro and Stoddard (1994:22) consumption is concentrated among 'males from late teens through their twenties'. This is not surprising, given the influence of Rastafari among artists and performers in the music industry, whose greatest supporters and consumers are young people. Whether the concert is 'Sumfest' in August in Montego Bay, or 'Sting' on Boxing Day in Kingston, or any of the hundreds of concerts and 'DJ sessions' that take place throughout the year, ganja smoking has become a normal activity. At football matches and street meetings of political parties ganja smoking is prevalent. Were the police to attempt to suppress its use in these environments not only would it damage their image but it would also create serious problems for crowd control.

Thus the society faces a serious problem. Thousands of young people are brought before the court for simple possession and for smoking, and thereby acquire criminal status. The damage criminalisation does to the young people, whose inclination everywhere is to experiment, is being seen as counterproductive. Both Stone and Dreher et al estimate that ever-use of ganja is in the region of forty-five per cent. Were the police to prosecute all who use it, the entire justice system would be unable to cope. But the fact that they cannot, even when the infractions are public, serves to undermine respect for the rule of law. In 2000, among over five thousand persons arrested for drug offences, one was an old man, about eighty years old, charged with simple possession of ganja. No society can tolerate such a large proportion of its citizens being branded as criminals. Hence, what has followed is a search for a way to decriminalise ganja use, while bearing in mind the country's obligations under international law.

The first serious attempt to decriminalise was made in 1978. The legislature at the time was influenced not only by the general appreciation of the cultural status of ganja among the population, but also by the serialisation in 1972 by *The Daily Gleaner* of the early findings of the Rubin and Comitas (1974) study of the effects of chronic use in Jamaica. Rubin and Comitas found no significant medical, psychological or social differences between the group of thirty chronic users, men who registered daily use over at least ten years, and the controls. While their study did not immediately influence any change to the legislation, it allowed for the first informed debate on the subject of use of a drug that was still 'officially' thought of as confined only to the marginalised and insane, helping set the stage for a Joint Select Committee of the Jamaican Parliament to study the issue and make recommendations. And so, in 1978, within a year of its appointment, the Committee unanimously recommended decriminalisation for medical and personal private use of up to two ounces. However, the report was shelved as political violence escalated over the next two years leading up to the general elections of October 1980. Two decades were to elapse before this matter again came before the legislature.

The second attempt, rather more one of amelioration than decriminalisation, has come about in more recent times as a result of international trends, which have shifted from treating drug consumption as criminal to treating it as a problem of health. Acting under the requirement of the 1988 United Nations Convention Against Illicit Traffic in Narcotic Drugs and Psychotropic Substances to provide alternatives to criminal conviction, the Government passed the Drug Court (Treatment and Rehabilitation of Offenders) Act, in force from 1999. The Act makes provisions for persons charged with using ganja, possession of up to eight ounces of ganja, or possession of ganja smoking implements, to be tried by a Resident Magistrate along with two Justices of the Peace in a new Drug Court. Prosecution of a case may be deferred if the person charged opts to undergo a treatment and rehabilitation programme. If the offender successfully completes the programme, the case is dropped; if not, the trial resumes.

Although it may be too early to assess the full impact of the Drug Court, there is every reason to doubt its effectiveness in curbing ganja use. In the first place, because Jamaicans do not perceive or classify ganja as a drug, most offenders would be unconvinced of the appropriateness of undergoing treatment and rehabilitation. Secondly, whereas addiction to crack/cocaine is strikingly visible in the number of once productive men and women reduced to petty criminality in support of their habit, to dereliction and vagrancy, the society has no experience of a similar kind attributable to ganja use. What they see instead are normal, functioning men, whose only nuisance is to those people who are unable to tolerate the acridity of smoke. Thirdly, many would argue that Bob Marley, Peter Tosh and other internationally famous role models not only had no need for rehabilitation but lent their artistic talent and their reputation to the call for the legalisation of ganja. In short, the Drug Court is likely to lack credibility as far as ganja is concerned.

The third attempt, which is currently underway, lies in the Prime Minister's appointment in 2000 of a National Commission on Ganja to consider and advise on a national approach to the matter of decriminalisation. As this represents the first time that the issue has been approached in this way, it is useful to examine it in some detail.

THE NATIONAL COMMISSION ON GANJA

In setting up the Commission, the Prime Minister was acting on the consensus of the Senate, following the introduction of a motion in response to the persistence of a national lobby calling itself the National Alliance for the Legalisation of Ganja, and of the House of Representatives. The Commission's Terms of Reference by omission and by implication made it clear that legalisation was not being contemplated. The first paragraph of the preamble referred to 'long and considerable debate in Jamaica regarding the decriminalisation or non-decriminalisation of ganja in well-defined circumstances and under specific conditions', and the penultimate to 'international treaties, conventions and regulations to which Jamaica subscribes that must be respected'. Since Jamaica could not legalise ganja without renouncing the conventions, decriminalisation in effect meant the personal or religious use in private, free of criminal sanction.

The Commission aroused wide interest in Jamaica and abroad. Its extensive consultation throughout the country and study of written submissions enabled it to identify the main arguments for and against decriminalisation. First, on the side of decriminalisation are the personal benefits that scores of people reported, such as the alleviation of colds, fevers, hypertension and ailments such as asthma and glaucoma, the healing of wounds, reduction of stress, and relief from nausea: 'The stories of the personalised benefits of ganja are so deeply entrenched in the folklore of the people that we do not think any warnings as to its danger or attempt to suppress its use by punitive sanction stand any chance of success' (National Commission 2001:16).

A second set of arguments focuses on God and the natural order. These see ganja as a creation of God for use by mankind, a plant whose seeds are eaten and spread by birds. 'If you are going to charge a man for it you have to charge God because God made it' (p.17). This line of reasoning formed the burden of the deposition made by the Roman Catholic Archbishop, head of his Church. In his and his bishops' view, the Creator of all things created them as good and for the benefit of mankind, and charges man with the responsibility of learning their qualities and using them in moderation. Abuse, he says, lies in excess.

In a third line of argument, people argue that ganja use is not criminal in the sense of it representing a breach of the moral order. It is a crime only because the law says so. But by criminalising ganja and lumping those who run afoul of the law against its use with other, sometimes hardened, criminals, the State itself undermines its own authority, turning the former into sympathisers of the latter and bitter opponents of the rule of law. Whereas ganja poses no threat to society, crack and cocaine do, and it is these that ought to be the focus of the justice system.

The final argument relates to the issue of equity and states that if alcohol and tobacco are not criminalized substances then ganja should be treated in the same way. Both alcohol and tobacco are leading causes of deaths, whereas no one dies of abusing ganja.

Also throwing their weight behind the proposal to decriminalise personal and religious uses are the National Council on Drug Abuse, the Medical Association of Jamaica, the Chief Medical Officer of Health, the Lord Bishop of Jamaica and the Independent Jamaica Council for Human Rights.

Arguments against any form of decriminalisation focus primarily on ill-effects such as hypoglycaemia, mood swings, negative personality change and loss of motivation, particularly among male adolescents. As with those in favour of decriminalisation, many base their objection on personal experiences.

A second line of opposing argument sees ganja as a gateway to other more harmful substances, particularly crack and cocaine. What is meant is not so much that its 'would-be' addictiveness could create higher levels of tolerance that require more potent drugs but that, as one substance in a multi-drug culture, ganja use will sooner or later cause people to experiment with and move on to others.

Thirdly, decriminalisation is expected to lead to the proliferation of abuse and an increase in the social disorder which many people feel has reached an intolerable level. In regard to the latter, the prospect of young males disrespecting their elders by smoking ganja in their presence, which is what they feel would happen once smoking was decriminalised, is too much to contemplate. Indeed, there are those who, if they could, would also ban the smoking of tobacco, which they regard as essentially harmful, physically and socially. The inequity in the legality of tobacco but illegality of ganja has little influence with those who proffer such reasoning in defence of the status quo.

Finding the arguments and authorities in favour of decriminalisation more compelling than the counter-arguments, and in light of the fact that most of those opposed were also in favour of some form or other of amelioration, the Commission reached 'the unanimous conclusion that ganja should be decriminalised for adult personal private use' (National Commission 2001: 38).

REACTIONS, RESPONSES AND RIGHTS

Immediately following the press reporting of the conclusions of the Committee, the Embassy of the United States rushed to issue a stern warning that decriminalisation of ganja could cause its Government to decertify Jamaica. Decertification deprives a country of all aid from the United States. This, in fact, may not be much but by obliging the U.S. to block all types of multilateral assistance, it in fact could spell severe isolation from the international community and exertion of serious economic pressures. A country will be decertified if, in the view of the US, that country is in breach of the international conventions or, more bluntly, adopts policies that the US sees as threatening to its own domestic security and welfare.

The Commission did take the conventions into account. The two relevant United Nations treaties are the *Single Convention on Narcotic Drugs, 1961*, and the *Convention Against Illicit Traffic in Narcotic Drugs and Psychotropic Substances, 1988*. Both these treaties oblige the signatory Parties to institute legislative and administrative measures to limit the use, possession and trafficking of drugs. The 1988 Convention more explicitly includes possession for personal consumption among those actions to be criminally sanctioned, but also, like the Single Convention, it steers clear of making the consumption itself a criminal offence. Thus, the act of smoking need not be criminal, though the possession of a small quantity for smoking would. This some would find unworkable.

However, in the Commission's view, the constitutional limitation clause worded into the Conventions ('Subject to its constitutional principles and the basic concepts of its legal system, each Party shall adopt such measures as may be necessary to establish as a criminal offence under its domestic law . . .') could, it felt, allow the State in its responsibility to safeguard the fundamental rights of its citizens, the latitude of freeing the private use of ganja from criminal sanction. The International Convention on Civil and Political Rights calls for, among other things, protection against invasion of privacy and protection of freedom of religion. If, therefore, the rights of privacy and freedom of religion were to be enshrined in the constitution, the private use of ganja could, in the Commission's thinking, fall within the constitutional limitation respected by the Drug Conventions.

That this is not so at present is due to a 'saving clause' in the Jamaican Constitution that allows all statutes in existence up to August 6th 1962, the day of Jamaica's political independence when its Constitution came into effect, to supersede the Constitution in cases where they conflict with the provisions of the Constitution. Thus, although the present Constitution acknowledges the rights of privacy and freedom of religion, in actual fact the Dangerous Drugs Law supersedes those rights, making it possible for the police to invade the privacy of a home in its prosecution. The amendments being proposed by both the ruling and opposition parties in Parliament would do away with the saving clause and guarantee protection of both religious freedom and privacy. It is not envisaged that such protection would be absolute. Laws that are required 'for the governance of the State in periods of public emergency' (National Commission 2001: 47) would obviously take precedence, and so would matters of public order, public safety, public health, and the rights and freedoms of others.

The recommendation of the National Commission to decriminalise the personal, private use of ganja, therefore hinges on Parliament protecting the country by applying the constitutional limitations of the International Conventions. Should it proceed thus to amend the present Constitution in the direction both parties are intending, Jamaica would find itself alongside Canada, where in July 2000 the Ontario Court of Appeal in handing down judgment that the country's marijuana laws infringed an appellant's security by preventing him from undertaking a safe medical treatment for his epilepsy, 'took note of the fact that the United Nations 1988 Convention had, as the Convention stipulated, to be subject to Canada's constitutional principles and basic concepts of its legal system' (National Commission 2001: 50). Two years later the Canadian Parliament made 'medical marijuana' legal.

CONCLUSION

This latest effort on the part of Jamaica to decriminalise ganja so far bears close resemblance to the first effort of 1978, in that the issue has gone the route of a Joint Select Committee of Parliament. The present Committee, which has achieved near unanimity to accept the recommendation of the Commission, is yet to report back to Parliament, where it will be debated before passage into law should Parliament accept the recommendation, or thrown out if it does not. The chances for the former are stronger than those for the latter, if the opinions of the Parliamentary Committee are anything to go by.[4]

But Parliament may not necessarily go the route of decriminalisation, in the sense understood and recommended by the Commission, which is to say the non-application of any sanction whatever for private and religious use. It may decide to go the way of the United Kingdom, which by declassifying cannabis to a Class C drug makes the possession and use of it a misdemeanour instead of a crime. Of course, a half loaf being better than no loaf at all, such a measure would spare thousands of Jamaicans, in particular young males, from criminal records, but it would bring little joy and make no difference to those who break the Dangerous Drugs Act in private and in public with impunity.

1   A labour shortage arose immediately after Emancipation when the newly freed Africans refused to work at the wage rates offered by the sugar planters, who turned to Indian indentured workers.
2   As a colony Jamaica had no international status therefore the local Legislative Council had to ratify the Convention signed by Britain.
3   As defined by an Act of that name.
4   As Chairman of the National Commission, the author was summoned before the Joint Select Committee on Wednesday November 12, 2003. Of the 14 members present only one felt that the recommendation to decriminalise private and religious use needed further discussion before he could assent. All the others indicated their readiness to support the recommendation.

REFERENCES

Campbell, S. (1988) *Caribbean Foodways*. (Jamaica: Caribbean Food and Nutrition Institute).

Chevannes, B. (1991) 'The Dreadlocks Rastafari', in Kortright Davis and Elias Farajaje-Jones (eds.), *African Creative Expressions of the Divine*, (Washington, D.C.: Howard University School of Divinity, pp. 37–52).

Dreher, M., Shapiro, D. and Stoddard, A. (1994) Drug Consumption and Distribution in Jamaica: A National Ethnographic Study, (Kingston, Jamaica: United States Embassy).

Knight, F. (1976) 'Role of Cannabis in Psychiatric Disturbance', *The New York Academy of Sciences*, Volume 282, pp. 64–71.

Lee, H. (1999) *Le Premier Rasta* (Paris: Flammarion).

Lewis, R. (1998) 'Marcus Garvey and the Early Rastafarians', in Nathaniel Murrell, William Spencer and Adrian McFarlane (eds.), *Chanting Down Babylon: The Rastafari Reader*, (Philadelphia: Temple University Press, pp. 145–158).

National Commission (2001) National Commission on Ganja Report, Kingston: Jamaica Information Service.

Rubin, V. and Comitas, L. (1974) *Ganja in Jamaica* (The Hague: Mouton).

Sloane, H. (1707) *A Voyage to the Islands Madera, Barbados, Nieves, S. Christophers and Jamaica*, (London).

Smith, M.G., Augier, R. and Nettleford, R. (1960) *The Rastafari Movement in Kingston*, (Kingston: Institute of Social and Economic Research, University College of the West Indies, Mona).

Stone, C. (1990) 'Extracts and Summary of the National Survey on Use of Drugs in Jamaica', *Jamaican Nurse*, 29 (1) 54–57.

Warner-Lewis, M. (2003) *Central Africa in the Caribbean: Transcending Time, Transforming Cultures*, (Barbados, Jamaica, Trinidad and Tobago: University of the West Indies Press).

Chapter Eleven

LIVING WITH HEROIN AT THE KENYA COAST

Susan Beckerleg

INTRODUCTION

Heroin has been a street drug at the Kenya coast since the 1980s, with its use spreading from a few large towns to many smaller settlements, including some rural villages. The increasingly easy availability of heroin is linked to the 1980s tourist boom when Italian investors set up businesses with local partners (UNODCCP, 1999). The Swahili community were particularly affected because they were in the forefront of the tourist industry and came into direct contact with Europeans requesting heroin (Beckerleg 1995 a). Before 1999, the supply of heroin to Kenya comprised 'brown sugar' from South Asia (UNDCP, 2000) that was mostly smoked or the vapour 'chased' on foil. From 1999, large amounts of 'white crest' appeared in Malindi. Heroin users and the police in Malindi suggest various supply sources for 'white crest', including that it is a synthetic substance manufactured by university students in Nairobi. However, it is more likely that this crystalline substance is white heroin from Thailand. 'White crest' cannot be 'chased' and many users have switched to injecting. 'White crest' can also be smoked with cannabis and in Malindi is then called a 'cocktail', or with tobacco when it is called a 'joint'.

Between 2000 and 2002 I led a study funded by the UK Economic and Social Research Council into heroin users, with a particular emphasis on women, in the Kenyan coastal town of Malindi. The research methods used were anthropological fieldwork including observation of heroin use and participation in the everyday lives of users; interviews with the families of users and key community members (Beckerleg and Lewando Hundt, forthcoming). In addition, a number of workshops with health workers, youth groups and concerned community members allowed participants to voice their views about heroin use in their town. This article presents the findings of the study to illustrate the ways that the heroin users and non-users live with the drug in the town of Malindi. The structure of the article is as follows: the main features of Swahili mainstream culture are outlined, before giving a more detailed description of the local heroin sub-culture. The following sections examine community responses to the heroin users in their midst. In the conclusion, the place of drugs in general, and heroin in particular, in contemporary Swahili culture is evaluated.

MAINSTREAM CULTURE

The origins of the Swahili along the East coast of Africa have been traced back over two thousand years (de vere Allen, 1993; Kusimba, 1999) and Islam in the region dates back to the eighth century (Horton and Middleton, 2000). Swahili culture incorporates elements drawn from Arabia and India, as well as from the West. The Swahili are urban-orientated traders and have a developed maritime culture. Since the 1960s Kenyan Swahili have been influenced by the growth of mass tourism in their midst. As part of globalisation, contemporary Swahili culture incorporates many diverse, and even contradictory elements, but still retains a clear identity, with distinctive modern dress, music and language styles (Beckerleg, 2004 a). One of the towns most affected by tourism is Malindi, an old Swahili settlement visited by Vasco da Gama over 500 years ago (Sharif, 1987). In the early 1980s Peake found Malindi to be a major tourist destination with a declining fishing industry (1989). Since then, the town has endured the Italian led tourist boom that started in the 1980s and involved the purchase of land and the development of hotels, restaurants, bars and casinos by Italian business people working with local partners who fronted the businesses. The economic downturn started gradually in the 1990s, and although some Italians remain, many businesses are failing and the town is now facing sharp declines in tourist numbers and revenue. Year-round fishing catches are reportedly reduced due to competition from commercial trawlers and because some fishing grounds are now part of the Marine National Park and therefore off-limits.

A second generation of Kenyan Swahili has now grown up in an area where tourism, with its associated easy but irregular money, is the main industry. A consumerist and hedonistic culture predominates at the Kenya coast whereby fortunes have been made through association with Europeans. Short-term conspicuous consumption has been a feature of everyday life in a culture familiar with the alternation of famine and feast. In the tourist season, high earnings can be obtained by money-changers, sex workers and others servicing tourists. During the off-season tourist period, when rough seas also limit fishing, many Swahili families go hungry in Malindi. Unemployment levels are high and the traditional escape routes for young Swahili men of signing-on as merchant sailors or migrating to Arabia for employment have become more difficult in recent years. Young women have even fewer avenues for employment.

Recreational drug use is a dominant feature of contemporary Swahili life. As Muslims, the Swahili stigmatize alcohol consumption but the majority see little harm in the use of cannabis and miraa (khat). Concern about drug use within the Swahili community is largely confined to the increasing numbers of young men and some women (Beckerleg and Lewando Hundt, 2004) who have become addicted to heroin.

Migration within the Swahili region and beyond has had an effect on families. Throughout the twentieth century, high rates of divorce and re-marriage (Mirza and Strobel, 1989), combined with the customary foster-ing of children within the extended family, has meant that many children are not brought up by two parents. There are also a growing number of Swahili women bringing up children alone. These trends towards fractured family relations are particularly pronounced amongst poor families who do not have the material resources or moral authority to care for, guide and regulate their members. This can be seen as an example of the kind of struc-tural violence identified in other contexts enduring similar social processes (Bourgois, 1995; Bourgois, 2001; Farmer et al, 1996; Farmer, 1999). For example, studies of Baltimore, USA in the 1960s provide interesting points of comparison with experience on the Kenya Coast from the 1980s onward. In Baltimore in the 1960s, increases in the heroin supply were combined with 'hope and despair' amongst young people (Agar and Schacht Reisinger, 2002, 115). Young black men derived hope from the civil rights movement but also became more aware of their disadvantaged position in society at the time. In Malindi, heroin became a street drug at a time that combined falling economic opportunities for young men with a local tourist boom that directly benefited few families.

HEROIN SUB-CULTURE

Heroin users in Malindi constitute a network of at least 600 individuals (Beckerleg and Lewando Hundt, 2004) who communicate using slang, interact on a daily basis and have developed a sub-culture that is repro-duced daily within the same physical spaces as mainstream Swahili society.

Language

The terminology used by members of the sub-culture of heroin users changes rapidly, so outsiders cannot readily gain entry to this group. As

Ramos (1990) found amongst Chicanos, the ability to converse in this semi-secret language confers an insider status. The use of obscure terminology also assists heroin users in conducting their illegal and socially sanctioned activities within the midst of mainstream society. Heroin users in this Kenyan setting use a mixture of Swahili and English loan words to talk about injecting in particular and heroin use in general (Beckerleg, 1995 b). Most of these terms are slang and are not readily understood by Swahili-speakers who are not part of the heroin-using sub-culture. However, some words such as 'junkie', 'shoot' or 'shooter' are understandable to drug users throughout the English-speaking world. Other terms are common to networks of heroin users within East Africa. Indeed, many words, such as *tapeli* (scam), *kubwenga* meaning 'to inject', or *noma* meaning a bad or dangerous incident such as being chased by the police, seem to originate from Tanzanian dialects of Swahili and to have been diffused into Kenyan drug slang. However, new terms are likely to spread quickly into general street talk (Bourgois, 1995).

User Etiquette

In Malindi many heroin users pair up with a 'partner' to raise cash, hang out and use together. For women especially, who usually earn money through sex work, having a male partner can be a useful security measure. Mixed pairs are sometimes though not always, sexual partners. However, the relationship is not primarily sexual and same-sex partners can be numerous but focussed on pairing to provide mutual support in the aim of getting and using heroin. Usually both partners are either smokers or injectors. If the pair are injecting, they may inject each other with separate or the same injecting equipment. Users all claim, and appear, to have their own equipment, but sharing also frequently occurs.

Within this sub-culture the ability to raise large amounts of money to purchase drugs by dealing, injecting other users for a fee, sex work (particularly with tourists), and confidence tricks are all acceptable activities. On the other hand, begging, sex work with local Africans and petty theft, such as taking clothes off the neighbours' washing lines, are not status enhancing. Once the money to buy heroin is raised, it is preferable to have sufficient funds to buy one's own supplies without resorting to sharing with others and be able to inject or smoke in a comfortable setting. High status injectors tend to use at home or at a friend's place. Amongst homeless users, heroin use takes place in derelict houses and on the streets in the open. Using heroin at home avoids inconvenience and reinforces the message that one has a place to live. Using alone denotes that one has sufficient funds and is therefore status enhancing, while not having one's own injecting equipment and borrowing or stealing from another user denotes a lack of control over one's life and a lack of autonomy (Beckerleg, 2004 b).

Many users who inject in semi-public settings are embarrassed by their injecting practices, perhaps sharing the widespread general aversion to needles and syringes or perhaps because they perceive injecting as denoting a deeper level of dependency than smoking. This embarrassment or shame concerning injecting practices is far from unique to the Malindi users and is well documented by researchers in other areas (Lockley, 1995). On the other hand, some users seek opportunities to inject in public settings or walk around the neighbourhood with a syringe sticking out of their arm. Once heroin has been consumed it is preferable not to display one's state of intoxication. In particular, sitting or standing in the semi-conscious state common to those who have consumed heroin in a public place is a practice that is looked down upon by other users.

The sub-culture of heroin users in Malindi draws on diverse elements. The injecting techniques adopted by heroin users in Malindi were learnt from European visitors and are therefore similar to the procedures of other drug sub-cultures. The borrowing of English language drug slang indicates European influence. Furthermore, heroin users in Malindi share many ideas concerning the significance of their behaviour with their counterparts in other parts of the world. For example, self-control is considered important in relation to drug use in both Malindi and in New Zealand (Plumridge and Chetwynd, 1999). In New Zealand, drug injectors who considered themselves recreational users spoke of themselves as heroic individuals who defied convention and 'prized self will and self control' (ibid: 334), while those who classified themselves as 'junkies' spoke of sensual hedonism as their motivating force in life. In Malindi no drug injector attempts to portray his or her drug use as recreational and it is universally accepted that those who inject heroin are physically dependent on the drug. Social status within the drug sub-culture comes from being seen to be in control. However, this stress on individual self-control is not a borrowed attribute but an expression of core Swahili values. Self-control in relation to heroin use is a key attribute of high status for heroin users, just as personal self-control is an important aspect of Swahili culture (Beckerleg, 1994; Parkin, 1995; Swartz, 1997). Within this drug sub-culture high consumption is usually associated with injecting and those that are able to consume large amounts while displaying autonomy and self-control gain status. Those that do inject with equipment that has been used by others have often borrowed or stolen it. Their use of that equipment demonstrates a lack of autonomy and a dependence on others, particularly if they are unable to inject themselves (Beckerleg, 2004 b).

Taking Care of Business

During their daily round of raising cash and using, heroin users in Malindi move between four types of spaces.

The Maskani

The term *maskani* is derived from the Arabic for 'place' (*maskan*) and in Swahili denotes meeting places, such as street corners and coffee stalls where young men congregate. Amongst heroin users in the town, the *maskani* is the setting for sharing information about the local supply of drugs and for negotiating deals either to fence stolen goods or to pool money for purchasing heroin. Most *maskani* are not exclusive to heroin users but are neighbourhood centres where street food is sold, people chew the legal drug *miraa* (khat) and news and gossip are exchanged.

The Base

Heroin users refer to locations on street corners within the town where dealers position themselves to sell as 'bases'. However, often heroin is purchased from the homes or business premises (disguised shops) of well-established dealers. Purchasing heroin is one of the most dangerous parts of users' lifestyles, as it is an interaction that could lead to arrest by police monitoring the 'base'.

The Chimbo

Once heroin has been purchased, users have to find a place to smoke or inject the drug. A location for using is referred to as a chimbo (sin) (pl: vyimbo), a Swahili word with the literal meaning of 'hole'. Some simply take the drug home and use openly in front of the family or lock themselves in the bathroom. But many users do not have the option of using at home, either because they do not have a home or because their families do not permit heroin use in the house. In addition, some users enjoy the street scene and prefer to smoke or inject in the company of other users. Quiet alleyways, boat shelters and derelict houses are some favourite spots. The location of vyimbo shift and are hidden from non-users.

The Kiwanja

After successfully purchasing and injecting or smoking heroin, users must turn their attention once again to raising money to buy the next supplies. Places where funds are raised (such as bars, the beach, the streets and markets), are referred to by users as the kiwanja, (pl: viwanja), a Swahili word denoting a ground, such as a sports field or plot for a house. At the kiwanja, petty trading is carried out, scams are deployed, pockets are picked, sex is sold, drugs are dealt and money begged. The viwanja consist of the public places of the town where users mingle with the majority population of non-users. The kiwanja is a conceptual term denoting the public spaces that users enter when they leave the more private space of the maskani and the chimbo and go 'out in the world'. Hence, there are viwanja all over the town. Users view the whole town as a large *kiwanja*, an arena where other roles, such as tour guide or sex worker or petty trader, are played out. Generally, users do not want potential customers, such as tourists, to know that they are heroin users. In addition, they are busy earning money and have no time to talk. They are, as Preble and Casey (1969) put it, energetically 'taking care of business'.

While the behaviour of users is usually predictable, the location of the key sites in users lives – the *maskani* meeting places, the *bases* where heroin is purchased, the *vyimbo* where it is smoked and even the specific *viwanja* where money is raised – all shift. Changes occur in use of spaces depending on level of community control/tolerance. Users must be constantly one step ahead of the police and local activist groups such as the Council of Imams and Preachers. Dealers shift premises or work from different street corners. Sometimes the *maskani* also becomes a *base*.

For users, compelled by their own drug use, the town is a place where they complete the cycle of raising money to buy heroin and use it. They live in a fast-growing, cosmopolitan tourist town, with its roots in Swahili culture and the economic activities of heroin users are, in fact, not atypical of much of the town's business activity. This reflection of the legal economy in the 'bazaar' of illicit enterprises has also been described in relation to the cities of the rich western world (Ruggiero and South, 1997).

JOINING AND LEAVING THE COMMUNITY

The heroin users refer to themselves as, and prefer non-users to call them, *wateja*, literally 'customers' or 'clients'. As well as having a partner, most *wateja* are part of a larger community of users. They congregate in the spaces they have made their own. Heroin use confers membership and overrides the ethnic and gender based barriers that apply to mainstream Swahili society and most other Kenyan social settings. With their private language, conventions and codes regarding the acquisition and use of heroin, they constitute what appears to be a tight knit and supportive community of perhaps 600 or more individuals in Malindi town (Beckerleg and Lewando Hundt, 2004). However, many members complain that they have no real friends and change using partners frequently. User/dealers attain high status within the community and may command considerable authority, provided their own use is seen to be under control. This is not easy to achieve and disputes, usually over money and the heroin supply, are an everyday occurrence. Violence amongst community members is not uncommon, with women being particularly vulnerable to attack from male users. In addition, some community members are tolerated although they are known to be police informers.

The imprisonment, hospitalisation or death of community members has little impact on the community of *wateja*. Indeed, absences are hardly mentioned, unless an arrest is thought to have possible repercussions on the safety of other members. Turnover of members is fairly rapid, so that the majority of individuals that meet at one *maskani* will change significantly within a year, or even six months. Nevertheless, it is not easy to voluntarily leave the community. One exit-route, located outside Malindi, is the Omari Project which has been providing free treatment services in the form of a six-month programme of detoxification and rehabilitation since 2000. In order to seek a place at the rehabilitation centre, potential clients must make the break from their partners and the community of users. Those that have completed the programme and have returned to Malindi are pursued by their former partners and peers, offered free samples and taunted that they can never stop being 'users'. Some successfully apply the relapse prevention techniques they have learnt during rehabilitation, resist and gradually form new friendships with non-users. But the pull of the subculture and its association with heroin that takes away emotional pain and confers confidence, can be irresistible. For individuals with poor family relationships and poorer employment prospects, the heroin community and its sub-cultural values is an enduring substitute to the task of finding a place in the mainstream.

COMMUNITY RESPONSES

Between 2000 and 2002 workshops in English and Swahili were held in Malindi for local health workers to raise awareness and increase knowledge about heroin use, community responses and reproductive health. The workshops were each attended by between 15–35 participants, some of whom lived in the nearby old town area that is dominated by the Swahili and has a reputation as a centre of drug dealing and use. When the workshops were being planned, local community members and health workers pointed out that few people could be expected to attend because no per diems or meals were on offer. However, attendance levels exceeded the numbers invited, as uninvited participants turned up having heard of the workshops through word of mouth.

Health workers

Health workers attending the workshops demonstrated their awareness of heroin use in the town. However, it was also clear that although heroin was being sold, smoked and injected in discreet locations all over the town, most participants had only vague notions of the extent and patterns of use. Most of the health workers had no interaction with heroin users seeking health care or help in stopping their use.

'The problem of heroin is recent. Before, it was brown sugar and now it is something else – something white that involves injecting.'

'Heroin has been around for ten years. It was hidden and now it is an open market. It is something called brown sugar. Girls use it in two districts of town.'

'Heroin has been around since before I came to the town in 1990. A lot of men are using and less women.'

The health workers mentioned the existence of 'brown sugar', 'white crest' and 'opium'. One participant said that cocaine is very expensive and therefore its availability is only for foreigners, and that he had only seen one local user through his work. The participants were of the opinion that in Malindi, unlike many towns in Kenya, glue sniffing amongst street children was not a big problem. There was also a short discussion at one of the workshops on the availability and use of various pills. One participant mused that 'Mandrax appeared not to have been available for a while, but tourists might be using it at their parties – or maybe it is amphetamines that are popular with Europeans'. Participants agreed that Diazepam use was more common than Rohypnol and that a variety of sleeping tablets were also popular.

Some of the health workers appeared knowledgeable about the mode of administration of heroin locally. They distinguished 'brown sugar', which could be sniffed, chased or injected, from 'white crest' which they said could be injected or smoked as a joint. Others had outdated information based on past observation of the use of 'brown sugar':

'They inject with lime after heating it on a spoon.'
'They use pills and grind them up with lime before injecting it.'

However, from many of the comments it was clear that some of the participants living in the old town area had first hand knowledge of heroin use in their community and its consequences:

'Some of them inject even in the genital area or into the penis.'
'I see them injecting in their legs in the alleyways.'
'There is a need to raise awareness of HIV amongst heroin users. There are many orphans. Young people are dying – like FH, and now his brother M is ill. They go to the hospital and are told they have TB. They may also have a skin rash. They die leaving young children. Also there is a tendency for heroin users to start younger and younger.'

Youth groups

The presence of members of voluntary youth associations at the workshops indicated an eagerness to gain a greater understanding of heroin use in the town. At the same time it was striking that these mostly non-Swahili participants had little first hand experience of heroin use and, unlike the health workers living in the old town, most did not know any users. They listened with rapt attention to descriptions of injecting practices and expressed the wish to meet and befriend heroin users who might want to stop. These youth inhabited the same town as the heroin users but were neither part of the drugs sub-culture nor participants in Swahili street culture. As members of youth and church groups they were unlikely to frequent the *maskani* where heroin users mingle with other Swahili men and youth buying street food, chewing *miraa* and, in the absence of employment, just pass the time. Those with regular jobs and little interest in the freelance deals that so many people rely on for survival are unlikely to spend much time with heroin users in their *viwanja* although it is here that opportunities for meeting heroin users arise: whether in the work place, particularly the market and bus station or places such as bars or the beach, where tourists are to be found. These venues, where money can be earned, the *viwanja* of user parlance, are bustling centres of the informal economy.

The situation concerning interaction with heroin users and knowledge of their way of life is different with many Swahili. In Malindi, the heroin sub-culture is an offshoot and product of mainstream Swahili culture. The majority Swahili non-users live with heroin in ways that most health workers and youth activists do not.

The Council of Imams and Preachers

Heroin abuse is perceived by Swahili elders to be overwhelmingly a problem affecting the Muslim population of Coastal Kenya (Beckerleg, 1995). In a number of coastal towns, including the port of Mombasa and the small tourist resort of Watamu, Islamic groups have taken action – some would say vigilantism – against drug dealers and users by beating them and reporting their activities to the police. In Malindi, a local branch of the Council of Imams and Preachers was formed with the aim of controlling the supply of heroin to the town (Nyahah, 2001). Some of their members attended the workshops.

The members comprise not only imams and preachers but also concerned Muslim men of the Swahili community, many of whom have family members who are heroin users. As such they know the identity of many users and dealers and the locations they frequent. In 2001, the Malindi branch of the Council hosted a Coast wide meeting to discuss their strategy towards drug abuse and in 2002 held a five-day seminar on the links between drug abuse and HIV. However, the group concentrates primarily on the eradication of heroin supply and work with the police to this end. Although they profess to target large scale dealers who they perceive as destroying their children, any user who also raises money by selling heroin is liable for arrest. They have also targeted users who inject in semi-public settings and have caused frequent shifts in the users' *maskani*. Members of the group have, with the police, raided known heroin dealers, with limited success. Their activities as a pressure group contributed to the arrest of three major dealers in 2002. Nevertheless, there is no indication that the supply of heroin to Malindi has been reduced. The price of a sachet of one tenth of a gram of 'white crest' has remained constant at Kenya Shillings 100 (about \$1.2 and £0.85) since 2000. The major result of their activities is that heroin users are less visible in the old town area where they previously congregated to buy and use, and have shifted to other neighbourhoods and to the beach.

Families

The activities of the Council of Imams and Preachers notwithstanding, heroin use is both condemned and tolerated by the Swahili community in Malindi (Beckerleg, 1995, a). The role of parents and the family in curbing or contributing to heroin abuse amongst family members is of particular interest. Interviews were carried out in 2001 with the family members or non-using boyfriends selected by 9 women users as supportive presences in their lives. A further 10 women were unable or unwilling to name a significant person in their life who was a non-user who could be interviewed. This illustrates that although many users live in the midst of mainstream society and interact with it on a daily basis, they are isolated and have no support system other than the heroin-user community.

Tolerance and accommodation of heroin use

The interviews that were carried out with family members and boyfriends of the women users reveal the extent to which heroin use is tolerated and accommodated in this culture. Some of the problems raised, such as theft of household items by the user, begging from the family, or conspicuous use of heroin, apply equally to male users and have been reported by their family members. These issues concern family members living with heroin users the world over (Dorn et al, 1994). However, although the families complained and some were clearly distressed by the drug use of their family member or girlfriend, the presence of the user was usually tolerated. Apart from one woman who lived with a family of heroin dealers who originated from another part of Kenya, all the family members interviewed were

Swahili or lived in close proximity to Swahili families and hence represented the dominant local culture.

The family homes that the users continue to occupy are busy households of extended families and, sometimes, lodgers. The occupants of these homes have become familiar with the patterns and signs of heroin use. They can identify when a heroin user has just smoked or injected or is sick from withdrawal of heroin. Some family members reported giving money to the user to buy supplies when she was in withdrawal, while others resisted ever giving any money. Family members also knew other members of the user network who visit the house and may smoke or inject there. In the close knit community of the old town and adjacent area where many of the users live, kinship and marriage bind the families of users in ways that complement the bonds associated with membership of the heroin sub-culture. Indeed, the activities of the users in their various buying and using locations, including homes, occur in spaces where the everyday life of mainstream society continues. Although users frequently complain that nobody trusts or respects them, they and their activities are tolerated.

However, a number of specific issues highlight the difficult situation of women users. Several family members complained that their heroin-using relative was incapable of looking after her children. Other complaints by family members centred on the dress code of Muslim women users. Of particular concern was whether she conformed to local standards of respectable dress by covering her hair when going out. Several female relatives of women users dwelt on the topic of dress while failing to mention that the user in question was going out in order to do sex work to raise money to buy heroin. Indeed, in Malindi, the accepted euphemism for sex work is to 'go out'. Hence a women who talks of not going out much means that she is not very active in the sex industry. It appears that discretion in 'going out' in terms of dress, counts for much in this setting, where there is both a local and tourist sex industry. In addition, many women users support their families as well as their heroin habit by sex work. In many poor families it would be both futile and counter-productive to complain too loudly about commercial sex work by heroin users.

CONCLUSION

Unlike the cultures of several other societies discussed in this volume, drug use has never been a feature of Swahili ritual. As Muslims, Swahili men and women are required to pray, fast and attend the Hajj to Mecca if such a journey is within their means. Local celebrations to mark the birth of the Prophet Mohammed (Maulidi) incorporate recitations of poems to praise the Prophet, the playing of tambourines and flutes and repetitive swaying movement (Topan, 1994). Some critics of the Maulidi claim that these expressions of religious fervour are un-Islamic because they can result in a trance state, similar to that achieved by exponents of Sufism or by users of drugs (see e.g. chapter by Schaefer, this volume). In many Swahili towns and villages though rarely in Malindi, spirit possession achieved through dance also puts people into a trance-like state without the aid of drugs (Topan, 1972; Caplan, 1997). At weddings and funerals, food, coffee and soft drinks are served but no intoxicants (Middleton, 1992). Sober, self-control is an aspiration of many Swahili and a means of demonstrating power and authority. On the other hand, for the past forty years the Swahili in Kenya have been absorbing new influences that emphasise the short-term pleasures of recreational drug use. With a trading and maritime background, people move frequently between the Swahili towns strung along the coast, exchanging ideas and influences. From the 1960s, in the larger town of Mombasa, Yemeni and Somali men introduced *miraa* to Swahili men meeting to drink coffee at roadside stalls or *baraza*, a more respectable version of the *maskani* favoured by contemporary youth. Tourism has subsequently provided the prosperity for some to indulge in recreational drug use on a scale that would have been impossible in earlier times. For example, in the 1970s in the northern island town of Lamu, hippy travellers came to 'drop out' and smoke cannabis in a tourist paradise. Although few independent travellers remain, the early European visitors stimulated the local trend for male youth to pursue short-term pleasures in an idyllic setting. Throughout the twentieth century, bars sprang up first to cater to sailors visiting the port of Mombasa, and later as part of the tourist industry. But alcohol has never become an accepted part of Swahili life, in the way that cannabis and khat have. Indeed, the Swahili have resisted the growth of bars and none exist within Malindi old town, although the area is ringed with them.

Although large scale trafficking in heroin between South Asia and East Africa is a recent phenomenon, dating from the late 1970s, there is a long history of contact between nations bordering the Indian Ocean. Heroin smoking and injecting are growing problems in many South Asian countries as well as in Tanzania and Kenya (Kilonzo et al, 2001;UNDCP, 2000; UNODCCP 1999). Heroin became widely available only recently and co-incided with the Italian–led tourist boom in Malindi and neighbouring Watamu. In the 1980s, in Watamu, many cannabis users moved onto smoking and chasing heroin. The new users and the wider community had no knowledge of the effects of heroin use or how it might differ from cannabis. The first heroin-related death occurred in Watamu in 1994 (Beckerleg, 1995, a). By then, a heroin sub-culture was developing and the community were learning to live with heroin. As suggested earlier, despite the distinctiveness of the Malindi and Watamu situations, their experience of the rise of a heroin and related drug sub-culture since the 1980s undoubtedly shares some characteristics with other countries. Notably, ignorance about the practice of 'chasing' heroin and its addictive potential was significant in the development of heroin cultures in the 1980s in both Kenya and the UK.

At the Kenya coast heroin users shift between the towns of Malindi, Watamu, Mombasa and Lamu. Heroin use is also growing in the areas south of Mombasa and spreading to smaller localities. The users from all these places share a common language, social conventions and values that are driven by the pursuit of heroin. The attributes of this heroin sub-culture also share many elements with other heroin using networks in other, richer parts of the world, including the UK, New Zealand and USA (Power et al, 1996; Plumridge and Chetwynd, 1999; Ramos, 1990). Indeed, many features of the Malindi centred heroin sub-culture were learnt from tourists. Heroin, as a substance that causes physical and emotional dependency and that requires ever increasing amounts to achieve the same effect, produces patterns of behaviour in its users that are replicated regardless of culture, social class, religion or ethnicity. Furthermore, the illegal nature of heroin use makes secrecy necessary and a private language aids discretion. As well as replicating patterns of use in other parts of the world, heroin users in Malindi draw on mainstream Swahili culture to create an identity and set of values that reflect both the local and the global values. Heroin use in this Swahili town and coastal area should be recognised as part of the process of economic and cultural globalisation. Importantly however, the globalisation of prohibition and of punitive policies aimed at drug supply and use must be sensitive not only to the nature of localised support for such measures *but also* to the factors underpinning the readiness of Swahili families and wider culture, to tolerate and accommodate heroin use. Heroin use at the Kenya coast is undoubtedly now a 'local' problem but its arrival reflects influences originating far away.

ACKNOWLEDGEMENTS

The research was funded by the UK Economic and Social Research Council (Grant number R000238392). The users who allowed me to follow them around and their families who allowed me to interview them are thanked.

REFERENCES

Agar, M. and Schacht Reisinger, H. (2002) 'A heroin epidemic at the intersection of histories: the 1960s epidemic among African Americans in Baltimore.' *Medical Anthropology* 21;115–156.

Beckerleg, S. (1994) 'Watamu: Lost Land, but a New Swahili Town.' in D. Parkin (Ed) *Continuity and Autonomy in Swahili Communities: Strategies of Self Determination.* Afro-Pub, Institute fur Afrikanistik, University of Vienna/ SOAS.

——(1995) (a) 'Brown Sugar or Friday Prayers: Youth Choices and Community Building in Coastal Kenya.' *African Affairs* 94, 23–38.

——(1995) (b) 'Heroin Inside-Out' *Anthropology in Action* Vol. 2, Number 2, 1995

——(2004) (a) 'Modernity has been Swahilized. The Case of Malindi.' In Eds P Caplan and F Topan, *Swahili Modernities: Identity and Power on the East African Coast*' USA: Africa World Press.

——(2004) (b) 'How 'cool' is heroin use at the Kenya Coast?' *Drugs: Education, Policy and Practice*. 11(1):67–77.

Beckerleg S. and Lewando Hundt G. (2004) 'The Characteristics and Recent Growth of Heroin Injecting in a Kenyan Coastal Town.' *Addiction Research and Theory*. 12(1):41–53.

Beckerleg S. and G. Lewando Hundt (forthcoming) 'Working with heroin users in an East African town' Eds L. Hume and J Mulcock *Awkward Spaces, Productive Places: Fieldwork in Difficult Conditions* Columbia University Press.

Bourgois, P. (1995) *In Search of Respect: Selling Crack in El Barrio* Cambridge: Cambridge University Press.

——(2001) 'The Power of Violence in War and Peace: Post-Cold War Lessons from El Salvador.' *Ethnography* 2(1): 5–34.

Caplan, P. (1997) *African Voices, African Lives: Personal Narratives from a Swahili Village*. London: Routledge.

De vere Allen, J. (1993) *Swahili Origins* London: James Currey.

Dorn, N., Ribbens, J. and South, N. (1994) *Coping with a Nightmare: Family Feelings about Long-term Drug Use*. London: ISDD/ADFAM National.

Farmer P., Connors M., Simmons J. (1996) *Women, Poverty and AIDS:. Sex, Drugs and Structural Violence*. Monroe: Common Courage Press.

——(1999) *Infections and Inequalities: The Modern Plagues* Berkeley: University of California Press.

Horton, M. and Middleton, J. (2000) *The Swahili: The Social Landscape of a Mercantile Society* Oxford: Blackwell Publishers.

Kilonzo, G. P., Mbwambo, J. K., Kaaya. S. F., Hogan, N. M. (2001) 'Rapid Situational Analysis for Drug Demand Reduction in Tanzania.' UNDCP.

Kusimba, C. M. (1999) *The Rise and Fall of Swahili States* London: Altamira Press.

Lockley, P. (1995). *Counselling Heroin and Other Drug Users*. London: Free Association Books.

Middleton, J. (1992) *The World of the Swahili* New Haven and London: Yale University Press.

Mirza, S. and Strobel, M. (1989) *Three Swahili Women: Life Histories from Mombasa, Kenya*. Bloomington: Indiana University Press.

Nyagah, R. (2001) 'Malindi People Winning the War against Drug Abuse.' *Daily Nation* 7 May 2001.

Parkin, D. P. (1995) 'Blank Banners and Islamic Consciousness in Zanzibar.' In A. P. Cohen and H. Rapport (eds.) *Questions of Consciousness* ASA Monograph 33. London and New York: Routledge.pp198–216.

Peake, R. (1989) 'Swahili Stratification and Tourism in Malindi Old Town, Kenya.' *Africa* 59 (2) , p209–220

Plumridge, E. and Chetwynd, J. (1999) Identity and the Social Construction of Risk: Injecting Drug Use. *Sociology of Health and Illness* 21(3):329–343.

Power R., Jones S., Kearns G., Ward J. (1996) An Ethnography of Risk Management amongst Illicit Drug Injectors and its Implications for the Development of Community-based Interventions. *Sociology of Health and Illness*. Vol. 18, No1, pp.86–106.

Preble, E. and Casey, J. J. (1969) Taking Care of Business – The Heroin User's Life on the Street. *International Journal of the Addictions* 4(1):1–24.

Ramos, R. (1990) 'Chicano Intravenous Drug Users' In E. Lambert *The Collection and Interpretation of Data from Hidden Populations*. NIDA Research Monograph Series 98. Rockville: NIDA.

Ruggiero, V. and South, N. (1997) The Late-modern City as a Bazaar: Drug Markets, Illegal Enterprise and the 'Barricades'. *British Journal of Sociology* 48(1):54–70.

Swartz, M. (1997) 'Illness and Morality in the Mombasa Swahili community: a Metaphorical Model in an Islamic Culture.' *Culture, Medicine and Psychiatry* 21(1): 89–114.

Shariff, A. (1987) *Slaves, Spices and Ivory in Zanzibar* London: James Currey.

Topan, F. M. T. (1972) 'Oral Literature in a Ritual Setting: the Role of Spirit Songs in a Spirit Medium-ship Cult of Mombasa, Kenya.' Unpublished PhD thesis, University of London.

——(1994) 'Song, Dance and the Continuity of Swahili Identity.' In Ed. Parkin D., *Continuity and Autonomy in Swahili Communities: Inland Influences and Strategies of Self-Determination*. Afro-Pub, Institute fur Afrikanistik, University of Vienna/ SOAS.

UNDCP (2000) *'The Eastern African Drug Beat' Importance of Data in Control of Illicit Drug Trafficking* Vol 2 No1, 13–14, January 2000.

UNODCCP (1999) *The Drug Nexus in Africa*, UN Office for Drug Control and Crime Prevention Monographs, Vienna.

INDEX

209

INDEX OF NAMES

215